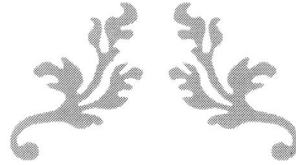

INTRODUCTION TO BUSINESS STATISTICS

A Simple Stepwise Approach to Basic Statistics

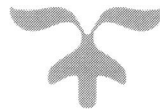

DR. KRUTI DHOLAKIA LEHENBAUER
Kruti.Lehenbauer@gmail.com

Table of Contents

Detailed Table of Contents

List of Figures

List of Tables

List of Examples

Introduction to the Book

In the modern world of computers, smartphones, and access to large scale datasets, most people do not realize how that data translates into real world decision-making and one tends to visualize computers making decisions based on the data that is being gathered from all around us. Many people imagine this process being like that of a calculator, where one inserts the problem that needs to be solved with the appropriate numbers and the answer pops up on its screen. However, this is not entirely accurate when it comes to using large scale data and how it helps businesses make the decisions regarding their costs, revenues, pricing structures, advertising strategies, and marketing methods. While ready-to-use software is available that translates this data into usable information, one of the most glaring discrepancies occurs when there is an inability on the part of a decision-maker to understand what the output truly means. It is essential for decision-makers to understand what the nuances of data are, in order to recognize how making any changes would impact future prospects of the business. This is one of the reasons why data literacy is a fundamental requirement of anybody who is either likely to make decisions for a business owned by someone else or even by themselves.

The general definition of statistics is "a branch of mathematics that deals with collection, analysis, interpretation, and presentation of numerical data." Statistics is split into two main parts: descriptive statistics and inferential statistics. Descriptive statistics consist of a variety of methods of collecting, describing, and presenting numerical data to understand existing trends in the data. Inferential statistics consist of analyzing and interpreting the data collected to enable drawing conclusions and using more accurate forecasting to improve future outcomes by a detailed study of existing data. Figure 1 shows how Descriptive Statistics and Inferential Statistics interact in order to contribute to the decision-making in a business.

This book covers descriptive statistics in Chapters 1 through 3 and thereafter focuses on the inferential statistics in Chapters 4 through 8. The first two chapters introduce basic types of functions, research methods, what hypothesis testing means, different types of data, how to present them in using tables and graphs, and how to describe data in numerical terms by focusing on the measures of central tendency and variability. Chapter 3 introduces the reader to the world of probability calculations before crossing over to the inferential world of statistics in the next section of the book. The inferential world of statistics allows one to enhance their decision-making skills, by learning about various types of distributions, sampling, and testing options armed with the descriptive statistical tools to draw meaningful inferences. The last three chapters of the book bring everything together as they explore the nuances of relationships between two or more variables and discuss methods to identify if and how they interact with each other.

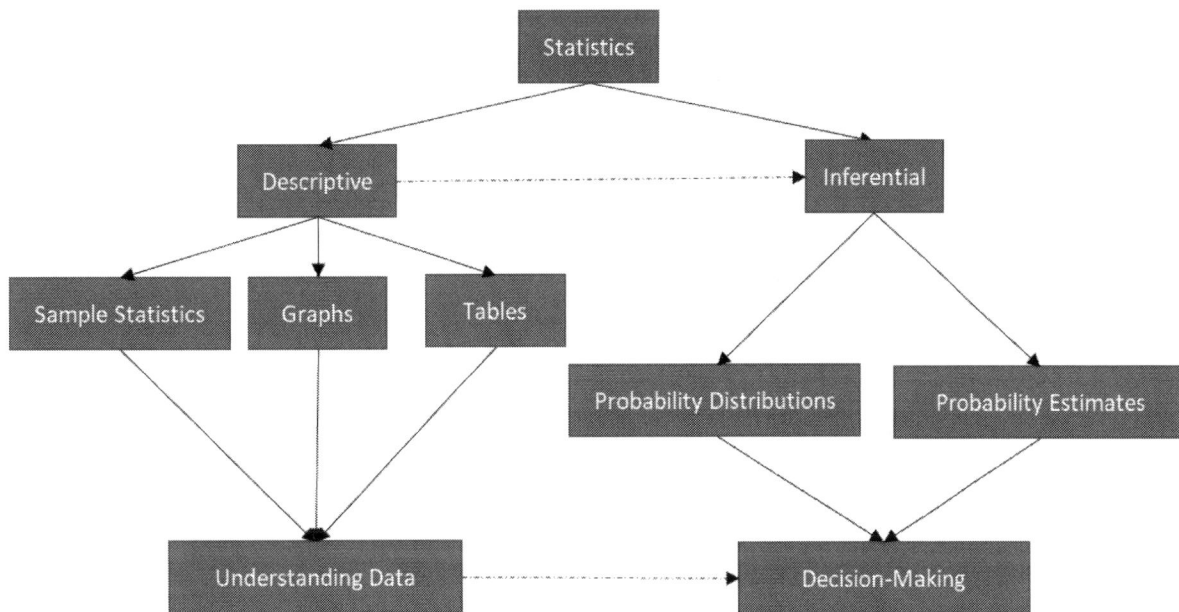

Figure.1. How Statistics Helps with Decision-Making

This book is primarily written for an undergraduate student who is being introduced to business statistics, with the assumption that either the individual will proceed to take more business classes or more statistics classes in their future. Theoretical derivations and proofs for various statistical concepts are deliberately not covered in detail in this book, because the purpose is to help the reader understand the basic concepts and to learn how to apply these concepts in the real world. In most chapters and sections of this book, a brief discussion of each concept is followed by a stepwise example (highlighted in gray) to demonstrate how a real-world problem can be solved using either manual or software-based calculations. The software of choice for this book is MS Excel and is referred to as just "Excel" in the text. It would be remiss to fail to note that the examples used to demonstrate solutions of basic statistical problems in this book are quite simple as compared to the real world and have limited sample sizes. The purpose of discussing and demonstrating the Excel solutions is to encourage the reader to start using Excel as an easy-to-access statistical tool which can save tremendous amounts of time with respect to calculations in the real world. The solutions also show the relevant formulas in the figures and tables to enable the reader to create their own Excel files.

Chapter 1.   Collecting, Organizing, and Displaying Data

The term "statistics" or "data" are often very liberally and interchangeably used in the real world. However, the casual usage of these terms is also often the reason most people do not realize or recognize the importance of clean data and clear estimates when faced with any decisions based on even a small level of uncertainty. The first thing to understand is why are statistics needed and what exactly "data" means in the context of statistics. Data (plural) or a *datum* (singular) typically refers to some type of a numerical value that is assigned to a specific characteristic of interest.

Thus, if one is interested in studying heights of 2-year-old children, then the value of the height (in inches or centimeters) of a child can be one data-point (also called a single *datum*). If the heights of 10 2-year-old children are collected, then it becomes a "*dataset*" consisting of 10 datapoints collected from 10 children. But what would be the point (no pun intended) of collecting this type of information in the real world? What if you knew that the expected height of an adult in inches is considered to be about double the height of that person in inches when they were 2 years old? Now, suddenly collecting and analyzing the heights of 2-year-olds might appear to be more interesting since the height at that age has a "predictive" power in terms of the expected adult height of those individuals. This is the "characteristic" that one might be interested in studying for making predictions or decisions. Moreover, it is usually not possible to get exact information for each individual in the entire population of 2-year-olds, which is why it is important to understand how collecting information on a sample can allow one to make decisions and predictions of the population.

This chapter lays out various methods by which data can be collected, organized, and displayed in order to get basic information about characteristics of interest. Each of these is presented in individual sections of this chapter with subsections devoted to understanding the various initial nuances of Descriptive Statistics. Since MS Excel is heavily used in this chapter and throughout this book, this playlist "Excel Basics by Kruti" on YouTube will help with getting familiar with the basic functions of Excel:
https://youtube.com/playlist?list=PLjc78F4DDADiCxMyo1mBWFNTdctmAiulB

1.1. Data Types and Collection

In mathematics, and therefore in statistics, the terms *constant* and *variable* are fairly commonplace, but many individuals do not necessarily recognize the differences and relationships between the two, except the obvious ones of "one is numbers" and "the other is letters." Similarly, the terms *hypothesis* and *research* are often used very loosely in common language but have specific meanings and implications in any type of scientific pursuit. The notion of *sampling* is well understood by most people but the context of sampling in statistics is more formalized. This applies to most of the descriptive statistics concepts covered in this chapter and beyond – that people know these concepts, people apply these concepts, but people do not necessarily know how to formalize these concepts in a manner that allows them to explicitly use these tools in formal decision-making.

1.1.1. Constants, Parameters, and Variables

The term *constant* refers to a fixed numerical value that can occur for an observation or in a functional relationship. A *parameter* is a constant that defines a whole class of equations but takes upon constant values for specific relationships and is usually indicated by small letters or Greek symbols. A *variable* is an element of an equation (or relationship or function) that can take upon multiple values in the relationship and is usually represented by capital letters. Usually, when a relationship is defined between two (or more) variables, one of them is expected to be *dependent* on the other *independent* variable(s) such that when the value(s) of the independent variable(s) change, the dependent variable value changes as a result of that change. The dependent variable is typically denoted by the letter Y (to indicate its placement on the vertical axis) and the independent variable(s), placed on the horizontal axis are denoted by the letter X (subscripts can be used to show more than one independent variable and each independent variable exists on its own axis).

The identification of dependent and independent variables correctly often poses a challenge because most people tend to get caught up in terminology instead of focusing on the concepts that these terms convey. To help the reader visualize the concept of dependent and independent variables a conceptual approach called the "Hot Air Balloon Approach" is demonstrated here. Say that one was interested in finding out how high a hot air balloon can rise, implying that the "height to which the balloon rises" is what the variable of interest is and by collecting various datapoints on heights achieved by different hot air balloons, one can get an idea of how high a hot air balloon is expected to rise. However, now consider what internal or external factors can impact this rising. Internal factors such as material from which the balloon is made, size of the balloon, weight of the basket attached to the balloon, temperature of the hot air that is blowing into the balloon are all expected to affect how high that balloon can go. On the other hand, external factors such as humidity in the environment, external temperature, speed and direction of wind, and location of the place from which balloon is sent off could also impact the vertical height of the balloon. These internal and external factors are all *independent* variables, some of which one can control (internal factors) and some of which one cannot physically control (external factors). But the dependent variable or the variable that one is interested in studying – height to which a hot air balloon rises – is what the researcher focuses on. The internal and external variables are held constant (controlled) to the best of one's ability when measuring the height to which the balloon rises. However, if the researcher wants to study what factors impact the rise of the balloon they would need to "tweak" or adjust one variable at a time. For instance, if researcher hypothesizes that bigger balloons will go higher than smaller balloons, they will keep all other internal and external factors constant and only change the size of the balloon. Similarly, if they hypothesize that the internal temperature of the hot air impacts the height to which a balloon can fly, the researcher will keep all other variables except the internal temperature constant and adjust the internal temperature to get various "readings" of the height to which the balloon rises. This process is called the research methodology that hinges upon the correct identification of dependent and independent variables and the ability to control at least some of the independent variables in order to study their specific impact on the dependent variable.

Using an example will help understand this difference a bit better in social sciences or business fields. Consider the relationship between the height in inches of a child at age 2 (X) and the expected height of that individual in inches as an adult (Y), which can be represented as: $Y = 2X$. In this equation, X and Y are variables because they will take on different values for different individuals and "2" represents a constant number that defines the relationship. Thus, if a 2-year-old's height is 36 inches, one can expect that child to be about 72 inches (6 feet tall) as an adult. In this case, the height as an adult is the dependent variable and the height at age 2 is the independent variable. Now, the relationship $Y = 2X$ is a fixed or established relationship but what if a relationship was defined in more general terms and the exact multiple (in this case, 2) was unknown such as $Y = bX$? Using measurements and statistical tools such as regression analysis, one can estimate that unknown parameter b which gives definition to the relationship of Y to the X.

The equation of a line is given by $Y = a + bX$, where a is called the "intercept" and b is called the "slope" of the line. This equation represents the entire set or population of all possible straight lines in a two-dimensional X-Y plane, and the values of the intercept and the slope, are parameters since they take on different values for each line. For instance, $Y = 5 + 2X$ is a different line than $Y = 10 - 2X$ because the parameters a and b have taken on different (but constant) values in each equation. Linear equations that are often used in statistical analysis will be discussed in more detail in the next sub-section.

1.1.2. Commonly Used Mathematical Functions in Statistics

A mathematical function is a statement that expresses a specific mathematical relationship between two (or more) variables such that the value of one variable is defined by the value of the other(s). For instance, if a dependent variable Y is a function of an independent variable X, it can be represented as $Y = f(X)$. Some commonly used mathematical functions in statistics are listed here with explanations on how they are interpreted.

1. **Linear Function and Lin-Lin relationships**: If variable Y is defined as a linear function of variable X, the equation is given by the following formula and it implies that when X changes by one unit, the change in Y is measured by the parameter b in the equation and the graph of the equation is a straight line:
$$Y = a + bX$$

    For any given real value of X, the corresponding value of Y can be calculated if the values of a and b are given. The following illustrations show two different linear relationships (or lines) $Y = 5 + 2X$ and $Y = 10 - 2X$, and their corresponding graphs in

Figure 1.1. The graphs also have tables on the right-hand side to indicate how different values of Y can be obtained by using the defined functions if the values of X are known.

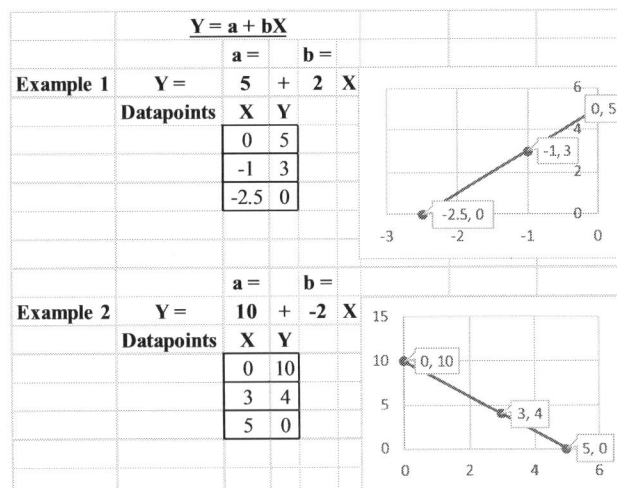

		Y = a + bX			
		a =		b =	
Example 1	**Y =**	5	+	2	**X**
	Datapoints	**X**	**Y**		
		0	5		
		-1	3		
		-2.5	0		
		a =		b =	
Example 2	**Y =**	10	+	-2	**X**
	Datapoints	**X**	**Y**		
		0	10		
		3	4		
		5	0		

Figure 1.1. Graphing Lines for lin-lin functions

As one can see in these linear equations, the values of both X and Y are in their basic form, with an exponent of 1 (i.e., higher powers or exponential forms or cross products such as X^2 or Y^3 or XY are not included in the equations). Straight lines such as these are often used for establishing or estimating linear relationships between two or more variables in Statistics and will be covered in Chapter 8 of this book. When all variables are in their basic form, the relationship is called a "Lin-Lin" relationship to indicate that the dependent as well as the independent variables are in a base "linear" form.

2. **Exponential and Logarithmic Functions and Log-Lin Relationships**: If variable Y is defined as an exponential function of variable X, the equation is given by the following formula where c is the parameter in the "base" of the exponent X:
$$Y = c^X$$

For any given real value of X, the corresponding value of Y can be calculated if the value of b is given. Consider two different exponential relationships $Y = 5^X$ and $Y = -5^X$, and their corresponding graphs obtained in Figure 1.2. The graphs also have tables on the right-hand side to indicate how different values of Y can be obtained by using the defined functions if the values of X are known. As can be seen in Figure 1.2, the general exponential function fluctuates as the value of the base parameter c changes.

If the base parameter c is equal to Euler's number e, defined as an irrational number rounded off to 2.718, then the relationship is a special type of exponential relationship that lends itself to various mathematical conversions in calculus. While those are not directly in the scope of this book, suffice it to understand that the base e is essential for being able to convert exponential functions into logarithmic forms, which can resemble linearity by changing the horizontal axis. This special case is written as follows and its graph is included as Example 3 in Figure 1.2. This special case exponent is used very often in statistics for probability distributions and logarithmic transformations.
$$Y = e^X$$

Notice how exponential distributions result in curves instead of straight lines when graphed. In statistics, a large portion of the estimations depend upon linearity for accuracy or for minimizing the errors of estimates. Moreover, the number values of some variables of interest can be large when compared to other variables (e.g., Revenues in millions of dollars when compared to number of years the firm has been in existence). These are the two main reasons why logarithmic functions can help with "linearizing" and "normalizing" the fluctuations in datasets. The logarithmic function is the "reverse" of the exponential function such that if $Y = c^X$ then the natural log of Y (lnY) also known as the "log of Y to base e" is defined as the product of natural log of c ($ln(c)$) and X:

$$lnY = X \times ln(c) = Xln(c)$$

If the same exponential functions as used earlier are converted into the logarithmic form, one would get $lnY = Xln5$ for example 1, $lnY = Xln(-5)$ for example 2, and $lnY = X$ for the special case example 3 covered in Figure 1.2 (left-hand side). Note that if base $c = e$, then $ln(c) = ln(e) = 1$ is the definition for natural logarithms. Refer to Figure 1.2 (right-hand side) and note how these same exponential relationships can now be visualized in linear form by adjusting the scale on the vertical axis.

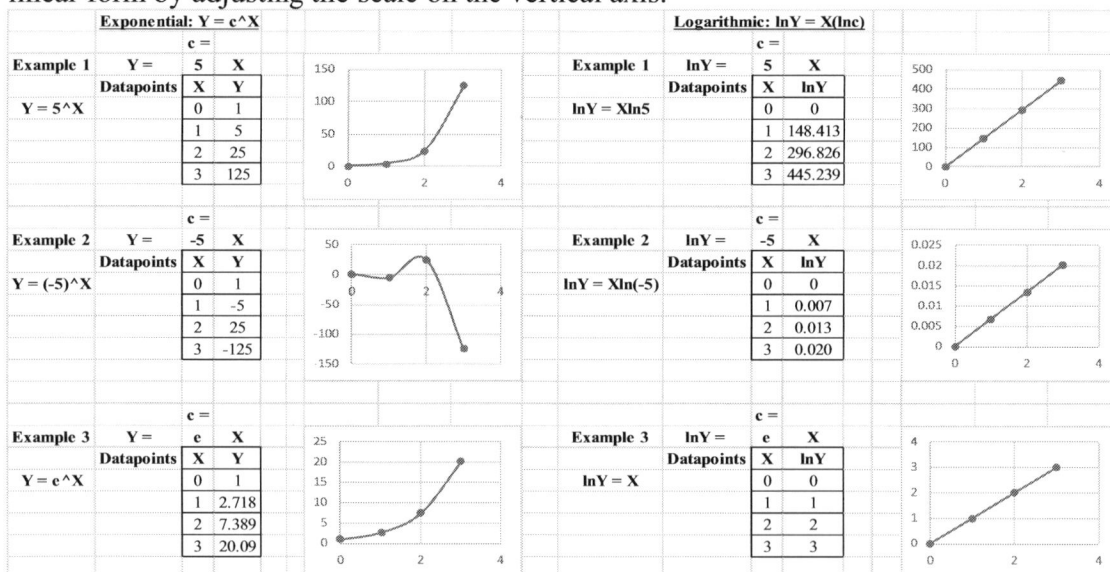

Exponential: Y = c^X					Logarithmic: lnY = X(lnc)			
	c =					c =		
Example 1	Y =	5	X		Example 1	lnY =	5	X
	Datapoints	X	Y			Datapoints	X	lnY
Y = 5^X		0	1		lnY = Xln5		0	0
		1	5				1	148.413
		2	25				2	296.826
		3	125				3	445.239
	c =					c =		
Example 2	Y =	-5	X		Example 2	lnY =	-5	X
	Datapoints	X	Y			Datapoints	X	lnY
Y = (-5)^X		0	1		lnY = Xln(-5)		0	0
		1	-5				1	0.007
		2	25				2	0.013
		3	-125				3	0.020
	c =					c =		
Example 3	Y =	e	X		Example 3	lnY =	e	X
	Datapoints	X	Y			Datapoints	X	lnY
Y = e^X		0	1		lnY = X		0	0
		1	2.718				1	1
		2	7.389				2	2
		3	20.09				3	3

Figure 1.2. Graphs for Exponential and Logarithmic Functions

The types of relationships where the dependent variable is in a logarithmic form (lnY) but the independent variable(s) is in a linear form (no exponents, powers, or logarithmic forms), are called Log-Lin relationships and are quite commonly used in statistical estimations. The only thing to remember is that when estimating parameters for Log-Lin relationships, interpretations of the intercepts and slopes need to be performed more carefully than what is done for linear relationships. A common form of Log-Lin relationship is shown in the following equation and Figure 1.3 shows two examples of this Log-Lin relationship and their respective graphs:

$$lnY = a + bX$$

Thus, in a Log-Lin relationship, the intercept a refers to the value of lnY when the value of X is 0 and the slope b refers to the change in the value of lnY when X changes by one unit. Another way to write this relationship would be $Y = e^{a+bX}$. Note that the graph only shows the Y output on the Y-axis and not the lnY, since the values of lnY are all going to be linear, which is precisely why this model is used for linear estimations even when the actual relationship between X and Y is non-linear.

3. **Lin-Log and Log-Log Relationships**: Two more types of similar relationships exist between dependent and independent variables in statistics and are commonly used in business and economic applications. These are defined based on whether the Y and X variables use either exponents or logarithms in the way they are defined. The first one is a Lin-Log relationship where Y is defined as a function of a logarithmic value of X. As one can see the relationship between X and Y is non-linear but the transformation of X in this manner allows for estimates of a linear relationship between Y and lnX.

$$Y = a + b\,lnX$$

	Log-Lin: $lnY = a + bX$				
		a =	b =		
Example 1	$lnY =$	5	2		
	Datapoints	X	lnY	Y	
$lnY = 5 + 2X$		0	5	148.4	
		1	7	1097	
		2	9	8103	
		3	11	59874	
		a =	b =		
Example 2	$lnY =$	10	-2		
	Datapoints	X	lnY	Y	
$lnY = 10 - 2X$		0	10	22026	
		1	8	2981	
		2	6	403.4	
		3	4	54.6	

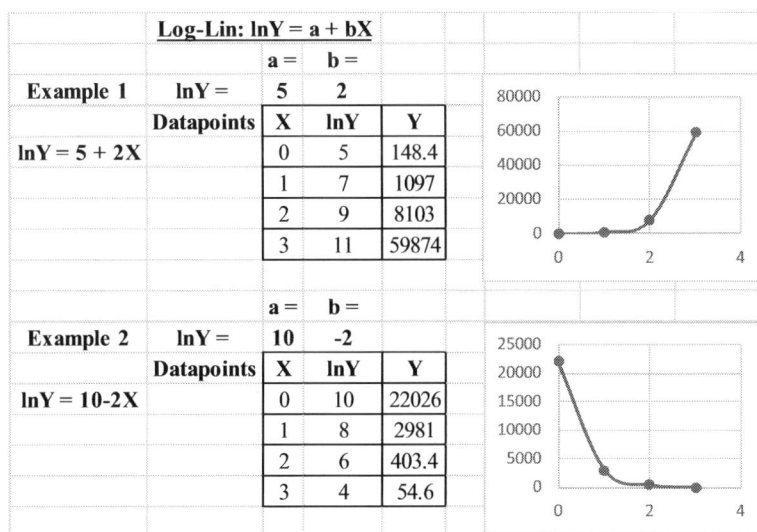

Figure 1.3. Log-Lin Functions

As seen in Figure 1.4, for a value of $X = 0$, the ln(0) is undefined, which is why one gets the "#NUM!" error in Excel. Here, when X changes by 1 unit, the change in Y is small and is calculated as b/X_{new}.

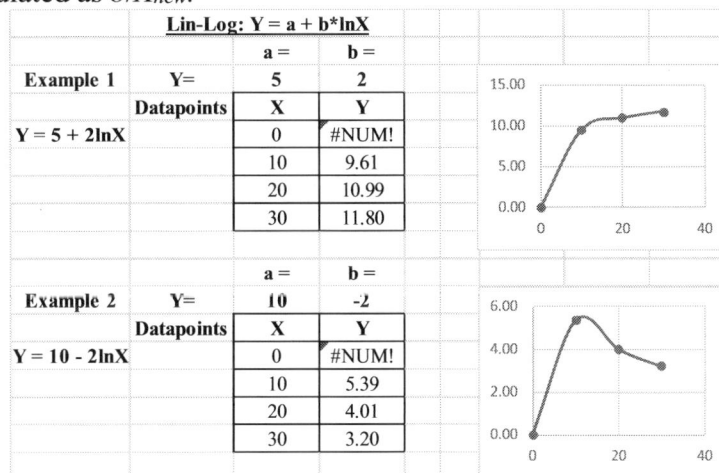

	Lin-Log: $Y = a + b*lnX$			
		a =	b =	
Example 1	$Y=$	5	2	
	Datapoints	X	Y	
$Y = 5 + 2lnX$		0	#NUM!	
		10	9.61	
		20	10.99	
		30	11.80	
		a =	b =	
Example 2	$Y=$	10	-2	
	Datapoints	X	Y	
$Y = 10 - 2lnX$		0	#NUM!	
		10	5.39	
		20	4.01	
		30	3.20	

Figure 1.4. Lin-Log Functions

The second relationship is the Log-Log relationship where both, the X and the Y terms use the logarithmic transformation in the following form:

$$lnY = a + blnX$$

This is one of the most useful relationships used in businesses and in economics and other policy-related fields because in this transformation, the slope b of this linearized estimate gives the value of the "elasticity" of variable Y with respect to variable X. To put it more simply, a one percent change in the value of the X variable results in a b% change in the value of the Y variable. The figure 1.5 shows the general relationship between X and Y (clearly non-linear) which can be estimated using linear estimation methods by simply using the log-log transformations.

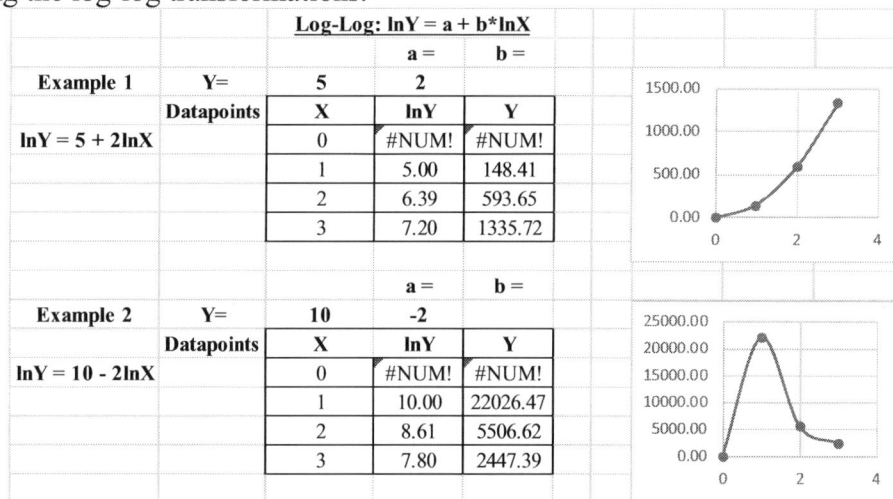

		Log-Log: lnY = a + b*lnX			
		a =	b =		
Example 1	**Y=**	5	2		
	Datapoints	X	lnY	Y	
lnY = 5 + 2lnX		0	#NUM!	#NUM!	
		1	5.00	148.41	
		2	6.39	593.65	
		3	7.20	1335.72	
		a =	b =		
Example 2	**Y=**	10	-2		
	Datapoints	X	lnY	Y	
lnY = 10 - 2lnX		0	#NUM!	#NUM!	
		1	10.00	22026.47	
		2	8.61	5506.62	
		3	7.80	2447.39	

Figure 1.5. Log-Log Functions

1.1.3. Hypotheses Testing and Research Methods

The goal of statistical sampling is typically to select a certain number of observations from the entire population for the variables of interest in order to test for the existence of some relationship. The hypotheses (notice *hypotheses* with an "e" is the plural of singular *hypothesis* with an "i") usually connect the dependent variable with the independent variable by assuming that there is no relationship (null hypothesis) and testing it against the notion that some relationship between the two variables exists (alternative hypothesis). It is not always possible in the real world to get information about all the existing observations in the population. The notion of testing samples in order to make decisions about the population is what drives statistical analysis. Samples can be taken by doing physical experiments, distributing surveys, analyzing content available in other studies, or doing a literature review, observing behaviors as a participant, or using data from existing sources in order to study or test the hypotheses. Chapter 6 exclusively deals with hypotheses testing, so more details will be covered in that chapter. However, hypotheses testing is the cornerstone of the scientific method, so it is essential to understand why the first five chapters of this book are devoted to learning the tools that are required to test hypotheses in statistics.

Research, in the scientific context, does not simply constitute an ability to search for information on internet engines such as Google or Bing; that is simply called a "search"! Research implies that there is an existing set of hypotheses (null and alternatives) that are being tested against each other using at least one instrument for data collection followed by the analysis of the collected data, interpretation of the results of the analysis, and a sound conclusion regarding which of the hypotheses is likely to hold at a given level of confidence in the process. Dependent and independent variables are clearly defined in any research methodology and the data is collected and analyzed using controls within the experiment (see the Hot Air Balloon in Section 1.1.1). In pure sciences, the experiments are often done by hand and controls can be set with precision. However, in social sciences and business, quasi-experimental designs are used where the control variables are often not directly within the researcher's control.

For instance, if one were to be interested in studying the differences in heights of teenagers, there might not be any way to physically control for gender or racial differences directly. However, by choosing a representative sample of the population of teenagers, with similar proportions of gender or racial diversity as exists in the population, one can "control" for the effects of either gender or race when studying the differences in heights of teenagers.

1.1.4. Statistics versus Parameters

Population	Sample
Characteristics of population are called *parameters* that are usually Greek letters such as μ for mean, σ for standard deviation, and ρ for proportions	Characteristics of sample are called *statistics* that are usually regular letters such as $\bar{X}$ for mean, s for standard deviation, and p for proportions.
Impractical to measure accurately because true population size might be unknown or infinite	Selected using random sampling methods from the population and is expected to be representative of the population.
Estimates of parameters are obtained through samples and confidence intervals are used to give strength to these estimates.	Allows one to make estimates about population parameters by using the values of the sample statistics
Homogenous populations can be easier to estimate parameters for, because small samples can work in a representative manner.	Better sampling methods lead to better data collection and more reliable results.

1.1.5. Types of Sampling

A sample should always be representative of the population from which it is drawn otherwise any conclusions about the population based on that sample will no longer be applicable to the population. For instance, if one is thinking about buying grapes at a store, tasting a sample of berries is not going to give them any information about the grapes! However, if one tastes a sample grape from a box of grapes, they can draw a conclusion about how the grapes taste and decide whether to buy them or not without having to taste each grape in the box. The sample gives one an idea of what the "population" of the grapes, which can be assumed to be homogenous (has same characteristics), is going to taste like. However, if instead of a box of grapes one picked up a box of mixed fruits, tasting the grape alone might not give one the full idea of what the rest of the contents of that box are going to taste like! Thus, samples should be taken randomly but in a manner that they truly represent the population in order to avoid errors in decision-making regarding the population.

The basic types of randomized sampling methods that are often used to collect statistics are simple sampling, stratified sampling, cluster sampling, systematic sampling, and convenience sampling. These are discussed briefly here but if a researcher wanted to actually implement any of these sampling methods, more study of each type is recommended:

- A *simple sample* is exactly what the name indicates – a simple method of randomly choosing a certain number of subjects to test out of the full population under the assumption that the population is truly homogenous (all characteristics are similar in all subjects).

- A *stratified sample* is one where a "strata" or characteristic is chosen and the proportions of selected subjects in the sample are held constant with the proportions of the population. For instance, if 20% of the population of a city is Hispanic, any sample chosen from that city should aim to consist of about 20% Hispanic people.

- A *cluster sample* is one where the grouping is done randomly into clusters and thereafter a cluster is selected for sampling in order to draw conclusions about the population.

- A *systematic sample* consists of choosing a random starting point in a large dataset (population) and choosing every n^{th} observation to be included in the sample, where n itself is randomly chosen.

- A *convenience sample* is one that consists of easily available participants or observations. Out of all the types of sampling, this is the one that is most often used these days on social media and is the one that is the most loaded with biases and errors because convenience samples often have no way to be truly randomized. For instance, if one were to hold a poll on FaceBook or Instagram, the responses one receives on that poll are less likely to be random, even though it is a highly convenient method of collecting information from others.

Remember that if the sample has errors in terms of collection of data, any results obtained from any amount of rigorous analysis of that data will still have errors in terms of their implications for decision-making regarding the population. Some of the most common issues with sampling and sampling biases are as follows:

1. **<u>Biased samples give biased results</u>** – if the sample was done with a strategy in mind to prove (or disprove) some hypothesis, that bias will impact any outcome of analysis.

2. <u>Self-selection can create biases</u> – if surveys are given out to people in general in order to collect specific information, only those that are willing to share that information will self-select to participate. This, in itself, causes a bias in the information that is collected because it might not be representative of the population. Now refer back to point 1!

3. <u>Sample size matters</u> – larger samples give more complete information about the population and are always preferred to smaller samples. Students often ask what the ideal sample size is and while there are statistical methods that allow one to identify the "minimum sample size" (see Chapter 5), there is no sweet spot for the ideal sample size. That being said, samples of less than 30 observations require special distributions to be used for analysis and often lead to results that are not highly generalizable.

4. <u>Influencing responses in surveys while sampling</u> – if a question is loaded in a manner that either confuses the responder or makes them lean one way or another in their response, the data collected might be meaningless. For instance, asking a leading question such as "Kids

who do not share their toys with other kids are evil. Does your kid share their toys with their friends?" is not going to result in a large number of people giving an honest answer since nobody wants to call their own child evil. Now refer back to point 1!

5. <u>Self-funded or special-interest studies</u> – large and small for-profit and non-profit organizations and even individuals are able to collect data very easily using polls and studying social media patterns and participation from people these days. One must be very cautious of accepting this data for analysis and more importantly, one must be cautious about any results coming out of such "research" analysis because… refer back to point 1!

6. <u>Misleading use of data</u> – it is said that there are three types of lies in this world – lies, damned lies, and statistics! This is because one can always select a sample non-randomly in order to demonstrate whatever it is that one wants to demonstrate. It is up to the audience to learn how to discern how dependable the results are by checking what methodology was used to collect data and analyze and interpret the results. Refer back to point 1, again!

7. <u>Confounding variables matter</u> – there could be hidden variables, also called confounding variables that impact the relationship between two variables X and Y that might not be considered when doing the analysis of the relationship. If the sample omits these variables, the results of the analysis will no longer be reliable. For instance, if a relationship between age and weight of teenagers is being considered, but there is no information collected about the height of the individuals, the results would not be accurate. This is also a bias so refer back to point 1!

8. <u>Correlation does not mean causation</u> – just because two variables appear to "move" together does not mean that they cause each other. Such correlations are called spurious correlations and are often confused as being causations. Thus, X and Y can both be increasing simultaneously but neither of them is actually impacting the other. These types of analysis often lead to biases and meaningless results from a real-world perspective. Here is a funny article that shows the extremes of causation being assumed based upon correlations between two random and unrelated variables: https://www.datasciencecentral.com/spurious-correlations-15-examples/

1.2. Organizing Data

It is important to take raw data and convert it into meaningful and organized set of measures by using formulas and statistical techniques in order to test some hypotheses as a part of a research methodology. Data can be categorized into two primary types: Qualitative and Quantitative data. Qualitative data is collected on either a nominal scale or an ordinal scale. A nominal scale refers to data that is described using "names" such as hair color being black, brown, red, blonde, or gray. An ordinal scale gives some type of a specific order to categories such as ranking satisfaction on a scale of 1 to 5. Here, even though the scale is numerical a person ranking satisfaction as being 2 is not saying that it is double the satisfaction at the rank of 1 or that 4 indicates double the satisfaction at the level of 2. It simply means that the higher number indicates a higher satisfaction without the numbers being significant in their numeric form. Qualitative data is often described using words or letters and the numerical meaning comes from the frequency of the occurrence of a particular value.

On the other hand, Quantitative data deals exclusively with numbers and all the characteristics of numbers in their innate arithmetical form. If age is the variable of interest, then an 8-year-old is double the age of a 4-year-old. Quantitative data can be discrete (disjoint; whole numbers only) or continuous (decimals and all real numbers are included in this data). Quantitative data is either a count or a measure of the variable and can be used in its raw form for drawing conclusions regarding the hypothesis being tested. This data is also called interval data because the differences between data can be observed and can also be represented in a ratio scale (proportions) when required.

1.2.1. Frequency and Cumulative Frequency Distributions

In the real world, data is often given in raw form with rows of observations, that can often lead into the thousands. This makes it essential to learn how to create shorter tables to understand how that data is distributed or to get a clearer "picture" of the data distribution. Frequency is defined as the number of times a specific value of data occurs in the sample. Cumulative frequency is an accumulation of all previous frequencies. When arranging data in frequency tables, it is helpful to maintain some type of order in the way the datapoints are listed in order to allow the cumulative frequencies to be properly calculated. The sum of all frequencies in the table is equal to the number of observations in the sample. Each row in a frequency distribution refers to a specific class or value of the dataset in the first column and the observed (or expected) frequency of its occurrence in the second column. The third column is usually created for cumulative frequency, if desired. The frequency distribution tables are often helpful for calculating measures of central tendency (covered in Chapter 2).

When intervals or groups are considered instead of the direct variable values, one can create frequency distributions for each interval or group called Grouped Frequency Distributions. For instance, if the variable of interest is household incomes, creating a frequency distribution using each value of household income might be just as large as the dataset itself. However, creating groups or intervals such as "less than 50K", "50K to 100K", "100K to 200K", "200K to 500K", and "above 500K" could allow one to see how the data is spread in an easier manner. Note that the intervals do not have to be of the same size and each interval should have a unique upper and lower limit. In the household income example, these limits would need to be specified to ensure that a household making exactly 100K does not get counted in two separate intervals. Before software became the standard method to analyze large scale data, specific intra-interval values were found as the midpoint of two consecutive interval limits, but since data is now analyzed using software, it is less relevant to be that specific in manual calculations in the business world.

Example 1:1. Creating a Frequency Distribution.

Suppose a researcher is interested in collecting data on the number of hours a student at XYZ school spends per day in doing homework, denoted by variable *X*, and takes a sample of 20 children who go to the school and obtains the following results (in hours): 3, 0, 2, 1, 5, 3, 1, 3, 5, 3, 5, 1, 0, 0, 1, 1, 3, 0, 1, 3. Create a Ungrouped frequency distribution followed by a Grouped Frequency distribution and include cumulative frequencies.

Solution: In order to create a frequency distribution, first find the lowest and highest value of the data given and it can be seen that the lowest value of X is 0 and the highest value is 5. Thus, the table should have 6 rows with values 0, 1, 2, 3, 4, and 5. Thereafter, tally the total number of each value to obtain the corresponding frequency. In this dataset, there are 4 children who spend 0 hours, 6 children who spend 1 hour, 1 child who spends 2 hours, 6 children who spend 3 hours, 0 children who spend 4 hours and 3 children who spend 5 hours doing their homework every day. Table 1.1 shows the values of X and the corresponding frequencies f for each value of X on the left-hand side.

Cumulative frequency is the response to the question of how many children do their homework for a specific value of X or fewer hours? Thus, for 0 hours, the answer would be 4 children. For 1 hour, the answer would be the 6 children who do homework for 1 hour and the 4 children who do homework for 0 hours resulting in a total cumulative value of 10 children who do their homework for 1 hour or less. For $X = 2$, the cumulative frequency consists of frequencies of $X = 2$, $X = 1$ and $X = 0$ for a total of 11 children. This is repeated for all values of X and is shown in the third column of Table 1.1. Notice that all 20 children in the sample show up in the cumulative frequency of the last value of $X = 5$ because all the children in the sample do homework for 5 hours or less. Also, note that Excel formulas for calculating the cumulative frequency are included in the table under the fourth column but one can always choose to do this by hand.

In order to create a Grouped Frequency Distribution, one can combine the data values of number of hours studied into class intervals of equal or unequal length, as desired. In this case, three classes have been chosen: 0 to 1 hours, 2 to 3 hours, and 4 to 5 hours of homework every day. Note that these are called "interrupted" class intervals since one is ignoring the values between 1 and 2 and between 3 and 4. This is because the data is discrete and does not include intermediate values. If one were to manually calculate the exact class intervals, they would need to be adjusted on each end by 0.5 hours in order to get continuous class intervals to yield "-0.5-1.5 hours", "1.5 to 3.5 hours," and "3.5 to 5.5 hours." The interval distribution or class distribution yielded in this example is shown in Table 1.1 on the right-hand side.

Table 1.1. Frequency and Cumulative Frequency Distributions from Raw Data

	A	B	C	D	Class	f	c.f.
1	X	f	c.f.				
2	0	4	4	=B2			
3	1	6	10	=C2+B3			
4	2	1	11	=C3+B4	Class	f	c.f.
5	3	6	17	=C4+B5	0-1	10	10
6	4	0	17	=C5+B6	2-3	7	17
7	5	3	20	=C6+B7	4-5	3	20
8	TOTAL	20			TOTAL	20	

1.2.2. Relative Frequency and Cumulative Relative Frequency

Creating frequency distributions also allows one to compare two different datasets based upon the frequencies of each value or class of a variable of interest. If one were to collect data for the Example 1.1 from 10 male and 10 female students separately and end up with something like the first three columns in Table 1.2, one can compare the number of hours spent by each gender of students directly because the sample size of both male and female students is the same. For instance, one can see that 3 out of 10 male students spend 0 hours on their homework as compared to 1 out of 10 female students.

However, if the sample size is not the same for male and female, one can always use a method to standardize the frequency in order to compare distributions. This is achieved by identifying what is called the relative frequency of each value or class by using the formula for proportion for frequency *f* of each class and sample size *n*. In Table 1.2, the last two columns show the relative frequencies for male and female students (even though in this case the sample size is the same) because the relative frequency gives the proportion information as well.

$$relative\ frequency = \frac{f}{n}$$

Now, the comparison of proportions becomes easier than raw frequencies. For instance, 0.4 or 40% of male students spend one hour doing their homework as compared to 0.2 or 20% of the female students (see row 2 in the Table 1.2). Cumulative Relative Frequency is defined as the cumulative frequency of a given class divided by the total number of observations in the distribution using the following formula:

$$cumulative\ relative\ frequency = \frac{c.f.}{n}$$

Table 1.2. Comparing Frequencies for Male and Female Students

X	f males	f females	Relative f males	Relative f females
0	3	1	3/10 = 0.3	1/10 = 0.1
1	4	2	4/10 = 0.4	2/10 = 0.2
2	1	0	1/10 = 0.1	0/10 = 0
3	1	5	1/10 = 0.1	5/10 = 0.5
4	0	0	0/10 = 0	0/10 = 0
5	1	2	1/10 = 0.1	2/10 = 0.2
TOTAL	10	10		

Example 1:2. Relative and Cumulative Relative Frequency Distribution.

Continuing with the Example 1.1, where one researcher is interested in collecting data on the number of hours a student at XYZ school spends per day in doing homework, denoted by variable *X*, and takes a sample of 20 children who go to the school and obtains the following results (in hours): 3, 0, 2, 1, 5, 3, 1, 3, 5, 3, 5, 1, 0, 0, 1, 1, 3, 0, 1, 3. Using the basic frequency table and the class frequency tables obtained in Example 1.1 find the relative frequencies and the cumulative relative frequencies.

Solution: The relative frequencies and cumulative relative frequencies for Table 1.1 can be seen in Table 1.3. While Excel formulas have been used for calculating, note that this can also be done manually using the actual values shown in the formulas:

Table 1.3. Relative and Cumulative Relative Frequencies

	A	B	C	D	E	F	G
1	**X**	**f**	**rel. freq.**		**c.f.**	**cumu. Rel. freq.**	
2	0	4	0.2	=B2/$B$8	4	0.2	=E2/$B$8
3	1	6	0.3	=B3/$B$8	10	0.5	=E3/$B$8
4	2	1	0.05	=B4/$B$8	11	0.55	=E4/$B$8
5	3	6	0.3	=B5/$B$8	17	0.85	=E5/$B$8
6	4	0	0	=B6/$B$8	17	0.85	=E6/$B$8
7	5	3	0.15	=B7/$B$8	20	1	=E7/$B$8
8	**TOTAL**	**20**					
9							
10	**Class**	**f**	**rel. freq.**		**c.f.**	**cumu. Rel. freq.**	
11	0-1	10	0.5	=B11/$B$14	10	0.5	=E11/$B$14
12	2-3	7	0.35	=B12/$B$14	17	0.85	=E12/$B$14
13	4-5	3	0.15	=B13/$B$14	20	1	=E13/$B$14
14	**TOTAL**	**20**					

1.2.3. Cross-Tabulations and Contingency Tables

If information is available (data is collected) on just one variable, frequency distributions are used to create a tabular presentation of the data. However, if data is collected on more than one variable from a population and at least one of the two variables is categorical, cross-tabulations of the frequencies are often helpful in understanding the distribution of observations in that sample.

Suppose data is collected on the frequency of seatbelts used (always, most of the time, some of the time, rarely, never) and the gender of the drivers in the USA on 900 drivers as shown in Table 1.4 and one is interested in studying whether seat belt use (*dependent* variable) varies by gender (*independent* variable). The actual test of this dependence will be a two-way Chi-Squared test, which is discussed in Chapter 8. However, this section discusses the various ways in which this data gives the reader information regarding the characteristics of seat belt usage by gender.

Table 1.4. Observed Values in a Cross-Tabulation

Observed Values						
	Seat Belt Use					
Gender	**Always**	**Mostly**	**Sometimes**	**Rarely**	**Never**	**TOTAL**
Male	105	65	58	39	59	**326**
Female	300	110	65	44	55	**574**
TOTAL	**405**	**175**	**123**	**83**	**114**	**900**

One can create "contingency tables" using these cross tabulations and Total Values using the following formulas to find Row Percentages, Column Percentages, and Total Percentages, O_i represents the number of people in each of the cells in the table above:

$$Row \ \% = 100 \times \frac{O_i}{n_{row}}$$

$$Column \ \% = 100 \times \frac{O_i}{n_{column}}$$

$$Total\ \% = 100 \times \frac{O_i}{n_{total}}$$

The row percentage helps with answering the question, "what is the percentage seatbelt use by gender?" For instance, of the total 326 males, 105 always wear seatbelts, 65 mostly wear them, 58 wear them sometimes, 39 rarely wear seatbelts and 59 never wear seatbelts. Converting this into row percentage, one can say that 105/326 = 0.322 or 32.2% of men always wear seatbelts, whereas 65/326 = 0.199 or 19.9% of men mostly wear it, and 59/326 = 0.181 or 18.1% of men never wear seatbelts. One can do this for all the categories as shown below to see the corresponding row percentages of each cell. Moreover, the last row of demonstrates that out of all the people, 45% always wear seatbelts, 19.4% mostly wear them, 13.7% wear them sometimes, 9.2% rarely wear them and 12.7% of the people never wear seatbelts while driving their car.

Row Percentages						
	Seat Belt Use					
Gender	**Always**	**Mostly**	**Sometimes**	**Rarely**	**Never**	**TOTAL**
Male	32.2%	19.9%	17.8%	12.0%	18.1%	**100.0%**
Female	52.3%	19.2%	11.3%	7.7%	9.6%	**100.0%**
TOTAL	**45.0%**	**19.4%**	**13.7%**	**9.2%**	**12.7%**	**100.0%**

The column percentage will help answer the question, "what is the percentage of males and what percentage of females in each seat-belt usage category?" Looking at the category of "Always," one can see that of the total 405 people who always wear seatbelts, 105 are men and 300 are women. Converting this into column percentage, one can say that 105/405 = 0.259 or 25.9% of people who always wear seatbelts are men, whereas 300/405 = 0.741 or 74.1% are women. One can do this for all the categories as shown below to see the corresponding column percentages of each cell. Moreover, of the total number of observations included in the study, 36.2% are males and 63.8% are females.

Column Percentages						
	Seat Belt Use					
Gender	**Always**	**Mostly**	**Sometimes**	**Rarely**	**Never**	**TOTAL**
Male	25.9%	37.1%	47.2%	47.0%	51.8%	**36.2%**
Female	74.1%	62.9%	52.8%	53.0%	48.2%	**63.8%**
TOTAL	**100%**	**100%**	**100%**	**100%**	**100%**	**100%**

The total percentages help one to represent what the relative frequency is of each cell in this cross-tabulation. So, the 105 males who always wear seatbelts are what percentage of the total number of observations? For this one would use the total percentage formula, which would result in 105/900 = 0.117 or 11.7%. One can do this for all the cells to get the corresponding percentages for each cell in the context of the total number of observations, 900. Notice that the Total percentages by gender are the same as the ones obtained in the Row Percentage calculations and the Total percentages by seat belt use are the same as the ones obtained in the Column Percentage calculations shown above.

	Total Percentages					
	Seat Belt Use					
Gender	Always	Mostly	Sometimes	Rarely	Never	TOTAL
Male	11.7%	7.2%	6.4%	4.3%	6.6%	36.2%
Female	33.3%	12.2%	7.2%	4.9%	6.1%	63.8%
TOTAL	45.0%	19.4%	13.7%	9.2%	12.7%	100.0%

1.3. Displaying Data Graphically

Sometimes the best way to represent data is by creating or demonstrating it in a graphical form, which allows the audience to visualize the pattern that exists in the dataset. Some of the most commonly used graphs are Pie Charts, Bar Graphs and Histograms, and Scatter Plots and Line Charts. While Pie Charts and Bar Graphs can be used for both Qualitative and Quantitative Data, the Scatter Plots and Line Charts make most sense when used for Quantitative Data. This section covers these basic types of graphs with extensive use of the Excel Software. Is it not difficult to create the graphs manually, but with the use of Excel (or other software), the process is easier, and the output is cleaner. For the sake of ease in comparing different graphical output, the data on number of hours of homework per day for a sample of 20 students from Example 1.1 and 1.2 will be used for Pie Charts, Bar graphs and Histograms. Since Scatter Plots and Line Charts make more sense with two variables included, a different dataset will be used for those.

1.3.1. Pie Charts

Pie Charts are circular and are named as such because of their shape, which looks like a pie with different "slices" representing different frequencies of occurrence of a particular category of a variable. The only requirement for creating a meaningful pie chart is that the total of all relative frequencies of all the categories should be 100%. The Pie chart of the X-variable can be created by following the given steps in Excel:
1. Highlight the Frequency Column (see Table 1.3, column B)
2. Go to the Insert Tab (next to the Home Tab) in Excel and click on "Recommended Charts" and select "Pie"

3. Once the "OK" button is clicked a Pie Chart similar to the following image on the left will pop up in the Excel worksheet

4. Notice that the categories are showing from 1 to 6 even though the data categories are 0 to 5, so the Values can be edited by going to the Chart Design Tab and clicking on Select Data option and editing the Category labels. Other cosmetic changes can also be made by using the Chart Styles options. The Chart Title can be edited as well. The way to edit the categories is shown in the above figure on the right-hand side. Figure 1.6 shows the final output of the Pie Chart that represents the Number of Hours spent in doing homework per day for the sample of 20 children. Note that the percentages of each category are included in the Pie Chart and are the same as the relative frequency values even though only the frequency column was selected.

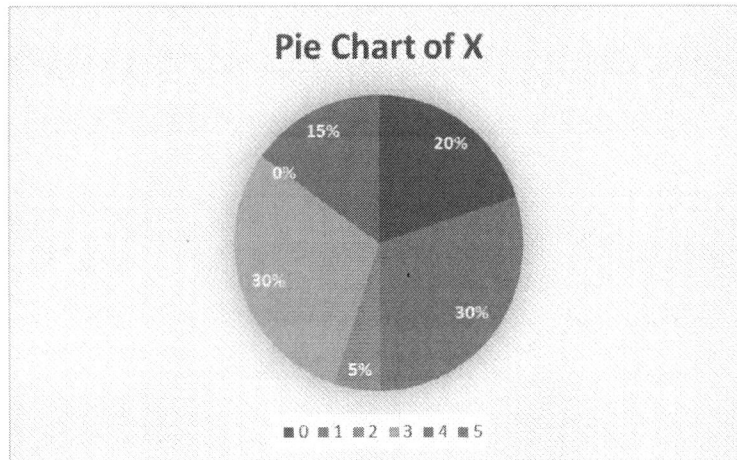

Figure 1.6. Pie Chart of Number of Homework Hours Per Day

1.3.2. Bar Graphs and Histograms

Bar Graphs typically refer to horizontal graphs with the observed categories on the vertical axis and the frequencies on the horizontal axis. The Column Graphs are the ones that most people associate with bar graphs with the categories laid on the horizontal axis and the frequencies on the vertical axis. See Figure 1.7. The image on the left-hand side is a Bar graph whereas the image on the right-hand side is a Column Graph. Both of these were created using the same steps as the steps for the Pie Chart with the difference that Bar Graph and Column Graph options were chosen instead of the Pie Chart option in Step 2.

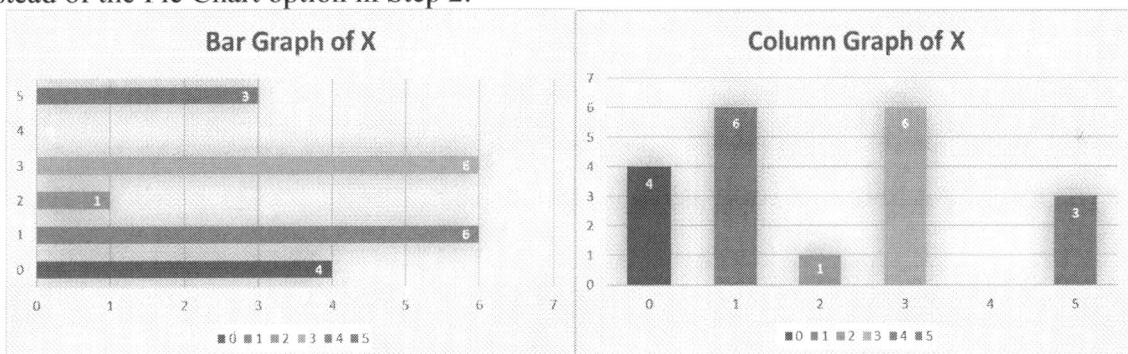

Figure 1.7. Bar and Column Graphs for Number of Homework Hours Per Day

A Histogram is a special type of a column graph that allows for the frequency distribution of the data to be presented without having to organize the data manually. There are two ways to create a histogram using Excel. First, highlight the values of X (either Raw X values or the organized values in column A of the Table 1.3 and go to Insert Tab and choose "Histogram." The default Histogram that will pop up is shown in Figure 1.8 on the top left-hand side. Notice that only two categories are shown on the horizontal axis. This can be edited manually by double-clicking on the axis and formatting it so that the "bin width" of the Histogram is set to 2 as shown in the figure on the top right-hand side. Once this number is changed to 2, and other edits are made, the bottom figure can be obtained.

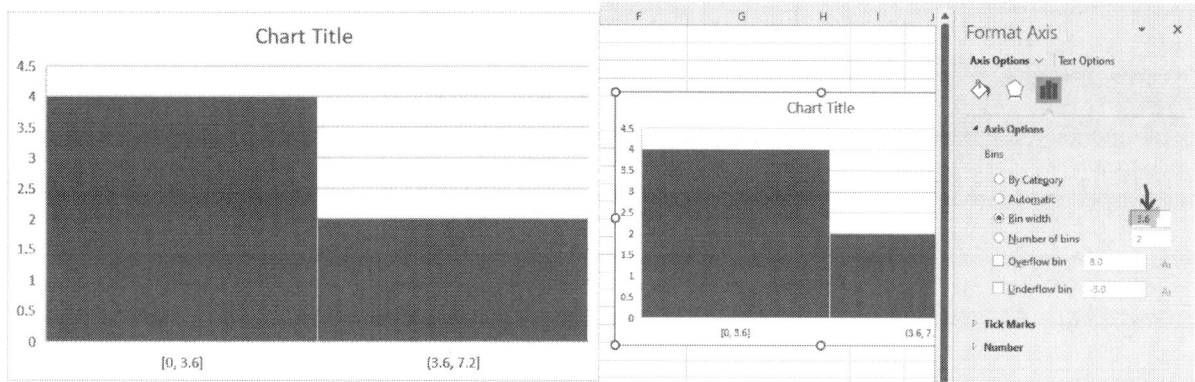

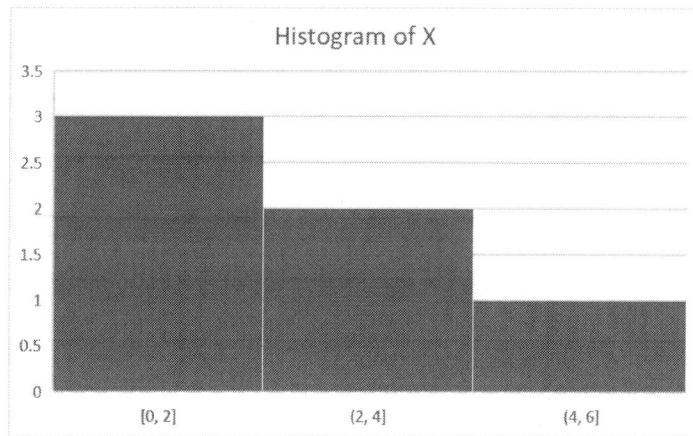

Figure 1.8. Histogram for Number of Hours of Homework Per Day

A slightly more complex method can be utilized for large scale datasets by going to the Data Tab and Selecting the Data Analysis Tab (if Data Analysis is activated in the Excel Options) to insert a Histogram. For instance, by using the raw data input, the following Histogram is created without having to adjust any bin (interval sizes) manually and the corresponding frequency distribution is also given as the output alongside the graph. More customizations can be made by adjusting the inputs in the Data Analysis tab for bins, if required.

Bin	Frequency
0	4
1.25	6
2.5	1
3.75	6
More	3

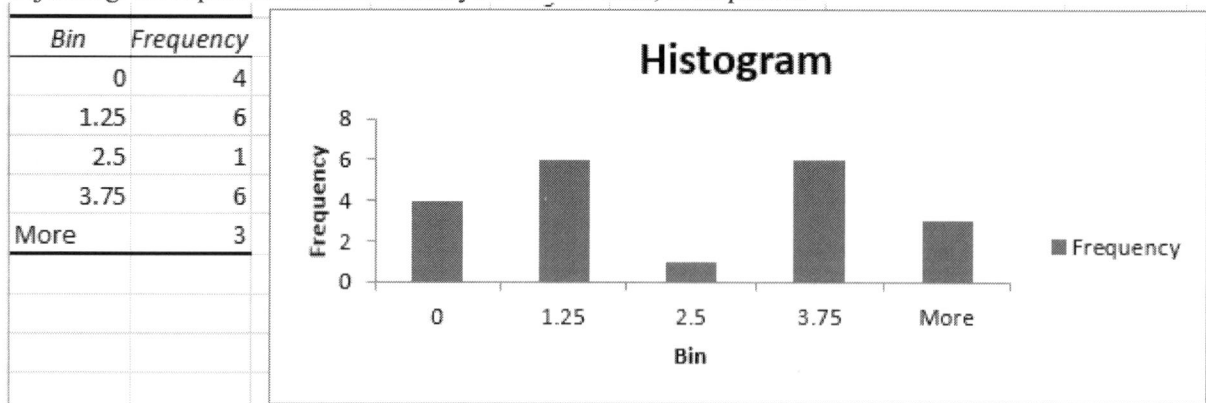

1.3.3. Scatter Plots and Line Charts

Scatter Plots make more sense when one either has a time series data where time is represented on the horizontal axis and a series of observations of a variable of interest over time are plotted on the vertical axis, or of if there is data available for any two variables that are expected to be related in some way, as seen in Section 1.1.2 for Commonly Used Mathematical Functions in Statistics. The process for creating the Scatter Plots (or Line Graphs) is similar to the process used for inserting Pie Charts and Bar Graphs in Excel. The only difference is that both the columns that have data in them are selected prior to choosing which type of Graph to insert.

If information is collected on two variables, say age of a teenager in years (X) and the weight of the teenager in lbs. (Y), these can be plotted using scatter plots (dots represent each point) to identify if there is a relationship between age and weight among teenagers. Note that line charts will not make much sense in this case because the data for both variables is randomized, even though it is easy to choose the line option from the Scatter Plot option if one chooses to do so. Also, important to note is that if the axes are not adjusted for the minimum and maximum options correctly, the relationship between the X and Y will not appear to be clear but can show up as being "clustered" since the numbers in both variables are significantly higher than single digits. Figure 1.9 shows the Scatter Plot for this dataset.

Scatter Plot for Age and Weight	
Age (Years)	Weight (lbs)
14.7	112
14.9	92
15.2	92
15.5	146
16.1	123
16.4	90
16.8	107
16.8	134
17.1	143
17.3	148
17.7	140
17.7	86
17.9	102
18.2	127
18.8	135
19.2	125
19.3	137
19.4	142

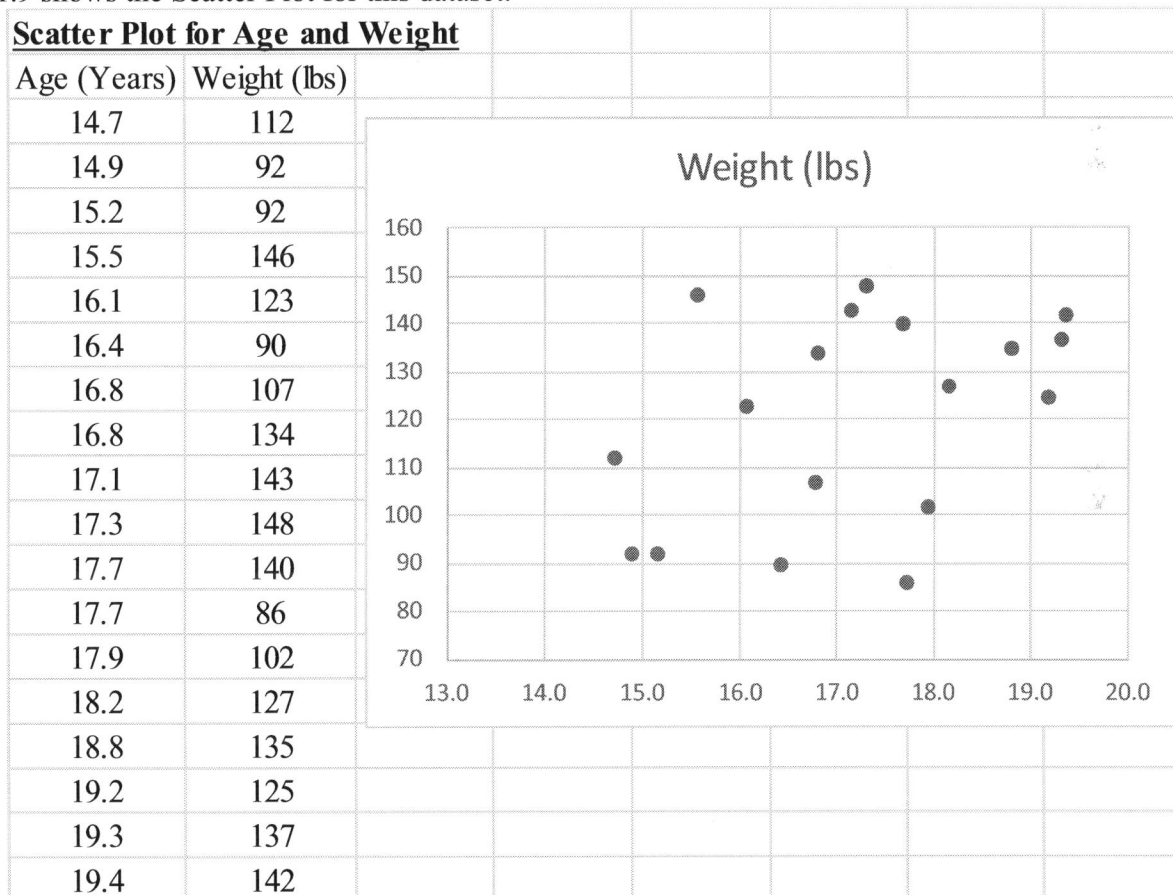

Figure 1.9. Scatter Plot for Age vs. Weight of Teenagers

On the other hand, if Monthly Inflation Rate data was collected from January 2021 to May 2022 (most current at the time of writing this book), a scatter plot (with the dots representing each point) might not be very useful but a line chart (with a line connecting the dots) can be created in Excel as shown in Figure 1.10 because the horizontal axis is not in a random order.

Time Series Line Chart										
Month	Inflation	Annual Est.								
Jan-21	0.43%	5.16%								
Feb-21	0.55%	6.60%								
Mar-21	0.71%	8.52%								
Apr-21	0.82%	9.84%								
May-21	0.80%	9.60%								
Jun-21	0.93%	11.16%								
Jul-21	0.48%	5.76%								
Aug-21	0.21%	2.52%								
Sep-21	0.27%	3.24%								
Oct-21	0.83%	9.96%								
Nov-21	0.49%	5.88%								
Dec-21	0.31%	3.72%								
Jan-22	0.84%	10.08%								
Feb-22	0.91%	10.92%								
Mar-22	1.34%	16.08%								
Apr-22	0.56%	6.72%								
May-22	1.10%	13.20%								

Monthly Inflation Rate in the USA

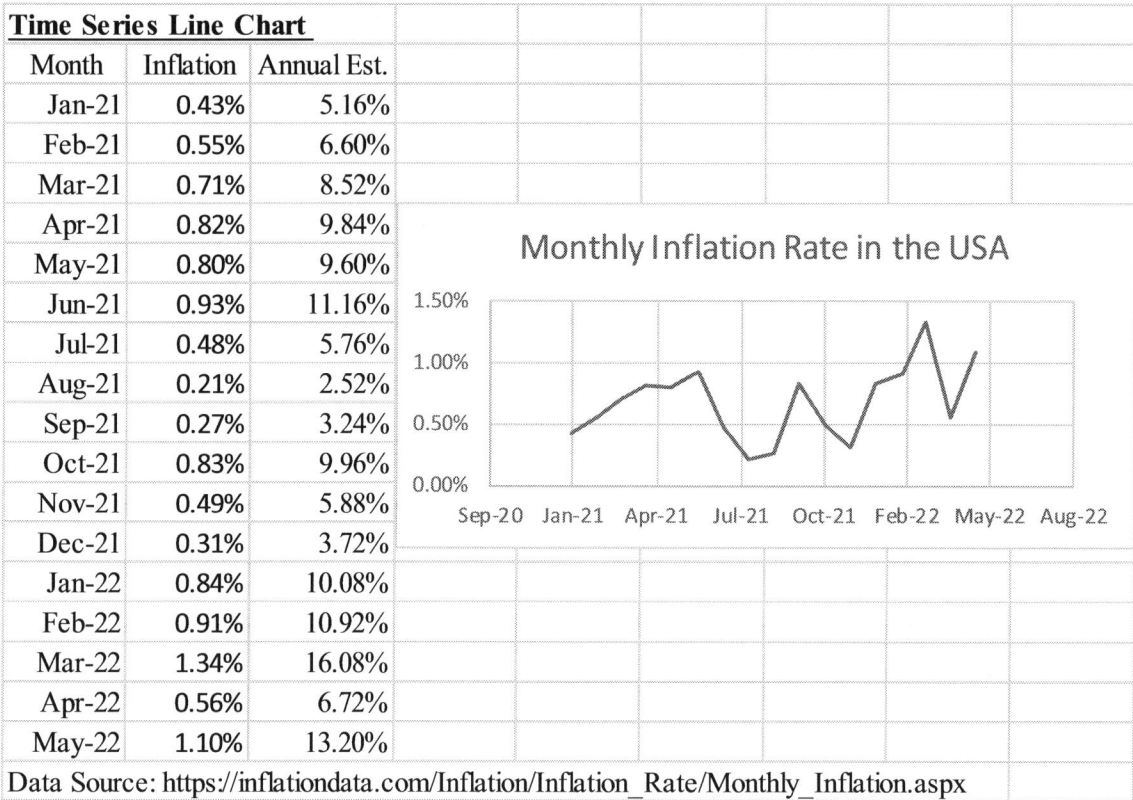

Data Source: https://inflationdata.com/Inflation/Inflation_Rate/Monthly_Inflation.aspx

Figure 1.10. Time Series Plot for Monthly Inflation Rate in the USA

Chapter 2. Measures of Central Tendency and Variability

The first question that new explorers of datasets often face is, "what is the purpose of all of this?" Chapter 1 described how data needs to be made meaningful by being presented in a manner that captures the essence of the dataset. While graphs allow one to see trends and patterns in the variable of interest, they do not always capture the intricacies and hidden information that can be extracted from the dataset to show how the variable of interest behaves or what its expected value could be. This is where statistics plays a crucial role because it allows one to break down the information in the datasets into bite-sized informational pieces. If only one variable of interest is studied at a time, "descriptive" analysis of that variable allows one to compare values obtained in different datasets or over time. Thus, only one variable will be focused upon at any given time in this chapter. Multiple variables considered simultaneously will be introduced in later chapters of this book.

Consider an example of two different statistics classes taught by Professor K and Professor L in the same institution. If the average student grade in both classes is discovered to be 85, should a student be indifferent in terms of which professor they register for? Now, instead of just the average, there should be an interest in the "spread" or the variability that occurs in each class. Thus, when one begins to look at statistics, they should want to focus on two primary aspects of any dataset – the average or the central tendency and the fluctuations within the dataset or the variability!

2.1. Measures of Central Tendency

A single number that represents what is typical or average of a given set of data is called a *Measure of Central Tendency*. When one hears the word "average," the natural assumption is that it refers to the midpoint of any data distribution. But there could be various types of midpoints – the three most common ones are the *Arithmetic Mean*, the *Median*, and the *Mode*. There are also other ways that data is often broken down into smaller clusters in order to convey pertinent information by using measures such as quartiles, percentiles, or the weighted mean. This section discusses all of these in some detail with their relevant mathematical formulas and conceptual descriptions.

Although the standard way to approach the values of the averages is to use the order of "mean, median, and mode," it is often easier to approach them in the order of "mode, median, and mean" when one first begins the journey into data and formulas. This section starts with the simplest "average" called the Mode, then proceeds to discussing the Median and related measures like quartiles and percentiles. Thereafter, the Arithmetic Mean and how it can be calculated in various types of quantitative datasets is discussed.

2.1.1. Mode

The Mode of a dataset (or distribution of all values of a variable) is defined as the value of the variable that occurs with the highest frequency in the dataset. In simpler terms, mode is the most frequent or most typical or most common value in a distribution. The symbol used for Mode is "Mo" and the advantage of mode is that it can be used for both quantitative and qualitative datasets.

Sometimes, a distribution has more than one mode, or in simpler terms there is more than one value that has the same higher frequency than the others. In that case, one can say that there are two (or more) modes in the distribution. Figure 2.1 shows the distribution with only one mode on the left-hand side and a bi-modal distribution on the right-hand side. It is crucial to remember that mode is NOT the *frequency* of the most frequent score but the *value* of the most frequent score in a dataset.

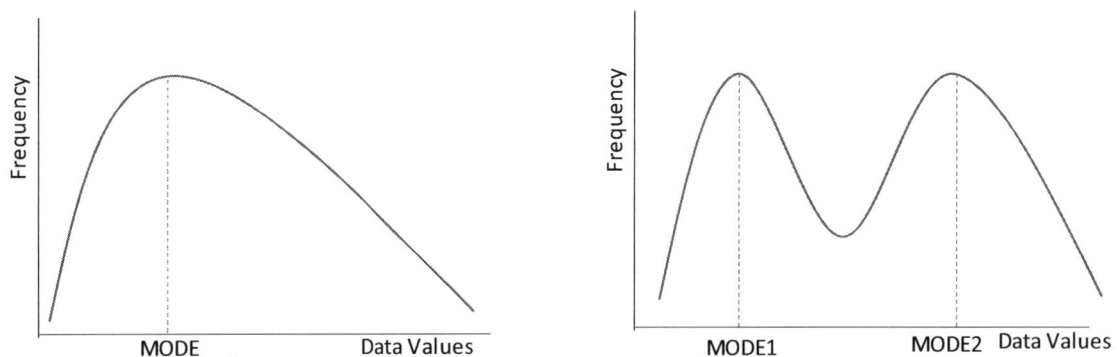

Figure 2.1. Representation of Mode in regular and bimodal distributions

Example 2:1 Qualitative Data.

What is the Mode of the race/ethnicity variable in a sample of 10 business owners in San Antonio if the following information is collected?

Table 2.1 Business Owner Race/Ethnicities in San Antonio Sample

Business #	Race/Ethnicity
1	non-Hisp Black
2	non-Hisp White
3	Hisp Black
4	Hisp White
5	non-Hisp White
6	Hisp White
7	Hisp White
8	Hisp Black
9	non-Hisp Black
10	Hisp White

Solution: In order to find the Mode, this data needs to be organized in a better way. Remember, that in this case, the numbers 1-10 are simply used to number the business and do not reflect any particular order. One can see that there are 4 categories of Race/Ethnicity combination that have been considered in Table 2.1. Thus, one can calculate the total number of businesses that fall into each of those categories as shown in Table 2.2.

Table 2.2 Frequency Distribution of Business Owner Race/Ethnicities

Race/Ethnicity	Frequency
Hisp Black	2
Hisp White	4
non-Hisp Black	2
non-Hisp White	2
TOTAL	10

Now that one can identify the frequencies of each type of business ownership, it is easy to see that 4 businesses out of the 10 are owned by Hisp White businesspeople. Thus, the MODE of this distribution is "Hisp White." (Caution: one of the stumbling blocks that students often face is that they say "4" is the mode but that is simply the highest occurring frequency value and not the mode.)

Example 2:2. Quantitative Data

What is the Mode of the age variable in a sample of 10 business owners in San Antonio if the information is collected as shown in Table 2.3?

Table 2.3 Business Owner Ages in San Antonio Sample

Business #	Age of Owner
1	45
2	52
3	25
4	32
5	55
6	56
7	55
8	29
9	31
10	55

Solution: In order to find the Mode, one needs to organize this data in a better way. Remember, that in this case, the numbers 1-10 are simply used to number the business and do not reflect any particular order. The easiest way to identify the mode in this case would be to sort the data for the variable "Age" in an ascending (or descending) order as shown in Table 2.4 below.

Table 2.4 Data Sorted by Age of Business Owners or Excel Method

Business #	Age of Owner
3	25
8	29
9	31
4	32
1	45
2	52
5	55
7	55
10	55
6	56

	A	B
1	Business #	Age of Owner
2	1	45
3	2	52
4	3	25
5	4	32
6	5	55
7	6	56
8	7	55
9	8	29
10	9	31
11	10	55
12		
13	Mode =	55
14	Formula -->	=MODE(B2:B11)

Now, one can see that the number "55" occurs with the highest frequency (3 times), implying that the Mode of Age for business owners in San Antonio is 55. Excel provides one with an easier way to find the mode for raw quantitative data as shown in the Table on the right.

It is important to note here that if the data is given in a frequency distribution format, Excel's "Mode" formula will not work. However, if the data is already in a frequency distribution, the value of the variable corresponding to the highest frequency will be the mode as shown in Table 2.5, and no formula will be necessary.

Table 2.5. Frequency Distribution of Ages

Age of Owner	Frequency	
25	1	
29	1	
31	1	
32	1	
45	1	
52	1	
55	3	MODE
56	1	
SUM	10	

2.1.2. Median, Quartiles, and Percentiles

Medians, Quartiles, and Percentiles offer a way to rank and split the distribution of values of a quantitative variable in different ways. The Median of a quantitative dataset (or distribution of all values of a variable) is defined as the value of the variable that splits the data evenly into two parts, 50% of the values being lower than the Median and 50% of the values being higher than the Median.

In a similar manner, quartiles (think about "quarters") divide the distribution of the values of the quantitative variable into 4 equal parts. The value of the first quartile (*Q1*) splits the distribution as 25% of the values being lower than *Q1* and 75% being higher. The second quartile (*Q2*) is the same as the Median since it has 50% of all values below and 50% of all values higher than the *Q2*. The third quartile (*Q3*) splits the dataset such that 25% of all values are higher than the *Q3* whereas 75% of the values in the distribution are lower than the *Q3*.

Percentiles also follow this general idea of splitting the distribution, but instead of two or four parts, percentiles divide the distribution of quantitative values into 100 equal parts, hence the term "per cent" or "per hundred" being a part of the percentile. In regular language, people often confuse the term *percentile* with *percentage* but that is an incorrect way to consider percentiles. For instance, a student can score a 65% on an exam but can have a percentile rank of 89%. This implies that the student's score of 65% is higher than 89% of the population of all students who take the exam. Percentiles are often used in large datasets to get a better grasp on what the data indicates.

Remember that in order to cut a piece of paper into two parts, one needs to only make ONE "cut" and to cut it up into four equal parts, one would need to make THREE "cuts." Similarly, in order to cut the paper into 100 equal parts, one would need to make 99 cuts. This is the reason there are only 3 values of the quartiles (*Q1*, *Q2*, and *Q3*) and 99 values of the percentiles. Figure 2.2 shows how the median and quartiles break up the dataset.

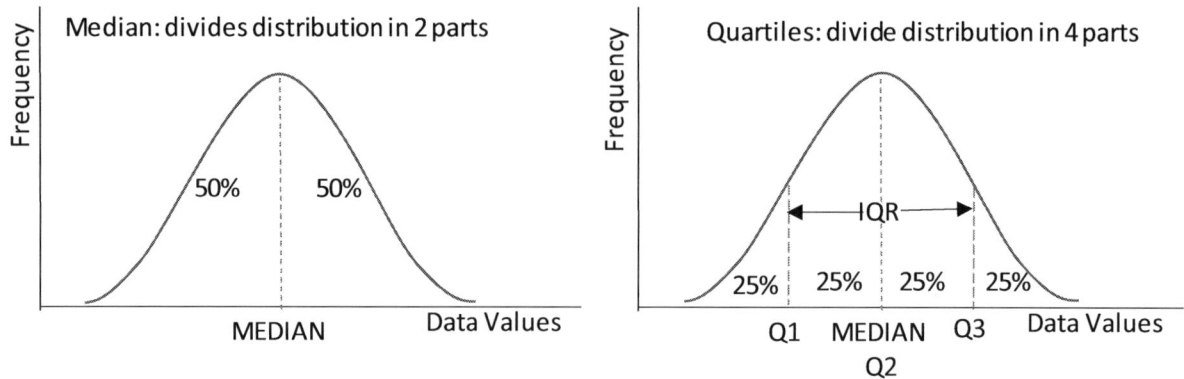

Figure 2.2. Visual Representation of Median and Quartiles

Now that the reader has a basic idea of what Median, Quartiles, and Percentiles are, they can proceed to understand how these can be calculated for actual values of a variable in a dataset. The basic formulas for calculating these are given below but note that the examples that follow the formulas are more likely to help understand how to apply these formulas correctly in the real world, and how Excel can help with identifying the correct values. It is also important to note that cumulative relative frequency tables (See Section 1.2.2 in Chapter 1) can help with identifying median, quartiles, and percentiles more efficiently.

Median Formula: If the total number of observations (n) in a dataset is an even number, and the data is sorted in an ascending manner, the *median is the value* of the $n/2^{th}$ observation. If n is an odd number, the *median is the value* of the $(n + 1)/2^{th}$ observation.

Quartile Formula: The "median" of the first half of the distribution is $Q1$ and the "median" of the second half of the distribution is $Q3$. The difference between the values of $Q3$ and $Q1$ is known as the Interquartile Range, which represents the "middle 50%" of the distribution.

$$IQR = Q3 - Q1$$

Percentile Formula: In order to find the kth percentile, where k is a number between 1 and 99, the value of the observation ($n \times k$) is used. If one is interested in calculating the percentile corresponding to a specific value in the dataset, and X represents the number of values lower than the value of interest, Y represents the frequency of the value of interest, and n is the total number of observations in the dataset, the percentile is obtained by using the following formula:

$$Percentile = \frac{(X + 0.5Y)}{n} \times 100$$

Example 2:3 Median, Quartiles, and Percentiles for Raw Data

A sample of 30 students is taken from one of the statistics classes offered at ABC university. A researcher is interested in studying their ages and the following values are observed. Answer the questions given below the values:
18, 21, 22, 25, 26, 27, 29, 30, 31, 33, 42, 32, 25, 22, 21, 18, 21, 22, 25, 26, 27, 29, 30, 31, 33, 42, 32, 25, 22, 21.
1. What is the median age in this distribution?

2. What are the quartiles for this distribution? What is the *IQR*?
3. Find the 65th percentile in this distribution.
4. What is the percentile rank of an individual who is 32 years old?

Solution: There are two approaches to solving this problem; one is to use raw data and the second is to create a frequency distribution table to calculate the relevant answers. Both methods are covered in this solution and will also allow for comparing the answers obtained using each method.

Method 1: Raw Data Method - As seen in Table 2.6, there are 30 observations in this dataset. To use Excel in-built formulas, there is no need to organize the data in an ascending form. However, if one were to manually calculate it, the data should be sorted in an ascending manner. The left-hand side shows how to calculate answers using the inbuilt formulas in Excel, whereas the right-hand side shows how to prepare the data for manual calculations. For the manual calculations, please refer to the ascending order sorted data including observation numbers on the right, in the Table 2.6.

1. *What is the median age in this distribution?* Since the total number of observations are 30, one can identify the middle observation, as the $30/2 = 15^{th}$ observation. The value of Age for the 15th observation is 26, so the median of this distribution is "26."

2. *What are the quartiles for this distribution? What is the IQR?* For *Q1*, one would find the "median" of the first half of the distribution. Since there are 15 observations in the top 50% of the data, one can identify the middle observation as the $(15 + 1)/2 = 8^{th}$ observation. The value of Age for the 8th observation is 22, so *Q1* is "22". Similarly, for *Q3*, one would find the "median" of the second half of the distribution. This portion refers to the 16th to the 30th observations. Thus, the middle observation is the $(16+30)/2 = 23^{rd}$ observation. The value of Age for the 23rd observation is 31, so *Q3* is "31." Notice that the Excel answer is a bit different, but since it rounds up to 31, there is no need to focus too heavily on the nuances of how the frequencies of ages can impact the calculations of *Q1* and *Q3*. Moreover, the value of the *IQR* $= Q3 - Q1 = 31 - 22 = 9$. Thus, one can say that the middle 50% of the class are between 22 and 31 years old.

3. *Find the 65th percentile in this distribution.* To find the 65th percentile, first multiply the total number of observations 30 with 0.65 to obtain 19.5. Since one cannot have a 19.5^{th} observation, it can be rounded up to go to the 20th observation. The value of Age for the 20th observation is 29 so one can say that the 65th percentile in this distribution is "29."

4. *What is the percentile rank of an individual who is 32 years old?* There are 24 people who are under the age of 32 in the dataset, so $X = 24$. The value 32 has a frequency of 2 in the dataset, so $Y = 2$. The $n = 30$ since that is the total sample size. Applying the formula for percentile, one can find that an individual aged 32 is at the 83rd percentile:

$$Percentile = \frac{(X + 0.5Y)}{n} \times 100 = \frac{(24 + 0.5 * 2)}{30} \times 100 \approx 83\%$$

Table 2.6. Using Excel to Calculate Median, etc. in Raw Data

	A	B	C
1	AGE		
2	18		
3	21		
4	22		
5	25		
6	26		
7	27		
8	29		
9	30		
10	31		
11	33		
12	42		
13	32		
14	25		
15	22		
16	21		
17	18		
18	21		
19	22		
20	25		
21	26		
22	27		
23	29		
24	30		
25	31		
26	33		
27	42		
28	32		
29	25		
30	22		
31	21		
32			
33	n =	30	=COUNT(A2:A31)
34	Median =	26	=MEDIAN(A2:A31)
35	Q1 =	22	=QUARTILE(A2:A31,1)
36	Q3 =	30.75	=QUARTILE(A2:A31,3)
37	IQR =	8.75	=B36-B35
38	65th Percentile =	29	=PERCENTILE(A2:A31,0.65)
39	Rank of Person Age 32 =	82.7	=PERCENTRANK(A2:A31, 32)*100

Observation #	AGE
1	18
2	18
3	21
4	21
5	21
6	21
7	22
8	22
9	22
10	22
11	25
12	25
13	25
14	25
15	26
16	26
17	27
18	27
19	29
20	29
21	30
22	30
23	31
24	31
25	32
26	32
27	33
28	33
29	42
30	42

Method 2. Frequency Distribution Method - Table 2.7 shows the data in the frequency distribution form, based on the raw data using the methods discussed in Section 1.2.1 of Chapter 1.

1. *What is the median age in this distribution?* One needs to identify the value for variable *AGE*, where the cumulative relative frequency is 50%. As one can see, value of 25 corresponds to a cumulative relative frequency of 46.67% that is less than 50%. However, the value of 26 corresponds to the cumulative relative frequency of 53.33% implying that the halfway point of the distribution would be Age of 26. Thus, 26 is the median.

2. *What are the quartiles for this distribution? What is the IQR?* For *Q1*, one would look for the cumulative relative frequency value of 25%. As one can see, the Age of 21 corresponds to 20.00% of the data whereas 22 corresponds with 33.33% of the data, implying that the 25% value falls into the group of Age 22. Thus, *Q1* is 22. In a similar manner, one can identify the

75% value as being in the group of Age 31, resulting in *Q3* being 31. One would calculate the *IQR* by simply taking the difference between *Q3* and *Q1*, which would be 9.

Table 2.7 Frequency Distribution Method

AGE	Frequency	Relative Frequency	Cumulative Relative Frequency
18	2	6.67%	6.67%
21	4	13.33%	20.00%
22	4	13.33%	33.33%
25	4	13.33%	46.67%
26	2	6.67%	53.33%
27	2	6.67%	60.00%
29	2	6.67%	66.67%
30	2	6.67%	73.33%
31	2	6.67%	80.00%
32	2	6.67%	86.67%
33	2	6.67%	93.33%
42	2	6.67%	100.00%
TOTAL	**30**		

3. *Find the 65th percentile in this distribution.* To find the 65th percentile, look at the column for cumulative relative frequency to find which group the 65% value falls into. One can see that it falls in the group of Age 29, implying that the 65th percentile *AGE* value in the distribution is "29."

4. *What is the percentile rank of an individual who is 32 years old? T*o calculate the percentile rank of an individual in the 32 group, look at the cumulative relative frequency of the Age group of 32, which is 86.67%. There are two people who are 32 years old in the table and the cumulative relative frequency of the lower group (Age 31) is 80%. Thus, one can find the midpoint between 80% and 86.67% for an approximate value of 83rd percentile.

Notice, that as data gets organized in different manners, going from raw data (using Excel functions) to data in ascending order (using manual formulas) to data in a frequency distribution (Method 2), one might be sacrificing some "accuracy" in the results. However, since the differences in answers are not large, it might be worth pursuing more efficient methods like the Frequency Distribution Method or even the raw data Excel method, whenever possible, as opposed to the manual method of calculations.

2.1.3. Mean and Weighted Mean

The Mean of a dataset typically refers to the arithmetic average of all values of a variable in the dataset. It is obtained by adding the set of all values of the variable and dividing the sum by the total number of observations of the variable. The standard representation of the arithmetic mean is $\bar{X}$ (read as X-bar) for the variable of interest X, or μ (Greek letter "mu"). The basic formula for the mean is:

$$\bar{X} = \frac{\sum X_i}{n} = \frac{sum\ of\ all\ values\ of\ X}{total\ number\ of\ values\ of\ X}$$

where X_i represents all the values of variable X and n represents the number of values of X available in the dataset. When using frequency distributions, the following formula can be used for finding the mean:

$$\bar{X} = \frac{\sum f_i X_i}{\sum f_i} = \frac{sum\ of\ product\ of\ frequency\ and\ value\ of\ each\ X}{sum\ of\ frequencies}$$

where f_i represents the frequency of each value X_i of variable X. When using grouped frequency distributions, if one assumes that "m" is the midpoint of each group, the following formula can be used for finding the mean:

$$\bar{X} = \frac{\sum f_i m_i}{\sum f_i} = \frac{sum\ of\ product\ of\ frequency\ and\ midpoint\ of\ each\ group}{sum\ of\ frequencies\ of\ all\ groups}$$

Weighted mean refers to the "mean of means" which allows one to find the overall average of a variable of interest X, for which multiple samples have been collected. The calculation of weighted mean for a variable of interest X, such that $\bar{X}_j$ represents the average of each of the j different samples collected and n_j represents the sample size for each of them uses the following formula:

$$\overline{X_w} = \frac{\sum n_j \bar{X}_j}{\sum n_j} = \frac{sum\ of\ product\ of\ average\ and\ sample\ size\ of\ each\ sample}{sum\ of\ all\ sample\ sizes}$$

A few examples will help with learning how to apply all these formulas correctly for different types of data distributions.

Example 2:4. Finding the Mean for Differently Organized Data

A sample of 30 students is taken from one of the statistics classes offered at ABC university. A researcher is interested in studying their ages and the following values are observed. Answer the questions given below the values:
18, 21, 22, 25, 26, 27, 29, 30, 31, 33, 42, 32, 25, 22, 21, 18, 21, 22, 25, 26, 27, 29, 30, 31, 33, 42, 32, 25, 22, 21.
1. Calculate the mean of the raw distribution of this data.
2. Calculate the mean using the frequency distribution of this data.
3. Calculate the mean using the grouped frequency distribution of this data (see Table 2.8) below:

Table 2.8. Example 2.4 Grouped Frequency Distribution

AGE Group	f = Frequency
18 to 21	6
22 to 25	8
26 to 29	6
30 to 33	8
34 to 37	0
38 to 42	2

Solution: In order to solve this problem (notice the numbers used are the same as the numbers used in the Example 2.3), one can use Excel or can manually calculate the answers. For each of the questions posed, answers are obtained using both these methods below:

1. Calculate the mean of the raw distribution of this data.

The manual calculation method for solving this is shown in the yellow-shaded area in Table 2.9 above the Excel solution using the direct formula in Table 2.9.

Table 2.9. Solving for Raw Data using Excel

	A	B	C	D
1	**RAW DATA METHOD**			
2				
3	**AGE**			
4	18	$\bar{X} = \dfrac{\sum X_i}{n} = \dfrac{sum\ of\ all\ values\ of\ X}{total\ number\ of\ values\ of\ X}$		
5	21			
6	22			
7	25	= 808/30		
8	26	= 26.93		
9	27			
10	29			
11	30			
12	31			
13	33			
14	42	**n =**	30	=COUNT(A4:A33)
15	32	**Total sum of X**	808	=SUM(A4:A33)
16	25	**Mean of X (X-bar)**	26.93	=AVERAGE(A4:A33)
17	22			
18	21			
19	18			
20	21			
21	22			
22	25			
23	26			
24	27			
25	29			
26	30			
27	31			
28	33			
29	42			
30	32			
31	25			
32	22			
33	21			

2. Calculate the mean using the frequency distribution of this data.

The method for manual calculations is shown in Table 2.10 on the right-hand side and the Excel method is shown on the left-hand side.

Table 2.10. Finding Mean for a Frequency Distribution

	E	F	G
	FREQUENCY DISTRIBUTION METHOD		
	X = AGE	**f = Frequency**	**f x X**
	18	2	36
	21	4	84
	22	4	88
	25	4	100
	26	2	52
	27	2	54
	29	2	58
	30	2	60
	31	2	62
	32	2	64
	33	2	66
	42	2	84
	TOTAL	**30**	**808**
	Mean X-bar =	26.93	=G16/F16

$$\overline{X} = \frac{\sum f_i X_i}{\sum f_i} = \frac{sum\ of\ product\ of\ frequency\ and\ value\ of\ each\ X}{sum\ of\ frequencies}$$

MANUAL CALCULATIONS

X = AGE	f = Frequency	f x X
18	2	18 x 2 = 36
21	4	21 x 4 = 84
22	4	22 x 4 = 88
25	4	25 x 4 = 100
26	2	26 x 2 = 52
27	2	27 x 2 =54
29	2	29 x 2 = 58
30	2	30 x 2 = 60
31	2	31 x 2 = 62
32	2	32 x 2 = 64
33	2	33 x 2 = 66
42	2	42 x 2 = 84
TOTAL	**30**	**TOTAL = 808**
Mean X-bar	=808/30 = 26.93	

3. Calculate the mean using the grouped frequency distribution of this data (see Table 2.8):

The first step for solving this problem is to identify the mid points of each of the groups. In this example, the groups are "non-continuous" since each group begins with the number that follows the whole number after the previous group. Moreover, the last group includes 5 different values of *AGE*, unlike the previous groups which only include 4 values. The frequencies of each group are based on the number of people that fall into each category (or group). It is essential to note that since one is "sacrificing" detailed information, this method of finding the mean is likely to result in a slightly different answer, because the sample size is small. The Table 2.11 shows the Excel method (on top) and the manual methods (on the bottom) for calculating the mean for a grouped frequency distribution.

Table 2.11. Calculating the Mean for a Grouped Frequency Distribution

J	K	L	M	N	O
GROUPED FREQUENCY DISTRIBUTION METHOD					
AGE Group	**f = Frequency**	**Lower End**	**Higher End**	**m = Midpoint**	**f x m**
18 to 21	6	18	21	19.5	117
22 to 25	8	22	25	23.5	188
26 to 29	6	26	29	27.5	165
30 to 33	8	30	33	31.5	252
34 to 37	0	34	37	35.5	0
38 to 42	2	38	42	40	80
TOTAL	**30**				**802**
Mean X-bar =	26.73	=O10/K10			

$$\overline{X} = \frac{\sum f_i m_i}{\sum f_i} = \frac{sum\ of\ product\ of\ frequency\ and\ midpoint\ of\ each\ group}{sum\ of\ frequencies\ of\ all\ groups}$$

MANUAL CALCULATIONS

AGE Group	f = Frequency	m = Midpoint	f x m
18 to 21	6	=(18 + 21)/2 = 19.5	= 6 x 19.5 = 117
22 to 25	8	=(22 + 25)/2 = 23.5	= 8 x 23.5 = 188
26 to 29	6	=(26 + 29)/2 = 27.5	= 6 x 27.5 = 165
30 to 33	8	=(30 + 33)/2 = 31.5	= 8 x 31.5 = 252
34 to 37	0	=(34 + 37)/2 = 35.5	= 0 x 35.5 = 0
38 to 42	2	=(38 + 42)/2 = 40	= 2 x 40 = 80
TOTAL	**30**		**TOTAL = 802**

Mean X-bar = 802/30 = 26.73

As one can see, the mean value for the grouped frequency distribution is different from the values obtained for the raw or the frequency distribution in questions 1 and 2. As discussed in the previous section, efficiency and accuracy are often trade-offs in the real world, and one needs to learn to determine, based on sample sizes and available information, which methods would be the most efficient. In any case, the manual calculations methods are often tedious and using Excel functions often proves to be the most efficient method in the real world.

Example 2:5. Finding Weighted Means

Dr. Elle wants to find out the average scores that her students make in the Basic Algebra course that needs to be taken before signing up for her Business Statistics course. She obtains the following information from various instructors who teach the Basic Algebra course. For Section 1, the average score of the class is 85 and the size of class is 25; for Section 2, the average score is 72 and the size is 12 and for Section 3, the average score is 79 and the class size is 20. Help Dr. Elle determine what the average math score is for a student entering her Business Statistics class.

Solution: First organize the information that has been given as follows

$$\overline{X_1} = 85\ and\ n_1 = 25$$
$$\overline{X_2} = 72\ and\ n_2 = 12$$
$$\overline{X_3} = 79\ and\ n_3 = 20$$

Using the formula for weighted mean, one gets:

$$\overline{X_w} = \frac{\sum n_j \overline{X_j}}{\sum n_j} = \frac{n_1\overline{X_1} + n_2\overline{X_2} + n_3\overline{X_3}}{n_1 + n_2 + n_3} = \frac{(85 \times 25) + (72 \times 12) + (79 \times 20)}{25 + 12 + 20} = \frac{4569}{57} = 80.16$$

Thus, Dr. Elle determines that the average math score for a student entering her Business Statistics class is 80.16. Direct Excel formulas to make calculations easier are shown in Table 2.12.

Table 2.12. Weighted Mean using Excel

	A	B	C	D
1	Weighted Mean			
2		X-bar Value	sample size n value	n x X-bar
3	Sample 1	85	25	2125
4	Sample 2	72	12	864
5	Sample 3	79	20	1580
6	TOTALS		57	4569
7				
8	Weighted Mean Xw-bar	80.16	=D6/C6	

2.2. Measures of Variability

Sometimes the value of the central tendency itself fails to give a clear idea of how data is spread out for the variable(s) of interest. Variability in the dataset refers to the way the data tends away from the central tendency values (such as mean, median, or mode). The most commonly used measures of variability are the *Range*, *Deviation*, and *Variance*. However, Box Plots can also often help with visualizing how the data is spread out by using *Quartiles* along with the *Range*. This section covers the three basic measures of variability along with a brief discussion on *skewness* and *kurtosis* values.

Consider a symmetrical distribution of data, which is defined as a distribution where the mean, the median, and the mode are one and the same value. This is most commonly recognized as an inverted-U shaped "bell curve." In Figure 2.3, one can see two symmetrical (both the left and the right sides are mirror images of each other) distributions. However, one can also observe that while both are symmetrical and have the same central tendency, they are quite different in terms of how they are spread out. Their "peaks" are not of the same height demonstrating that at least one of them has a *kurtosis* value that is not line with the expected "normal distribution" assumptions. If the kurtosis value is equal to "3," the "peak and tails" of the distribution are close to a normal distribution. If the value of kurtosis is greater than 3, the "peak" is taller and the tails are narrower than a normal distribution and if the value of kurtosis is less than 3, the "peak" is flatter, and the tails are wider than a normal distribution curve. The Normal Distribution and its nuances are covered in later chapters but suffice it to say that normal distribution assumptions are some of the most common assumptions made in the real world when using large datasets to make business decisions. This is why it is important to note the value of the kurtosis to determine how closely the sample data reflects the expected assumptions and behaviors of the population.

Frequency

X-bar = Median = Mode   Data Values

Frequency

X-bar = Median = Mode   Data Values

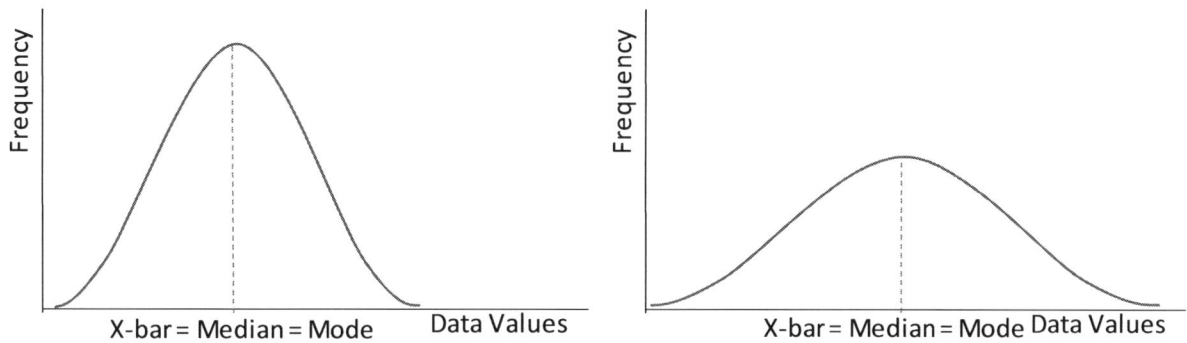

Figure 2.3. Symmetrical Distributions Spread Differently

Now, consider an asymmetrical distribution of data where the measures of central tendency (mean, median, and mode) yield different values as seen in Figure 2.4. The image on the left shows the left-skewed or negatively skewed distribution (the tail is on the left side of the "bump") and the image on the right shows the right-skewed or positively skewed distribution (the tail is on the right side of the "bump.") In cases like these, the Mean (X-bar), the Median, and the Mode (*Mo*) do not have the same values. In a left-skewed distribution the Mean is less than the Median and both of them are less than the Mode (highest point of the curve), whereas in the right-skewed distribution, the Mode (highest point of the curve) is less than the Median, and the Mean is greater than both of them. Thus, an additional variability measure called "skewness" needs to be considered. Note that if the value of skewness is negative, the distribution is left-skewed and if the value of skewness is positive, the distribution is right-skewed.

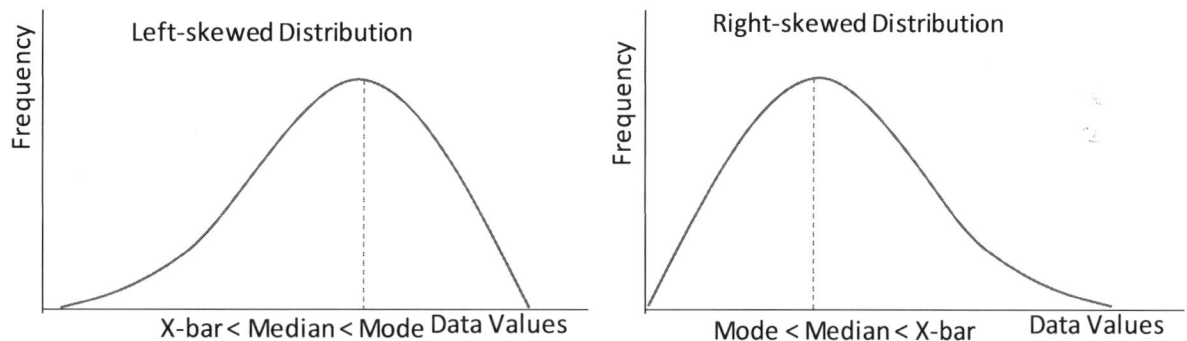

Frequency

Left-skewed Distribution

X-bar < Median < Mode   Data Values

Frequency

Right-skewed Distribution

Mode < Median < X-bar   Data Values

Figure 2.4. Asymmetrical Distribution of Data – Left-skewed and Right-skewed

For the sake of simplicity and recognizing that measures such as skewness and kurtosis are easily obtained by using modern software, the manual calculations of these two measures are not covered in this chapter. However, it is important to note that unlike the mean and the standard deviation, skewness and kurtosis are unit-free measurements of the asymmetrical tendency or the "peakedness" respectively of the variable.

2.2.1. Range

The easiest way to understand how widely the data is spread is to identify the smallest value and the largest value in the dataset and to find the difference between the two numbers. This value, called the *Range* identifies the most extreme values in the dataset. In the real world, this can be helpful to know, especially in cases where the mean, median, or mode values are not hovering around the middle of the Range because it indicates that there could be outliers in the dataset that are affecting the distribution.

$$Range = Maximum\ value\ of\ X - Minimum\ value\ of\ X$$

2.2.2. Box Plots

Before proceeding with deviations and variances, an example of the efficiency of box plots in presenting information visually is covered below using the same dataset as the previous example.

Example 2:6. Drawing a Box Plot

A sample of 30 students is taken from one of the statistics classes offered at ABC university. A researcher is interested in studying their ages and the following values are observed. Answer the questions given below the values:
18, 21, 22, 25, 26, 27, 29, 30, 31, 33, 42, 32, 25, 22, 21, 18, 21, 22, 25, 26, 27, 29, 30, 31, 33, 42, 32, 25, 22, 21.
1. Find the values of the Range and Quartiles for this dataset
2. Draw a Box Plot to show the distribution of this dataset.

Solution: To find the Range, identify the smallest and largest values in the dataset, which are 18 and 42, respectively. Thus, *Range* = 42 – 18 = 24 years. The Quartiles (based on calculations in Example 2.3) are 22, 26, and 31 for *Q1*, *Q2*, and *Q3*, respectively. One can use this information to create a Box Plot manually as shown in Figure 2.5.

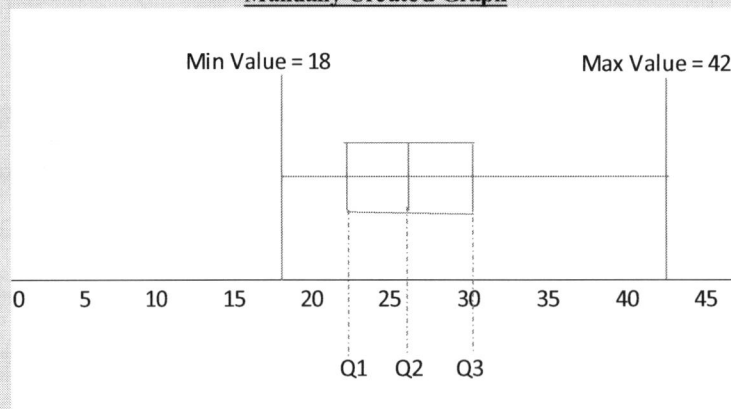

Figure 2.5. Manually created Box Plot for Example 2.6

However, using the Excel function for Box-and-Whisker Plots, available under Recommended Graphs section, the Box Plot can be obtained directly. Excel standard is to put the *AGE* variable on the vertical axis instead of the horizontal axis as can be seen in Figure 2.6.

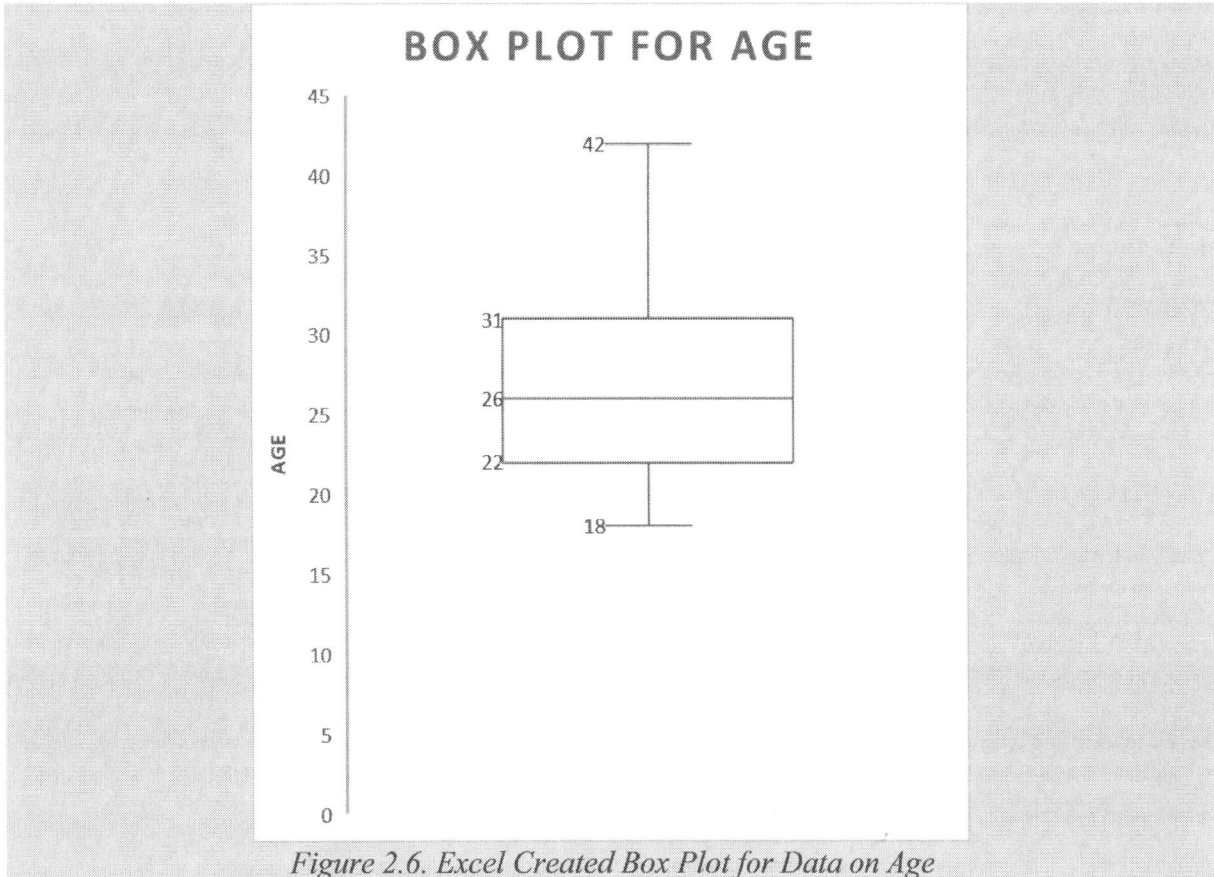

Figure 2.6. Excel Created Box Plot for Data on Age

2.2.3. Deviations and Variance

How many times have you found yourself using terminology like "I can be at the destination in 15 minutes, give or take 5 minutes?" That "give or take" is referring to the deviation or the interval between 10 minutes and 20 minutes that you expect to take in reaching your destination. Human brains innately approximate how much time one would need to complete a task successfully, based on previous experiences of the individual and automatically give an interval during which one is most likely to finish the task. When one has to go to a destination that they have not been to before, they tend to give themselves more time to get there versus going to a frequently visited destination. This is because when one has collected enough "observations" on how long it would take them to reach somewhere, one is able to "narrow" the interval of time expectations but if one is unfamiliar or have only been somewhere once or twice, one tends to have a more generous allocation of time to ensure they get there as planned. This type of variability from the measure of central tendency can be captured by using deviations and variances in mathematical form and helps one to identify quantifiable intervals for datasets.

The word "deviation" refers to the distance and direction of any raw score from the Mean in a dataset. Thus, if one wants to find the deviation of a specific score X_i from the Mean $\bar{X}$ for a variable of interest X, the general deviation can be written as:

$$D_i = X_i - \bar{X}$$

Thus, for each value of X_i, one can calculate the corresponding Deviation D_i. If the value of a given deviation, D_i is positive, one can say that the value of X_i is greater than the mean of the distribution and if the deviation D_i is negative, one can say that the value of X_i is less than the mean of the distribution. Example 2.7 demonstrates the calculations of deviations using the same dataset as the previous examples.

Example 2:7. Calculations of Deviations

A sample of 10 students is taken from one of the statistics classes offered at ABC university. A researcher is interested in studying their ages and the following values are observed: 18, 21, 22, 25, 26, 27, 29, 30, 31, 33. Calculate the deviation of each value from the Mean of the *AGE*.

Solution: Table 2.13 shows how to calculate the Mean and the corresponding deviations for each value of X.

Table 2.13. Example for Deviation Calculation

Obs. #	X = AGE	Di = Xi - X-bar	Deviation Di
1	18	= 18 - 26.2	-8.2
2	21	= 21 - 26.2	-5.2
3	22	= 22 - 26.2	-4.2
4	25	= 25 - 26.2	-1.2
5	26	= 26 - 26.2	-0.2
6	27	= 27 - 26.2	0.8
7	29	= 29 - 26.2	2.8
8	30	= 30 - 26.2	3.8
9	31	= 31 - 26.2	4.8
10	33	= 33 - 26.2	6.8
TOTAL	262		0

Mean X-bar = 262/10 = 26.2

One can see that the observations below the mean (26.2) have a negative value of deviation, whereas the observations above the mean have a positive value of the deviation. More importantly, since the Mean is the "middle" value in the distribution, the total sum of all deviations Di is 0 since the positive and negative values "cancel" each other out.

Now, what if one wants to find the average distance of each observation from the mean? The mean formula of "sum of all values divided by the number of values" would always yield a zero, since the sum of all deviations is always zero in a distribution. Thus, there is a need to get creative. One option is to take the absolute value of the deviations and find their average. This yields the formula for the Mean Deviation (MD), which is defined as the average deviation of each value from the overall Mean of the distribution of the variable of interest, as follows:

$$MD = \frac{\sum |X_i - \bar{X}|}{n} = \frac{\sum |D_i|}{n}$$

Example 2:8. Mean Deviation

A sample of 10 students is taken from one of the statistics classes offered at ABC university. A researcher is interested in studying their ages and the following values are observed: 18, 21, 22, 25, 26, 27, 29, 30, 31, 33. Calculate the Mean Deviation of the *AGE*.

Solution: Table 2.14 shows how to calculate the Mean, the corresponding deviations, and the corresponding absolute values of deviations for each value of X. As seen in Table 2.14, the Mean Deviation of this sample is 3.8 and the value of the Mean is 26.2.

Thus, in words, the description of the sample would be: "The sample of the ages of 10 students shows that the mean age of students in the statistics classes offered at ABC university is 26.2 with a mean deviation of 3.8". This means that on an average students are either 3.8 years younger or older than 26.2 or between 22.4 and 30 years old.

Table 2.14. Mean Deviation Calculation

Obs. #	X = AGE	$D_i = X_i - \bar{X}$	Deviation D_i	Absolute Deviation
1	18	= 18 - 26.2	-8.2	8.2
2	21	= 21 - 26.2	-5.2	5.2
3	22	= 22 - 26.2	-4.2	4.2
4	25	= 25 - 26.2	-1.2	1.2
5	26	= 26 - 26.2	-0.2	0.2
6	27	= 27 - 26.2	0.8	0.8
7	29	= 29 - 26.2	2.8	2.8
8	30	= 30 - 26.2	3.8	3.8
9	31	= 31 - 26.2	4.8	4.8
10	33	= 33 - 26.2	6.8	6.8
TOTAL	262		0	38

Mean X-bar = 262/10 = 26.2

Mean Deviation = 38/10 = 3.8

However, this type of Mean Deviation calculation results in issues on a bigger scale because it over generalizes the distribution or the "spread" of the data, and the use of absolute values prevents meaningful analysis of more complex probability distributions such as the Normal distribution, which require calculus in order to derive formulas. Thus, a slightly different approach can be used in order to identify what the general deviation of a sample or population would be. The approach is to take the squared value of the deviations (note that square of a number is always a positive number) and then later to find the square root in order to establish the units correctly.

The concept of Squared Deviations enters the picture now. Instead of finding the absolute deviation value, one would find the squared deviation for each unique value X_i in order to find the Mean of the Squared Deviations. Another, more commonly used term for the Mean of the Squared Deviations is "Variance." Note that the value of the Variance is always in "squared units." Thus, if the variable of interest in measured in meters, the value of the Variance would be in squared-meters; if the variable is measured in years, the value of the Variance would be in squared-years. There is also a difference in the calculation of Variance when considering the entire population of individuals versus when a sample is considered. The concept of the Population (generalized) Variance is considered first. The symbol for Population Variance is Var or σ^2 and the formula for Population Variance (Mean Squared Deviation) is:

$$Var = \sigma^2 = \frac{\sum(X_i - \bar{X})^2}{n} = \frac{\sum D_i^2}{n}$$

If one wanted to calculate the Variance of a Sample (limited size) drawn from the general population, one uses the denominator of $(n-1)$ instead of the total number of observations, n. This is done to adjust for any potential errors in measurements by reducing "one degree of freedom." The symbol for Sample Variance is s^2 and the formula is:

$$s^2 = \frac{\sum(X_i - \bar{X})^2}{n-1} = \frac{\sum D_i^2}{n-1}$$

The square root of Variance is referred to as the "Standard Deviation" of the distribution and the units of Standard Deviation are the same as the units of the variable of interest allowing the visualization of the movement on the number line. If one is using Population Variance, its square root will yield the value of the Population Standard Deviation, and if one is using the Sample Variance, its square root will yield the value of the Sample Standard Deviation. The symbol for Population Standard Deviation is σ and symbol for Sample Standard Deviation is s but in general, it is best to remember the value of standard deviation (S.D.) as being the square root of the Variance.

$$S.D. = \sqrt{Var}$$

Using the same data as previous examples, the Variance and the Standard Deviation of a raw data distribution are discussed in Example 2.9 before proceeding to the applicable formulas for frequency distributions.

Example 2:9. Variance and Standard Deviation

A sample of 10 students is taken from one of the statistics classes offered at ABC university. A researcher is interested in studying their ages and the following values are observed: 18, 21, 22, 25, 26, 27, 29, 30, 31, 33. Calculate the Variance and the Standard Deviation of *AGE*.

Solution: This dataset is a ***sample*** of 10 students, so one should use the Sample Variance formula which has the $(n-1)$ correction in the denominator. Table 2.15 shows how to calculate the Mean, the corresponding deviations, and the corresponding squared values of deviations for each value of *AGE* in order to calculate the Sample Variance and the Standard Deviation of *AGE*. The yellow-highlighted portion shows how to directly calculate Mean, Variance, and Standard Deviation using Excel formulas without having to calculate the Deviations manually for a Sample. The solution shows that the *AGE* variable is distributed with a mean of 26.2 years with a standard deviation of 4.78 years in the provided sample.

Table 2.15. Variance and Standard Deviation Calculations

	A	B	C	D	E	F
1	**Obs. #**	**Xi = AGE**	**Di = Xi - X-bar**	**Deviation Di**	**Squared Deviation**	**Di^2**
2	1	18	= 18 - 26.2	-8.2	= -8.2 x - 8.2	67.24
3	2	21	= 21 - 26.2	-5.2	= -5.2 x -5.2	27.04
4	3	22	= 22 - 26.2	-4.2	= -4.2 x -4.2	17.64
5	4	25	= 25 - 26.2	-1.2	= -1.2 x -1.2	1.44
6	5	26	= 26 - 26.2	-0.2	= -0.2 x -0.2	0.04
7	6	27	= 27 - 26.2	0.8	= 0.8 x 0.8	0.64
8	7	29	= 29 - 26.2	2.8	= 2.8 x 2.8	7.84
9	8	30	= 30 - 26.2	3.8	=3.8 x 3.8	14.44
10	9	31	= 31 - 26.2	4.8	= 4.8 x 4.8	23.04
11	10	33	= 33 - 26.2	6.8	= 6.8 x 6.8	46.24
12	**TOTAL**	**262**		**0**		**206**
13						
14	**Mean X-bar =**	262/10 =	26.2	26.2	=AVERAGE(B2:B11)	
15	**Sample Variance =**	206/(10-1) =	22.84	22.84	=VAR.S(B2:B11)	
16	**Standard Deviation =**	Sqrt of Var =	4.78	4.78	=STDEV.S(B2:B11)	
17						
18	**EXCEL Direct Formulas for population:**					
19	**Population Variance =**	20.56	=VAR.P(B2:B11)			
20	**Standard Deviation =**	4.53	=STDEV.P(B2:B11)			

In the last 2 lines of the Table the Excel formulas for Population Variance and Standard Deviation are shown. One should avoid using population formulas when using a "Sample," since one can observe that the answers indicate that the Population Variance and Standard Deviation provide a smaller "spread" of the data (both values are smaller than the values of the Sample calculations). Since samples are used to make decisions about entire populations, the formula correction for sample is essential to avoid costly mistakes in the real world, particularly when the sample size is less than 50 observations.

If, instead of raw data, the data for a variable of interest is given in the frequency distribution form, where f_i represents the frequency of each value of X_i, the formula used to calculate the Sample Variance is as follows:

$$s^2 = \frac{\sum f_i (X_i - \bar{X})^2}{n - 1} = \frac{\sum f_i D_i^2}{n - 1}$$

If the data for a variable of interest is given in the grouped frequency distribution form, where f_i represents the frequency of each group and m_i represents the mid-point of each group, the formula used to calculate the Sample Variance is as follows:

$$s^2 = \frac{\sum f_i (m_i - \bar{X})^2}{n - 1} = \frac{\sum f_i D_i^2}{n - 1}$$

As seen in Example 2.4, the calculations for both of these types of distributions are similar if one remembers that for the groups, the midpoint m_i for each group represents the "average" value of the entire group.

Example 2:10. Standard Deviation for Grouped Frequency Distribution

A sample of 10 students is taken from one of the statistics classes offered at ABC university. A researcher is interested in studying their ages and the following Table 2.16 is provided to show grouped frequency distribution. Calculate the Variance and the Standard Deviation of *AGE*.

Table 2.16 Example of Grouped Frequency Distribution

AGE Group	fi = frequency
18-21	2
22-25	2
26-29	3
30-33	3

Solution: The manual calculation for this example is done in a manner similar to the one used in Example 2.4 in terms of creating the columns for the calculations. The Excel solutions is as shown in Table 2.17 below:

Table 2.17. Variance and Standard Deviation for Grouped Frequency Distribution

	A	B	C	D	E	F	G	H	I
1	AGE Group	fi = frequency	Lower end	Higher end	mi = Midpoint	fi x mi	Di = mi - X-bar	Di^2	fi x Di^2
2	18-21	2	18	21	19.5	39	-6.8	46.24	92.48
3	22-25	2	22	25	23.5	47	-2.8	7.84	15.68
4	26-29	3	26	29	27.5	82.5	1.2	1.44	4.32
5	30-33	3	30	33	31.5	94.5	5.2	27.04	81.12
6	TOTAL	10				263			193.6
7									
8	X-bar =	26.3	=F6/B6						
9	Variance =	21.51	=I6/(B6-1)						
10	Std. Dev. =	4.64	=SQRT(B9)						

2.2.4. Coefficient of Variation

The Coefficient of Variation (*CV*) allows one to control for different sizes of samples by finding the ratio of the standard deviation to the mean. This coefficient does not have any units and therefore allows comparisons across different samples that are derived either from the same population or from different populations. If the value of the *CV* is less than 100, it indicates that the standard deviation value is less than the value of the mean in the distribution. If the value is close to 100, it indicates that the dataset is very widely spread out since the value of the standard deviation is very close to that of the mean. The formula for *CV* is as below:

$$CV = \frac{s}{\bar{X}} \times 100$$

In **Example 2:10** above one can see that the mean is 26.3 years, and the standard deviation is 4.64 years. Thus, the Coefficient of Variation would be 17.64 indicating that the distribution of the data is not very wide.

$$CV = \frac{s}{\bar{X}} \times 100 = \frac{4.64}{26.3} \times 100 = 17.64$$

2.3. Measures of Central Tendency and Variability in Practice

Having learned about measures of central tendency and the measures of variability, the question remains on how one can use these to get an idea of the "distribution" of a variable of interest in a dataset. There are two main rules that can be easily applied for considering the distributions: Chebyshev's Rule and the Empirical Rule. Chebyshev's Rule is more general and does not make any assumptions about the type of distribution that a variable has in the population, whereas the Empirical Rule is primarily used when one either knows or expects that the variable of interest is Normally distributed (has an inverted U-shaped curve).

2.3.1 Chebyshev's Rule

This rule is based upon the Chebyshev Inequality Theorem that was proven by Russian Mathematician Pafnuty Chebyshev. It allows one to generalize the expectations or the probability of a certain portion of the dataset falling within a particular range. Thus, if one knows the mean ($\bar{X}$) and the standard deviation (s) for any dataset, one can make the following assumptions about the observations of the variable of interest (X), which are also demonstrated in Table 2.18:

1. 75% of the values of the variable of interest (X) lie within 2 standard deviation distance from the mean.
2. 89% of the values of the variable of interest (X) lie within 3 standard deviation distance from the mean.
3. 95% of the values of the variable of interest (X) lie within 4.5 standard deviation distance from the mean

Table 2.18. Chebyshev's Rule Formulation

General Table for Chebyshev's Rule		
Interval lower end	**Interval Upper End**	**Percent Data Contained**
Xbar - 2s	Xbar + 2s	75%
Xbar - 3s	Xbar + 3s	89%
Xbar - 4.5s	Xbar + 4.5s	95%

Example 2:11. Chebyshev's Rule Application

A sample of 10 students is taken from one of the statistics classes offered at ABC university. A researcher is interested in studying their ages and the following values are observed: 18, 21, 22, 25, 26, 27, 29, 30, 31, 33. Find the Chebyshev's Intervals for this dataset and confirm if they are accurate.

Solution: As seen in Example 2.9, the mean $\bar{X}$ for this example is 26.2 years and the standard deviation s is 4.78 years. The Chebyshev's intervals can be calculated as shown in Table 2.19 below. The formulas used are also shown in the table. These results show that at least 75% of all people in the sample will fall between 16.64 and 35.76 years of age. Now, it turns out that since there is a limited sample size, all observations fall within this age range. But the method of calculation would remain the same even if one had a much larger dataset. Similarly, 89% of all observations are expected to fall within 11.86 and 40.54 years of age and 95% of all observations are expected to fall within 4.69 and 47.71 years of age.

Table 2.19. Solution for Chebyshev's Intervals

	A	B	C
1	X-bar =	26.2	
2	s =	4.78	
3	**Interval lower end**	**Interval Upper End**	**Percent Data Contained**
4	16.64	35.76	75%
5	11.86	40.54	89%
6	4.69	47.71	95%
7	Formulas used:		
8	=B1 - 2*B2	=B1 + 2*B2	
9	=B1 - 3*B2	=B1 + 3*B2	
10	=B1 - 4.5*B2	=B1 + 4.5*B2	

If one pays attention to the ranges of the intervals, one will notice that the intervals get much wider (and sometimes can yield meaningless results from a real-world perspective) as there is a tendency to include more data within the interval. Bigger sample sizes often yield more meaningful results since the mean and the standard deviation are affected by the size of the sample, n.

2.3.2 Empirical Rule

This rule is based upon the assumptions of a symmetrical, Bell-curved Normal Distribution. It allows one to generalize the expectations or the probability of a certain portion of the dataset falling within a particular range if one expects (or knows) that the variable of interest is distributed normally. Unlike the Chebyshev's Rule, the Empirical Rule yields narrower intervals and covers a larger portion of the data. Thus, if one knows the mean ($\bar{X}$) and the standard deviation (s) for any dataset, one can make the following assumptions about the observations of the variable of interest (X):

1. 68% of the values of the variable of interest (X) lie within 1 standard deviation distance from the mean.
2. 96% of the values of the variable of interest (X) lie within 2 standard deviation distance from the mean.
3. 99.99% of the values of the variable of interest (X) lie within 3 standard deviation distance from the mean

Figure 2.7 shows the visual representation of the Normal Distribution spread using the Empirical Rule and the table for the Empirical Rule in formula form:

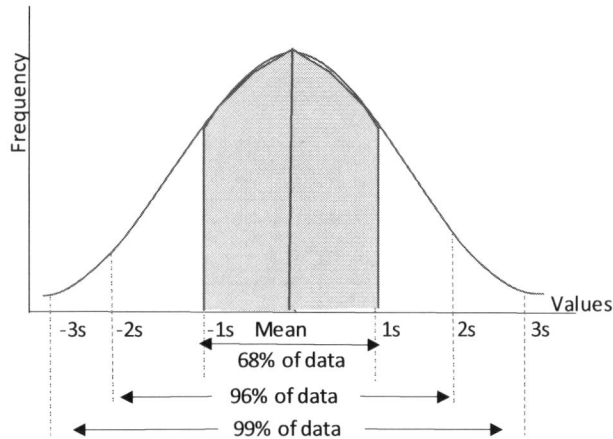

General Table for Empirical Rule		
Interval lower end	Interval Upper End	Percent Data Contained
Xbar - 1s	Xbar + 1s	68%
Xbar - 2s	Xbar + 2s	96%
Xbar - 3s	Xbar + 3s	99.99%

Figure 2.7. Empirical Rule Visual Representation and Table

Example 2:12. Empirical Rule Application

A sample of 10 students is taken from one of the statistics classes offered at ABC university. A researcher is interested in studying their ages and the following values are observed: 18, 21, 22, 25, 26, 27, 29, 30, 31, 33. Find the Empirical Intervals for this dataset and confirm if they are accurate.

Solution: As seen in **Example 2:9**, the mean $\bar{X}$ for this example is 26.2 years and the standard deviation s is 4.78 years. The Empirical intervals can be calculated as shown in Table 2.20 below. The formulas used are also shown in the Table. These results show that at least 68% of all people in the sample will fall within 21.42 and 30.98 years of age. As one can see in the raw data, the people who are aged 18, 31, and 33 are not a part of this interval (3 out of 10 observations is 30%), implying that the estimate of 68% (close to 70%) of the dataset falls in the first interval! Similarly, at least 96% of all observations are expected to fall within 16.64 and 35.76 years of age and almost all (99.99%) observations are expected to fall within 11.86 and 40.54 years of age.

Table 2.20. Solution for Empirical Intervals

	A	B	C
1	**X-bar =**	26.2	
2	**s =**	4.78	
3	**Interval lower end**	**Interval Upper End**	**Percent Data Contained**
4	21.42	30.98	68%
5	16.64	35.76	96%
6	11.86	40.54	99.99%
7	Formulas used:		
8	=B1 - 1*B2	=B1 + 1*B2	
9	=B1 - 2*B2	=B1 + 2*B2	
10	=B1 - 3*B2	=B1 + 3*B2	

Again, as intervals increase to accommodate more data, the results can be made to become as meaningful (or meaningless) as one wants them to be! For instance, making a claim like almost all students in this college are between 11 and 40 years old is true, but it does not hold any meaning in terms of understanding the composition of the population. On the other hand, smaller intervals such as the first standard deviation one (21.42, 30.98) indicate that 68% (or approximately 2/3rd of all people in this sample) are between 21 and 31 years of age! Thus, bigger sample sizes often yield more meaningful results since the mean as well the standard deviation are both affected by the size of the sample, n.

2.3.3. Comparing Two Different Datasets

In order to compare two values from different datasets, a Z-value is calculated and used to find the relative placements of a certain value of interest. Z-value refers to the distance measured as the "number of standard deviations" between a given value of X and the mean and the formula is as follows:

$$Z = \# \ of \ std.dev. = \frac{Given \ value \ of \ X \ - \ Mean \ of \ Xi}{std.dev.of \ Xi} = \frac{X - \bar{X}}{s}$$

Example 2:13. Professor K or Professor L?

Now it is time to revisit the original question that was posed at the beginning of this chapter. Consider the example of two different statistics classes taught by Professor K and Professor L in the same institution. If the average student grade in both classes is discovered to be 85, should a student who expects to score a 90 in statistics be indifferent in terms of which professor they register for? Assume that the standard deviation in Professor K's class is 3 points and the standard deviation in Professor L's class is 5 points. Identify which class is the student likely to do better in.

Solution: The values of the means and the standard deviations for the classes taught by Professor K and Professor L are given are as follows:

$$\overline{X_K} = 85$$

$$\overline{X_L} = 85$$
$$s_K = 3$$
$$s_L = 5$$

Now, one can calculate the Z-value for the student who is expecting to make a 90 in their statistics class for each professor

$$Z_K = \frac{X - \overline{X_K}}{s_K} = \frac{90 - 85}{3} = 1.67$$

$$Z_L = \frac{X - \overline{X_L}}{s_L} = \frac{90 - 85}{5} = 1$$

As one can see, the value of 90 is 1.67 standard deviations away from the mean in Professor K's class but is exactly 1 standard deviation away from the mean in Professor L's class. The spread of Professor K's class is narrower than the spread of grades in Professor L's class. Thus, the student who expects to get a 90 would find it easier to do well in Professor L's class as compared to Professor K's class.

Table 2.21. Professor K vs. Professor L Z-value Calculations

	A	B	C	D	E	F
1	**Comparing Two Distributions**					
2		**X-value**	**X-bar**	**Std. Dev.**	**Z-value**	
3	**Professor K**	90	85	3	1.67	=(B3-C3)/D3
4	**Professor L**	90	85	5	1	=(B4-C4)/D4

NOTE: Based on the Empirical Rule, one can say that 68% of the students in Professor K's class score between 82 and 88 (1 std. dev. distance from mean in either direction), and 96% of students score between 79 and 91. However in Professor L's class, 68% of the students score between 80 and 90 and 96% of the students score between 75 and 95 implying that a student who expects to do well in statistics is likely to do better than expected in Professor L's class as compared to Professor K's class. If a student expects to struggle with a good grade in statistics, the narrower spread of Professor K's class is a better solution for that student.

Example 2:14. Identify the better player

Sam and Dave play on two separate soccer teams. Sam is on the 5th grade team and typically scores 5 goals per game. Dave is in the 8th grade team and typically scores 3 goals per game. The 5th grade team has a mean of 4 goals per player per game and a standard deviation of 2 goals whereas the 9th grade team has a mean of 2 goals per player per game and a standard deviation of 1.5 goals. Which one of the two boys is a better soccer player?

Solution: The values of the means and the standard deviations for the two teams are given are as follows:

$$\overline{X_{5th}} = 4$$
$$\overline{X_{9th}} = 2$$
$$s_{5th} = 2$$

$$s_{9th} = 1.5$$

Now, one can calculate the Z-values for Sam and Dave

$$Z_{Sam} = \frac{X - \overline{X_K}}{s_K} = \frac{5 - 4}{2} = 0.5$$

$$Z_{Dave} = \frac{X - \overline{X_L}}{s_L} = \frac{3 - 2}{1.5} = 0.67$$

One can see that both, Sam and Dave perform better than their respective team averages. However, the Z-score for Sam is lower than the Z-score for Dave. This implies that Dave outperforms Sam when their performances are compared to their respective teammates.

Table 2.22. Sam vs. Dave's performance in Soccer Teams

	A	B	C	D	E	F
1	**Comparing Two Distributions**					
2			**Team Values**			
3		**X-value**	**X-bar**	**Std. Dev.**	**Z-value**	
4	**Sam**	5	4	2	0.50	=(B4-C4)/D4
5	**Dave**	3	2	1.5	0.67	=(B5-C5)/D5

List of Formulas for Chapter 2

Mode: Mode is the most frequent or most typical or most common value in a distribution

Median Formula: If the total number of observations (n) in a dataset is an even number, and the data is sorted in an ascending manner, the *median is the value* of the n/2th observation. If n is an odd number, the *median is the value* of the $(n+1)/2^{th}$ observation.

Quartile Formula: The "median" of the first half of the distribution is *Q1* and the "median" of the second half of the distribution is *Q3*. The difference between the values of *Q3* and *Q1* is known as the Interquartile Range, which represents the "middle 50%" of the distribution.
$$IQR = Q3 - Q1$$

Percentile Formula: In order to find the kth percentile, where k is a number between 1 and 99, and X represents the number of values lower than the value of interest, Y represents the frequency of the value of interest, and n is the total number of observations in the dataset, the kth percentile is obtained by using the following formula:
$$k^{th}\ Percentile = \frac{(X + 0.5Y)}{n} \times 100$$

Mean of Raw Data: If Data is in raw form
$$\bar{X} = \frac{\sum X_i}{n} = \frac{sum\ of\ all\ values\ of\ X}{total\ number\ of\ values\ of\ X}$$

Mean from Frequency Distribution: If Data is given as a frequency distribution
$$\bar{X} = \frac{\sum f_i X_i}{\sum f_i} = \frac{sum\ of\ product\ of\ frequency\ and\ value\ of\ each\ X}{sum\ of\ frequencies}$$

Mean from Grouped Frequency Distribution: If Data is given with intervals or groups
$$\bar{X} = \frac{\sum f_i m_i}{\sum f_i} = \frac{sum\ of\ product\ of\ frequency\ and\ midpoint\ of\ each\ group}{sum\ of\ frequencies\ of\ all\ groups}$$

Weighted Mean for multiple samples: If means for multiple samples are given and a total mean needs to be calculated
$$\overline{X_w} = \frac{\sum n_j \bar{X}_j}{\sum n_j} = \frac{sum\ of\ product\ of\ average\ and\ sample\ size\ of\ each\ sample}{sum\ of\ all\ sample\ sizes}$$

Range of Data: *Range = Maximum value of X – Minimum value of X*

Deviation of Specific Point from Mean: $D_i = X_i - \bar{X}$

Mean Deviation: For finding mean deviation for all points of dataset
$$MD = \frac{\sum |X_i - \bar{X}|}{n} = \frac{\sum |D_i|}{n}$$

Variance of Population and Sample: adjustment for sample size required.

$$Var = \sigma^2 = \frac{\Sigma(X_i - \bar{X})^2}{n} = \frac{\Sigma D_i^2}{n}$$

$$s^2 = \frac{\Sigma(X_i - \bar{X})^2}{n-1} = \frac{\Sigma D_i^2}{n-1}$$

Standard Deviation formula: $S.D. = \sqrt{Var}$

Variance for frequency distribution: Note that std.dev. is always square root of variance

$$s^2 = \frac{\Sigma f_i (X_i - \bar{X})^2}{n-1} = \frac{\Sigma f_i D_i^2}{n-1}$$

Variance for grouped frequency distribution: f_i represents the frequency of each group and m_i represents the mid-point of each group

$$s^2 = \frac{\Sigma f_i (m_i - \bar{X})^2}{n-1} = \frac{\Sigma f_i D_i^2}{n-1}$$

Coefficient of Variation: Ratio of standard deviation to the mean

$$CV = \frac{s}{\bar{X}} \times 100$$

Z-values: Distance of a point in terms of number of standard deviations from mean (Z)

$$Z = \# \, of \, std.dev. = \frac{Given \, value \, of \, X - Mean \, of \, Xi}{std.dev. \, of \, Xi} = \frac{X - \bar{X}}{s}$$

Chapter 3. Probability Theory

Probability is a term that measures the likelihood of an event occurring, mathematically. People use it in their routines very comfortably, without necessarily being aware that they are using probability or rather, expected probability of a specific event. Saying things such as "there is a 20% chance of rain today" or "there is a 70% chance that Team A will win against Team B in today's game" reflect that ability of the human mind to translate the likelihood of an event into a quantifiable number based on previous experiences with a particular event. However, if one had to place a bet on the event actually occurring, one would likely modify their expectations! Before defining Probability formally, some pertinent terminology should be considered:

1. An *Experiment* is defined as a controlled operation that yields a set of results.

2. A *Trial* is each iteration of the Experiment.

3. *Outcome* refers to each result of an Experiment.

4. *Sample Space S* is defined as a set of all outcomes of an experiment.

5. An *Event* is defined as the subcollection of specific outcomes of an experiment.

6. *Empirical Probability* is the observed relative frequency of the Event of interest.

7. *Theoretical Probability* is the Expected relative frequency of the Event.

8. The *Law of Large Numbers* indicates that as the number of Trials increases, the more accurately does the Empirical Probability mimic the Theoretical Probability.

Empirical Probability, P_E, is defined as the relative frequency of an Event when an Experiment is taking place. The general formula for Empirical Probability is given as follows:

$$P_E = relative\ frequency = \frac{Number\ of\ times\ an\ Event\ occurs}{Total\ number\ of\ Trials\ of\ the\ Experiment}$$

For defining the Theoretical Probability, P_T one assumes that all the *Outcomes* of a given *Experiment* are equally likely to occur and that there is no bias in the *Experiment*. Thus, the formula for Theoretical Probability is as follows:

$$P_T = \frac{Number\ of\ outcomes\ favorable\ to\ an\ Event}{Total\ number\ of\ possible\ Outcomes\ of\ the\ Experiment}$$

For the sake of simplicity, Probability, in general is referred to as P, but it is important to keep in mind that the observed probabilities might be quite different from the expected probabilities. However, in the long run the relative frequency of observed probability is close to the theoretical probability so one can define Probability in general as "the long-term relative frequency of a specific outcome."

Here is how one can visualize the difference between observed and theoretical probabilities. Say that one wants to toss an unbiased coin, what would one expect the probability of getting Heads to be? Most people would realize that since there are only two outcomes (Heads or Tails), the expected probability of getting Heads is ½ or 50%. Now, an Experiment can be performed to see if this theoretical expectation of getting Heads (Event of interest) is met or not. Table 3.1 shows the number of Trials performed (tossing a coin) and the number of Heads that were obtained in each Experiment.

In this illustration, one can see that each "Experiment" of coin tossing consisted of a specific number of Trials (10, 50, 100...). For each Trial, the Sample Space S = (Heads, Tails) and the Event of interest was defined as getting Heads as a result of the coin toss. In the first Experiment, with 10 trials, 3 Heads were obtained out of the 10 tosses resulting in the observed probability of 3/10 = 0.3 or 30%. In the second experiment, with 50 trials resulted in 30 Heads out of the 50 coin tosses implying that the observed probability is 30/50 = 0.6 or 60%... and similarly, in the sixth experiment with 1000 trials, 510 Heads were obtained resulting in a probability of 51%. One can see that when only 10 trials were conducted, the observed probability of getting Heads was only 3/10 or 0.30 or 30%. However, as the number of Trials increases, the empirical (or observed) probability of getting Heads increases and eventually starts tending towards the theoretical probability of 0.5 or 50%, which is what one would expect when tossing a random coin!

Table 3.1. Experiments with Tossing a Coin

Experiment #	1	2	3	4	5	6
Number of Trials	10	50	100	250	500	1000
Number of Heads	3	30	58	140	260	510
P(Heads) observed	0.3	0.6	0.58	0.56	0.52	0.51

3.1. Defining Events accurately

The identification of an Event is critical in measuring the probability of the Event occurring (or failing to occur). So, it is essential to understand the various ways that one can define events based upon what one is interested in studying or learning more about. A series of illustrations will help to learn how to properly define Events.

Illustration 1. If one tosses an unbiased six-faced dice, one expects the Sample Space $S = (1, 2, 3, 4, 5, 6)$ and note that all outcomes are equally likely with a probability of 1/6. If one defines variable A as the outcome of the dice toss, one can say that the probability of A being equal to 1 is the same as the probability of A being equal to 2 is the same as the probability of A being equal to 3 and so on.

$$P(A = 1) = P(A = 2) = \ldots = P(A = 6) = \frac{1}{6}$$

Now, one can define the Event of interest as desired. Let E be defined as the outcome of rolling <u>at least a 5</u> on the dice. Thus, the Set of $E = (5, 6)$ since if the dice rolls to a 5 or a 6, it is a desired outcome. To clarify, the set of Events E has 2 possible outcomes whereas the Sample Space has 6 possible outcomes. Thus, the theoretical Probability of Event E occurring can be written as:

$$P(E) = \frac{2}{6} = 0.33$$

Illustration 2. Consider a deck of cards, and one wants to draw a single card out of the deck, implying that the Sample Space consists of 52 different outcomes and all the outcomes have an equal probability of 1/52. Defining the Event of interest as the outcome of getting a "picture" card (Jacks, Queens, or King). Typically, there are four suits (hearts, spades, diamonds, and clubs) each consisting of 13 cards of which three are "picture cards." Thus, the Event E has a total of 12 outcomes possible and the theoretical probability of Event E of drawing a picture card at random can be written as:

$$P(E) = \frac{12}{52} = 0.231$$

Illustration 3. Suppose a Middle School in San Antonio has 300 children enrolled in 6th grade. Thus, the Sample Space has 300 outcomes. Let 20% of them be enrolled in one or the other team sport. Let the Event of interest E be defined as "children not playing any team sport," since those are the students that one is seeking to study in the analysis. In this case, the Probability of Event E **not** occurring is equal to the 20% of the children that are enrolled in sports.

$$P(E') = \frac{students\ playing\ team\ sports}{total\ number\ of\ students} = 20\% = 0.20$$
$$By\ Rule\ 4\ of\ Probability: P(E) = 1 - P(E')$$
$$\therefore P(E) = 1 - 0.20 = 0.80$$
$$\therefore 0.80 = \frac{students\ not\ playing\ team\ sports}{300}$$
$$\therefore students\ not\ playing\ team\ sports = 300 \times 0.80 = 240$$

Another way to interpret probability is to say that if a random child is selected from the Middle School in San Antonio, there is a 20% chance that the child is enrolled in a team sport or conversely, there is an 80% chance that the child is not enrolled in a team sport.

3.2. Rules of Probability

There are some basic Rules of Probability that guide how the assumptions and calculations work when using Probability. These are presented in two parts, the first part being the Basic Rules and the second part being the Advanced Rules, but they are numbered in sequential order for ease of understanding.

3.2.1 Basic Rules of Probability

1. Probability of an Event that CANNOT occur is always equal to 0. In the case of the coin, the possible outcomes are only two – either Heads or Tails. Thus, the probability of getting neither Heads nor Tails would be zero.

2. Probability of an Event that MUST occur is always equal to 1. In the case of the coin, if one defines the Event of interest as getting either Heads or Tails, the probability of getting either Heads or Tails is equal to 1, since at least one of the two outcomes has to occur. Thus, it is essential to define Event of interest accurately.

3. The Probability of any Event is always a number between 0 and 1. Probability is defined as a ratio of number of favorable outcomes for an event to the total possible outcomes of the experiment. Thus, $0 \leq P \leq 1$. It is important to note that if the Probability of an event is 0.34, the corresponding percentage (34%) is simply a way of writing it differently. 0.34 is NOT equal to 0.34%!!

4. <u>Complement of an Event</u>: The sum of probabilities of all possible outcomes of a Trial is always equal to 1. If one defines the probability of drawing a Queen out of a deck of cards as $P(Q)$, then the probability of not getting a Queen can be written as $P(Q')$ or the Complement to getting a Queen.
$$P(Q) + P(Q') = 1$$
$$P(Q') = 1 - P(Q)$$

5. <u>Odds against an Event</u> is the ratio between the Probability of failure of the Event to occur and the Probability of the Event occurring:
$$Odds\ Against\ Event\ = \frac{P(Event\ fails\ to\ occur)}{P(Event\ occurs)} = \frac{P(failure)}{P(success)}$$

If the Event of interest is drawing a Queen out of a deck of cards and ran 10 trials where one obtained a Queen 4 times out of the 10 trials, the Odds against getting a Queen would be:
$$Odds\ Against\ Queen\ = \frac{P(Event\ fails\ to\ occur)}{P(Event\ occurs)} = \frac{6/10}{4/10} = 1.5$$

<u>Odds in Favor of an Event</u> is the ratio between the Probability of the Event occurring and the Probability of the Event failing to occur:
$$Odds\ in\ Favor\ of\ Event\ = \frac{P(Event\ occurs)}{P(Event\ fails\ to\ occur)} = \frac{P(success)}{P(failure)}$$

For the example of drawing a Queen used above, the Odds in Favor of Queen would be:
$$Odds\ in\ Favor\ of\ Event\ = \frac{P(Event\ occurs)}{P(Event\ fails\ to\ occur)} = \frac{4/10}{6/10} = 0.67$$

6. Counting Rule 1. Principle for Multiple Experiments: If an Experiment 1 has m outcomes and Experiment 2 has n outcomes, then the two experiments in that specific order can have a total of m x n outcomes.

If one tosses a coin as Experiment 1 and tosses a six-faced unbiased dice as Experiment 2, one can expect that the total number of outcomes would be 2 x 6 = 12 outcomes
Experiment 1 coin toss: Two outcomes (Heads, Tails)
Experiment 2 dice toss: Six outcomes (1, 2, 3, 4, 5, 6)
Total Outcomes Possible: (Heads, 1), (Heads, 2), (Heads, 3), (Heads, 4), (Heads, 5), (Heads, 6), (Tails, 1), (Tails, 2), (Tails, 3), (Tails, 4), (Tails, 5), (Tails, 6) or 12 outcomes.

7. Counting Rule 2. For Experiment with multiple steps: If an experiment has k steps and n_1 is the number of outcomes for Step 1, n_2 is the number of outcomes for Step 2, ..., n_k is the number of outcomes for Step k, the total number of experimental outcomes is given by (n_1)x(n_2)x...x(n_k).

This is just a slight difference in words from the Counting Rule 1 in the sense that instead of running two different experiments in a given order, one is simply following different steps as a part of the same experiment. If a coin is flipped once, the two expected outcomes are (Heads and Tails). If an experiment requires one to toss the same coin 3 times in sequential order, there are 3 steps ($k = 3$) with 2 outcomes each (Heads, Tails). Thus, k =3 and $n_1 = 2$, $n_2 = 2$, and $n_3 = 2$ and the total number of outcomes for the 3-toss Experiment are = n_1 x n_2 x n_3 = 2 x 2 x 2 = 8 outcomes. This can be verified as follows:
(Heads, Heads, Heads); (Heads, Heads, Tails); (Heads, Tails, Heads); (Heads, Tails, Tails); (Tails, Heads, Heads); (Tails, Heads, Tails); (Tails, Tails, Heads); (Tails, Tails, Tails) or 8 total outcomes.

For a twist on this example, suppose that one wanted to do a two-step experiment ($k = 2$) where one tosses a coin first ($n_1 = 2$ outcomes) and a dice next ($n_2 = 6$ outcomes) the total number of outcomes would be 2 x 6 = 12 outcomes. This can be verified as follows:
(Heads, 1); (Heads, 2); (Heads, 3); (Heads, 4); (Heads, 5); (Heads, 6); (Tails, 1); (Tails, 2); (Tails, 3); (Tails, 4); (Tails, 5); (Tails, 6) or 12 outcomes total.

8. Counting Rule 3. Combinations of selections. The number of combinations of x items that can be selected from n items, without regard to arrangement, is denoted as $\binom{n}{x}$ or $_nC_x$ that represents the total number of combinations possible.
$$\binom{n}{x} = \frac{n!}{x!\,(n-x)!}$$
The "!" sign represents "factorial" such that:
$$X! = (X) \times (X\text{-}1) \times (X\text{-}2)...3 \times 2 \times 1.$$

Suppose that one was interested in choosing 3 marbles out of a bag that has 6 marbles in it at random. The Counting Rule 3 allows one to determine how many different ways one could choose $x = 3$ marbles out of the bag of $n = 6$ marbles by using the formula as below:

$$\binom{6}{3} = \frac{6!}{3!\,(6-3)!} = \frac{6 \times 5 \times 4 \times 3 \times 2 \times 1}{(3 \times 2 \times 1) \times (3 \times 2 \times 1)} = \frac{720}{36} = 20$$

3.2.2. Advanced Rules of Probability

Probability concepts such as Complement, Union, Intersection, Conditional Probability, and Independent Events are often easier understood with the help of visualizations using Venn Diagrams along with their formulas. Before continuing with the Rules of Probability, it will help to understand how Venn Diagrams can be used to represent the outcomes of an experiment and the events of interest. The Sample Space S is defined as all possible outcomes of an experiment and usually denoted in a Venn Diagram as a "Box." The Events of interest A, B, C, ... are denoted by capital letters and are denoted in a Venn Diagram as circles. Thus, if one is drawing a Venn Diagram of outcomes of a dice toss, the Sample Space $S = (1, 2, 3, 4, 5, 6)$ and if the events of interest are defined as $A = (5, 6)$ and $B = (3, 4)$, Figure 3.1 demonstrates what the diagram should look like. The outcomes (1, 2) are neither in Event A or in Event B but since they are a part of the Sample Space they are shown in the white area of the Venn Diagram.

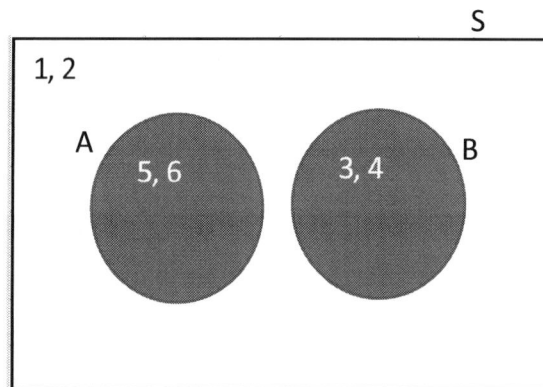

Figure 3.1. Venn Diagram General Presentation

9. Complement Set: Referring back to Probability Rule number 4, if Event A is the event of interest drawn from the Sample Set S of all possible outcomes of an experiment, then all the outcomes that are not in the Event A belong to the Complement set of A known as A' (A prime) and $P(A) + P(A') = 1$. Using the same illustration of picking a Queen from a deck of cards (total of 4 Queens in each deck), one can represent the Complement Set Q' as the Blue-shaded area of Figure 3.2. Moreover, one can write the formulas as:

$$P(Q) = \frac{total\ number\ of\ Queens}{total\ number\ of\ cards} = \frac{4}{52}$$
$$P(Q') = 1 - P(Q)$$
$$P(Q') = \frac{total\ number\ of\ non - Queen\ cards}{total\ number\ of\ cards} = \frac{52 - 4}{52} = \frac{48}{52}$$

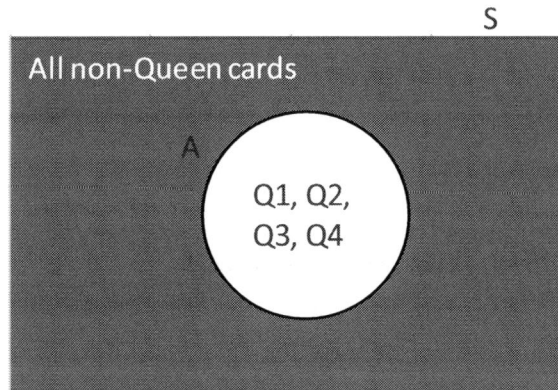

Figure 3.2. Venn Diagram for Complement of Queen Selection in a deck of cards

10. <u>Intersection Set and Multiplication Rule</u>: If two events A and B are defined as a part of an experiment with Sample Space S, the Intersection Set consists of the outcomes that occur in **both** A and B and is represented as "$A \cap B$." The key word that describes the Intersection set is "AND" and is often used in the applications of Logic as such. The "and" refers to something that occurs in both spaces and in just one or the other.

If the Sample Space S is defined as the outcome of a dice toss and Event A is defined as a set of all even outcomes (2, 4, 6) and Event B is defined as a set of all outcomes that are perfect squares (1, 4), then one can see that the outcome (4) is common to both Events, A and B. Thus, the intersection of A and B consists of a single outcome, 4. Figure 3.3 shows the intersection region shaded in gray, where the regions of Events A and B intersect.

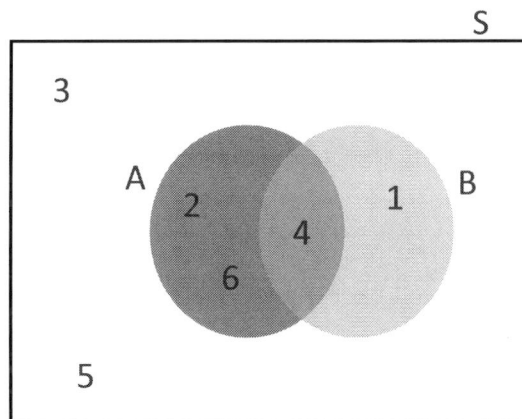

Figure 3.3. Intersection Regions of A and B

While the formula for the intersection requires more clarification in the context of the meaning of independent and dependent events, both the formulas presented here show the <u>Multiplication Rule of Probability</u> for now:

$$P(A \cap B) = P(A) \times P(B|A) = P(B) \times P(A|B) \; general \; formula$$
$$P(A \cap B) = P(A) \times P(B) \; if \; events \; A \; and \; B \; are \; independent \; of \; each \; other$$

In order to assess whether two events are independent of each other or not, one can apply the formulas directly. Thus, in the illustration of the dice, one knows that the probability of A, P(A) = 3/6 = 1/2 since Event A includes three out of the six possible outcomes of a dice toss. Similarly, the probability of B, P(B) = 2/6 = 1/3 since Event B includes two of the six possible outcomes of the dice toss. Thus,

$$P(A) \times P(B) = \frac{1}{2} \times \frac{1}{3} = \frac{1}{6} = 0.167$$

Now note that the probability of the intersection set P($A \cap B$) = 1/6 since only one outcome occurs in both A and B. Thus, the product of the probabilities of Events A and B is equal to the probability of the intersection set, implying that Events A and B, in this case, can be considered to be independent of each other, or the occurrence of one does not impact the occurrence of the other.

11. <u>Union Set and Addition Rule</u>: If two events A and B are defined as a part of an experiment with Sample Space S, the Union Set consists of the outcomes that occur in either A or B or in both and is represented as "$A \cup B$." The key word that describes the Intersection set is "OR" and is often used in the applications of Logic as such. The "or" refers to something that occurs in either or both spaces of interest.

If the Sample Space S is defined as the outcome of a dice toss and Event A is defined as a set of all even outcomes (2, 4, 6) and Event B is defined as a set of all outcomes that are perfect squares (1, 4), then the outcomes of (1, 2, 4, 6) occur in either A or in B or in both A and B. Thus, the union of A and B consists of four outcomes. Figure 3.4 shows the union region shaded in blue, which covers all outcomes of A and B together.

The formulas for Union of two sets, also known as the <u>Addition Rule of Probability,</u> are given as follows. The reason to subtract the intersection area in the formula is that since that portion occurs in both A and in B, it is double counted when one adds the A and B outcomes. Moreover, if there is no intersection region for A and B, one can use the second formula.

$$P(A \cup B) = P(A) + P(B) - P(A \cap B) \; general \; formula$$
$$P(A \cup B) = P(A) + P(B) \; if \; events \; A \; and \; B \; are \; mutually \; exclusive$$

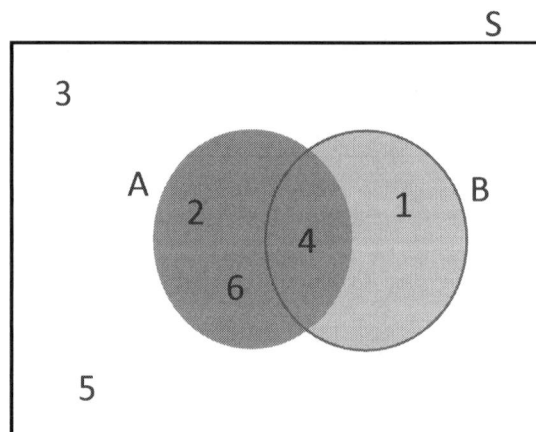

Figure 3.4. Union Region of A and B

In order to assess whether two events are mutually exclusive of each other or not, one can apply the formulas directly. In the illustration of the dice, the probability of A, $P(A)$ = 3/6 = 1/2 since Event A includes three out of the six possible outcomes of a dice toss. Similarly, the probability of B, $P(B)$ = 2/6 = 1/3 since Event B includes two of the six possible outcomes of the dice toss. Thus,

$$P(A) + P(B) = \frac{1}{2} + \frac{1}{3} = \frac{5}{6} = 0.833$$

Now note that the probability of the intersection set $P(A \cup B)$ = 4/6 =0.67 since a total of four outcomes occurs in the union set of A or B. Thus, the sum of the probabilities of Events A and B is NOT equal to the probability of the union set, implying that Events A and B are not mutually exclusive of each other.

12. Conditional Probability: When A and B are not independent of each other, or when the occurrence of one of the events impacts the occurrence of the other, one can use conditional probability. It is helpful to try to visualize what this would mean in the real world before exploring the formulas.

Say that one defines Event A as drawing a Queen of Hearts from a deck of cards. The probability of A occurring is 1/52. Now, suppose one defines Event B as drawing a King of Hearts from the same deck without putting the first card back (without replacement, in technical terms). The probability of B occurring is 1/51 if the first card was not a King of Hearts and if the first card was a King of Hearts, then the probability of pulling another King of Hearts would be 0. As you can see, the probability of B occurring was affected by the fact that the first card was not replaced into the deck. If one were replacing the card back into the deck before pulling out more cards, then each card would maintain its unique probability of 1/52 since there would be 52 steady outcomes. The formula for Conditional Probability is given as follows:

$$P(B|A) = \frac{P(A \cap B)}{P(A)}; \; P(A) \neq 0$$

The Conditional Probability of B given A is defined as the ratio of the probability of the intersection of A and B to the probability of A occurring. It is especially important to note that ***Independent Events are DIFFERENT from Mutually Exclusive Events***! In fact, if two Events A and B are mutually exclusive, they cannot be independent of each other. Think about a coin toss. There are only two outcomes (Heads, Tails) in the Sample Set. If one defines Event A as getting Heads and Event B as getting Tails on a coin toss, one knows the probability of each is ½ or 0.5. However, if the coin has already been tossed and it landed on Heads, one knows that the probability of getting Tails now is zero. So, $P(A)$ is 0.5 and $P(B)$ is 0.5. However, $P(B|A)$ = 0, because both B and A cannot occur at the same time and $P(A \cap B)$ would always be 0.

Example 3:1. Applying Some Rules of Probability.
Coach Ortiz is interested in identifying which parks the cross-country runners on the team prefer to practice at. Coach also wants to keep in mind that female runners might have different preferences than male runners based on upon safety and other considerations such as the early

dawn practice time. He collects the following information from his players by asking them to choose one of the three options for practice. Help him answer the questions given below Table 3.2.

Table 3.2. Coach Ortiz's Cross Country Team Preferences

Gender	Harberger Park	Valero Trail	Mission Trail	TOTAL
Female	5	8	2	15
Male	8	6	4	18
TOTAL	13	14	6	33

1. If a random student is picked out of the group, what is the probability that they like to run at Valero Trail?
2. What is the probability of a random student in the group being Female?
3. What is the probability that a random student chosen from the group likes to run at either Harberger Park or Mission Trail?
4. What is the probability that a Male student prefers to run at Valero Trail?
5. Are "being female" and "Mission Trail" independent events?

Solution: The Table 3.2 is a Contingency Table because it has two different variables that are being simultaneously considered: gender and preference of location of practice. The answers to the questions and their explanations are given below:

1. *If a random student is picked out of the group, what is the probability that they like to run at Valero Trail?*

The total number of students is 33 and 14 of those students prefer to run at Valero Trail. Thus, the Sample Space has 33 observations, and the Event *VT* defined as running at Valero Trail has 14 observations. So, the probability of *VT* would be:

$$P(VT) = \frac{14}{33} = 0.424$$

2. *What is the probability of a random student in the group being Female?*

If one defines Event *F* as a student being female, one can see that the total number of observations is 15. Thus, the probability of *F* would be:

$$P(F) = \frac{15}{33} = 0.455$$

3. *What is the probability that a random student chosen from the group likes to run at either Harberger Park or Mission Trail?*

If one defines Event *HP* as preference to run at Harberger Park and Event *MT* as preference to run at Mission Trail, one can see that Event *HP* has 13 observations and Event *MT* has 6 observations. There are no common observations (students who like to run at both places) Using the Union Set Rule #11 for Mutually Exclusive events, one can calculate the that the probability that a randomly chosen student likes to run at either location is 0.576 or 57.6%

$$P(HP) = \frac{13}{33} = 0.394$$

$$P(MT) = \frac{6}{33} = 0.182$$

$$P(HP \cup MT) = \frac{13 + 6}{33} = 0.576$$

4. *What is the probability that a Male student prefers to run at Valero Trail?*

Let Event M be defined as the student being Male. Now, it is already known that the student is a Male, so one should not consider the entire group of students when calculating the probability of Event VT (preference to run at Valero Trail). It is a conditional probability of VT given M that is being calculated. Table 3.2 shows that out of all the Males, 6 like to run at Valero Trail so one can calculate the probability as:

$$P(VT|M) = \frac{6}{18} = 0.333$$

A more complex method of solving this problem would be:

$$P(VT|M) = \frac{P(VT \cap M)}{P(M)} = \frac{6/33}{18/33} = 0.333$$

5. Are "being female" and "Mission Trail" independent events?

In order to test for independence, one can find the $P(F)$ and $P(MT)$ first. Then, one can find the $P(F \cap MT)$ to see if the product of $P(F)$ and $P(MT)$ is equal to the probability of the intersection set to determine whether the gender and preference for Mission Trail are independent events or not.

$$P(F) = \frac{15}{33} = 0.455$$

$$P(MT) = \frac{6}{33} = 0.182$$

$$P(F) \times P(MT) = \frac{15}{33} \times \frac{6}{33} = 0.083$$

$$P(F \cap MT) = \frac{2}{33} = 0.061$$

As one can see, the value of $P(F \cap MT)$ is 0.061 whereas the product of $P(F)$ and $P(MT)$ is 0.083. Since these are not equal to each other, one can say that "being female" and "Mission Trail" are not independent events.

3.3. Joint Probabilities, Tree Diagrams, and Bayes' Theorem

When an experiment is repeated over multiple trials, it becomes necessary to calculate the joint probabilities of the outcome of interest for each trial. There are formulas that allow one to calculate these probabilities and one can also use the visual aid of Tree Diagrams if the number of trials are manageable. The Bayes' Theorem uses Tree Diagrams and the conditional probability rules in order to calculate the posterior probabilities of an event of interest, which will be discussed in more detail in this section as well.

3.3.1. Joint Probabilities

In an *Experiment*, one tries to perform *Trials* that are independent of each other to avoid running into the issue of Conditional Probabilities. Moreover, one assumes that the outcomes of each Trial are mutually exclusive. Thus, if one tosses a dice three times in a row, one can expect the probability of an Event A being the face-value of 2 to remain constant at 1/6 or 0.167 in each Trial. The Complement of A would be any face-value other than 2. Thus, Trials 1, 2, and 3 are independent of each other and for each Trial A and A' are always mutually exclusive of each other. This allows one to get the Joint Probability of getting all three face-values of 2 as follows:

$$P(A_1 \cap A_2 \cap A_3) = P(A_1) \times P(A_2) \times P(A_3) = 0.167^3 = 0.0047$$

One can create various combinations of getting 2 or not getting 2 and calculating the probability of those Joint events. For instance, if one wanted to get the joint probability of getting a 2 on first trial or $P(A_1) = 0.167$, not getting a 2 on the second trial pr $P(A_2') = 0.833$, and getting a 2 on the third trial or $P(A_3) = 0.167$, one can obtain it by using the following formula:

$$P(A_1 \cap A'_2 \cap A_3) = P(A_1) \times P(A'_2) \times P(A_3) = 0.167 \times 0.833 \times 0.167 = 0.0232$$

3.3.2. Tree Diagrams

A better way to visualize Joint Probabilities is available through the use of Tree Diagrams as shown in Figure 3.5 The first trial can result in A or in A' resulting in two alternatives for where Trial 2 would occur. Similarly, there are four alternatives for where Trial 3 would occur depending on what the outcomes for Trials 1 and 2 were.

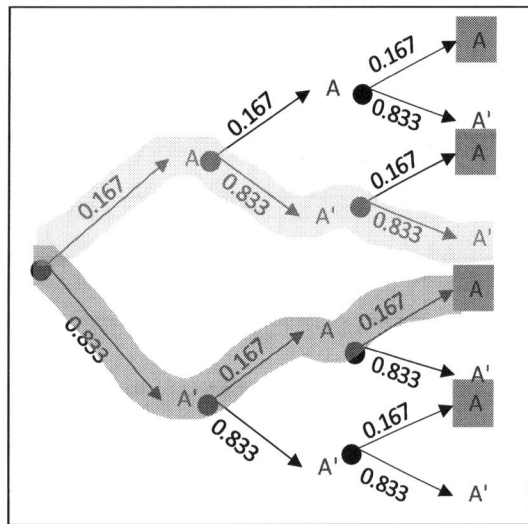

Calculations using Tree Diagram

P(2, 2, 2) = 0.167 x 0.167 x 0.167 =	0.0047
P(2, 2, not 2)= 0.167 x 0.167 x 0.833 =	0.0232
P(2, not 2, 2)= 0.167 x 0.833 x 0.167 =	0.0232
P(2, not 2, not2)= 0.167 x 0.833 x 0.833 =	0.1159
P(not 2, 2, 2)= 0.833 x 0.167 x 0.167 =	0.0232
P(not 2, 2, not 2)= 0.833 x 0.167 x 0.833 =	0.1159
P(not 2, not 2, 2)= 0.833 x 0.833 x 0.167 =	0.1159
P(not 2, not 2, not 2)= 0.833 x 0.833 x 0.833 =	0.5780

Total Probability of getting 2 in third trial	
P(2, 2, 2) + P(2, not 2, 2) + P(not 2, 2, 2) + P(not 2, not 2, 2)=	
=0.0047 + 0.0232 + 0.0232 + 0.1159 =	0.167

Figure 3.5. Tree Diagram for Joint Probabilities

The pathways demonstrate what outcomes are possible and their related probabilities. The highlighted portions correspond to the formulas that are highlighted on the right-hand side which shows the calculations using pathways. The biggest issue with the Tree Diagram method is that as the number of Trials increases, it becomes more complex. For instance, the Figure 3.5 only shows 3 Trials, and it already has 8 pathways. If one refers to the Counting Rule 2 under the Section 3.2.1 Basic Rules of Probability one can see that since there are 2 possible outcomes and 3 total trials, the number of pathways would be $2^3 = 8$. Similarly, if there were 4 Trials, one would have 2^4 or 16 pathways to consider.

3.3.3. Bayes' Theorem and Probability Application

Bayes' Theorem, discovered by statistician Thomas Bayes in 1763, is a mathematical formula to compute the conditional probability of a given event based on previous knowledge or assumptions of conditions that could impact the event itself. It is increasingly being used in subjectivist statistical methodology which relies on revisiting assumptions of data as more data is collected in order to make predictions more accurate.

Let S_1 and S_2 be two mutually exclusive events, where one of them must be true. Moreover, let $P(S_i)$ refer to the posterior probability of the specific event of interest (either S_1 or S_2) and an

Event E be defined as a particular outcome of an Experiment, then the Conditional probability of S_i given the event E is defined as the Bayesian Probability of S_i and the formula is:

$$P(S_i|E) = \frac{P(S_i) \times P(E|S_i)}{P(S_1) \times P(E|S_1) + P(S_2) \times P(E|S_2)}$$

Example 3:2. Bayesian Probability for Gestational Diabetes

Suppose it is known that 12% of expectant mothers typically develop Gestational Diabetes (GD) in the third trimester of their pregnancy. The test done at Week 27 or 28 of the pregnancy is reasonably accurate but is not entirely foolproof. If the expectant mother has GD, the test is positive 90% of the time. However, the test is positive 15% of the time for expectant mothers who do not have GD for various reasons. What is the probability that an expectant mother does not have GD if she gets a positive test result? (Note that these values are based on suppositions made by the author and are not reflective of the actual accuracy of any medical test).

Solution: Start by listing out all the relevant details and comparing the values with the Bayes' Theorem formula.
- $P(S_1) = P(GD) = 0.12$ (posterior probability of developing GD during pregnancy)
- $P(S_2) = P(GD') = 0.88$ (posterior probability of not developing GD during pregnancy)
- $E = POS$ = positive result on the GD test during Week 27 or 28 of pregnancy
- $P(E|S_1) = P(POS|GD) = 0.90$ (probability that the test is positive for women who have GD)
- $P(E|S_2) = P(POS|GD') = 0.15$ (probability that the test is positive for women who do not have GD)

Find the conditional probability $P(GD|POS)$, also known as the Bayesian Probability of having GD if the test is POS. Figure 3.6 demonstrates the Tree Diagram Pathways

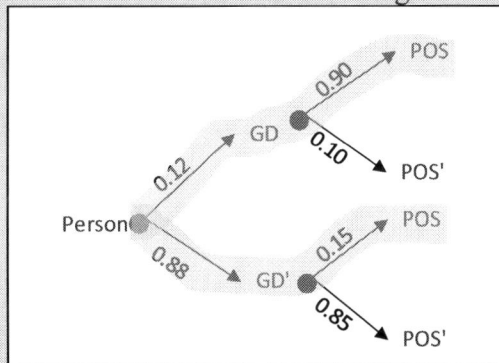

Figure 3.6. Tree Diagram for Bayes' Theorem Calculations

$$P(GD|POS) = \frac{P(GD) \times P(POS|GD)}{P(GD) \times P(POS|GD) + P(GD') \times P(POS|GD')}$$
$$= \frac{(0.12) \times (0.90)}{(0.12 \times 0.90) + (0.88 \times 0.15)} = \frac{0.108}{0.108 + 0.132} = 0.45$$

Thus, there is a 45% probability that an expectant mother has GD if she tested positive for it in the Week 27 or 28 Gestational Diabetes test. There is less than a 50% chance of a person testing positive for GD to actually have GD. This is one of the reasons why if a woman tests positive during the GD screening test, the doctor will often require additional testing before recommending a plan for monitoring it during the remaining weeks of her pregnancy.

List of Formulas for Chapter 3

$$P_E = relative\ frequency\ = \frac{Number\ of\ times\ an\ Event\ occurs}{Total\ number\ of\ Trials\ of\ the\ Experiment}$$

$$P_T = \text{Theoretical Probability} = \frac{Number\ of\ outcomes\ favorable\ to\ an\ Event}{Total\ number\ of\ possible\ Outcomes\ of\ the\ Experiment}$$

Complementary Events and Total Probability: If A is the event of interest
$$P(A) + P(A') = 1$$
$$P(A') = 1 - P(A)$$

Odds: Ratio of two probabilities

$$Odds\ Against\ Event\ = \frac{P(Event\ fails\ to\ occur)}{P(Event\ occurs)} = \frac{P(failure)}{P(success)}$$

$$Odds\ in\ Favor\ of\ Event\ = \frac{P(Event\ occurs)}{P(Event\ fails\ to\ occur)} = \frac{P(success)}{P(failure)}$$

Counting Rule 1. If an Experiment 1 has *m* outcomes and Experiment 2 has *n* outcomes, then the two experiments in that specific order can have a total of *m* x *n* outcomes.

Counting Rule 2. If an experiment has *k* steps and n_1 is the number of outcomes for Step 1, n_2 is the number of outcomes for Step 2, ..., n_k is the number of outcomes for Step *k*, the total number of experimental outcomes is given by $(n_1)x(n_2)x...x(n_k)$.

Counting Rule 3. Combination rule for *x* events out of *n* total outcomes
$$\binom{n}{x} = \frac{n!}{x!\,(n-x)!}$$

Multiplication Rule of Probability General formula and formula if *A* and *B* are independent
$$P(A \cap B) = P(A) \times P(B|A) = P(B) \times P(A|B)\ general\ formula$$

$$P(A \cap B) = P(A) \times P(B)\ if\ events\ A\ and\ B\ are\ independent\ of\ each\ other$$

Addition Rule of Probability General formula and formula if *A* and *B* are mutually exclusive.
$$P(A \cup B) = P(A) + P(B) - P(A \cap B)\ general\ formula$$

$$P(A \cup B) = P(A) + P(B)\ if\ events\ A\ and\ B\ are\ mutually\ exclusive$$

Conditional Probability. Probability of B occurring given that A has already occured:
$$P(B|A) = \frac{P(A \cap B)}{P(A)};\ P(A) \neq 0$$

Bayes' Theorem: Let S_1 and S_2 be two mutually exclusive events, where one of them must be true. Moreover, let P(S_i) refer to the posterior probability of the specific event of interest (either S_1 or

S_2) and an Event E be defined as a particular outcome of an Experiment, then the Conditional probability of S_i given the event E is defined as the Bayesian Probability of S_i and the formula is:

$$P(S_i|E) = \frac{P(S_i) \times P(E|S_i)}{P(S_1) \times P(E|S_1) + P(S_2) \times P(E|S_2)}$$

Chapter 4. Probability Distributions

Before discussing the Probability Distributions that are based on the Joint Probabilities similar to what was covered in the previous chapter, it is necessary to define what a *Random Variable* means and how to present the values of a *Random Variable* when building distributions. This will help to keep track of how formulas can be "read" or interpreted when taking different types of probability distributions into account.

A *Random Variable* (*RV*) is defined as a variable that can take on the values of all the outcomes of an experiment and is always associated with a specific probability distribution. It is just another name for the "Events" that were covered in the previous chapter. It is usually represented with a capital letter such as A, B, C, …, X, Y, Z. The values of the *RV* can vary with each trial or observation and each value is a number. For general formulas, these values are represented with small letters such as "x," "y" or "z" to refer to a numeric value. To illustrate, if one defines X as the number of Heads when 2 coins are flipped, then the values that X can take on would be (0, 1, 2) depending upon how many Heads show up. One can write X as the variable "X_i" where "i" refers to each specific outcome possible. Thus, X_i = Total number of Heads when 3 coins are tossed and $x_i = 0, 1 , 2$. ***The subscripts are often omitted in general usage, but they are used in formulas in different books and sources, which is why the reader will see this book switching back and forth between the two depending upon how relevant they are in terms of generalizability.***

If the values of a *RV* are countable, random, and whole numbers then one can say that the *RV* is a "*discrete*" random variable. If the values of a *RV* are measurable and continuous, then one can say that the RV is a "*continuous*" random variable. Discrete *RVs* are often associated with probability distributions such as Binomial, Poisson, Hypergeometric, and Geometric distributions. Continuous *RVs* are associated with parametric (symmetrical) probability distributions such as the Uniform, Exponential, Normal distributions, and with non-parametric (asymmetrical) distributions such as Chi-Squared and F-distributions. Most of these distributions are covered in more detail in subsequent chapters. But first it is essential to understand what a Probability Distribution is and what are the key elements to construct one.

Probability Distributions are always constructed based upon the Theoretical Probabilities and are not based on Empirical Probabilities. The distribution function for probability of any *RV* is called the *Probability Density Function* (PDF) and is based on the assumptions of the Section 3.2. Rules of Probability # 3 and # 4 that the probability of each outcome is between 0 and 1 and the sum of all probabilities of outcomes of a *RV* is equal to 1. The expected value of the *RV* is called the "Mean" (μ) of the PDF and the expected "Variance" (σ^2) of the PDF can be calculated based on the mean and probabilities of each outcome using the following formulas:

$$E(X_i) = \mu = \sum X_i \cdot P(X_i)$$

$$Var(X_i) = \sigma^2 = \sum (X_i - \mu)^2 \cdot P(X_i)$$

$$Std. Dev. (X_i) = \sigma = \sqrt{\sum (X_i - \mu)^2 \cdot P(X_i)}$$

Example 4:1. Probability Distribution for tossing 2-coins

Create a Probability Distribution identifying the total number of Heads that can be obtained when two coins are tossed simultaneously and find the Mean and Standard Deviation values for the distribution.

Solution. First, define *H* as the Random Variable that shows the number of Heads obtained when two coins are tossed. Thus, the set of $H = (0, 1, 2)$ where either none of the coins end up with Heads ($h_1 = 0$), only one of the coins ends up with Heads ($h_2 = 1$), and both coins end up with Heads ($h_3 = 2$). Using the Combination Formula from the Probability Rule #8 (Counting Rule #3), $n = 2$ (because 2 coins are being tossed) and x takes the different values of h_1, h_2, and h_3, one can find the following:

$$\binom{n}{x} = \frac{n!}{x!\,(n-x)!}$$

$$\binom{2}{0} = \frac{2!}{0!\,(2-0)!} = \frac{2 \times 1}{(1) \times (2 \times 1)} = \frac{2}{2} = 1$$

$$\binom{2}{1} = \frac{2!}{1!\,(2-1)!} = \frac{2 \times 1}{(1) \times (1)} = \frac{2}{1} = 2$$

$$\binom{2}{2} = \frac{2!}{2!\,(2-2)!} = \frac{2 \times 1}{(2 \times 1) \times (1)} = \frac{2}{2} = 1$$

Thus, if the two coins were tossed simultaneously for 4 times (sum of all the combination outcomes $= 1 + 2 + 1 = 4$), one can expect 0 Heads to occur one time, 1 Heads to occur 2 times, and 2 Heads to occur 1 time. Table 4.1 shows the Relative frequency of each outcome, which is defined as the Probability P(*H*) for each outcome:

Table 4.1. Probability Distribution of Tossing 2 coins simultaneously

Tossing 2 coins

N = 2
n = h = 0, 1, 2

# of Heads	Expected Frequency	Relative Expected Frequency	For Mu	Squared Deviations	For Variance
H	fe	P(H)	H.P(H)	(H - mu)^2	P(H)*(H - mu)^2
0	1	0.25	0	1	0.25
1	2	0.5	0.5	0	0
2	1	0.25	0.5	1	0.25
TOTAL	**4**	**1**	**1**		**0.5**

Using the formula for the Mean or the Expected average value of Heads, one can get:

$$E(H_i) = \mu = \sum H_i \cdot P(H_i) = (0)(0.25) + (1)(0.5) + (2)(0.25) = 0 + 0.5 + 0.5 = 1$$

Using formula for Variance, one gets:

$$Var(H_i) = \sigma^2 = \sum (H_i - \mu)^2 \cdot P(H_i) = (1)(0.25) + (0)(0.5) + (1)(0.25) = 0.5$$

Standard Deviation is always the square root of the Variance, so

$$Std.\,Dev. = \sqrt{Var(H_i)} = \sqrt{0.5} = 0.7071$$

Under certain given conditions the empirical or observed frequency distributions can be approximated by well-known theoretical distributions. There are about five key theoretical probability distributions, which occupy a central position in statistics, and this book will focus on those. In this chapter Discrete Probability Distributions such as the Binomial and Poisson Distributions and Continuous Probability Distributions such as the Uniform and Exponential Distributions are discussed. The next chapter (and beyond) will heavily focus on the Normal Distribution since it plays a crucial role in a variety of business applications of statistics.

4.1. Discrete Probability Distributions

If the values of a *RV* are countable, random, and whole numbers then one say that the *RV* is a "*discrete*" random variable. This section focuses on the Binomial and the Poisson Distributions due to their popularity in statistical calculations in the real world. Hypergeometric and Geometric Distributions are not discussed in this book but are also two other types of distributions for discrete *RVs*.

4.1.1. Binomial Distribution

James Bernoulli discovered the Binomial Distribution in 1700 CE and this distribution has some very particular characteristics. In the case of a Binomial Distribution, the Random Variable (*RV*) is measured in a manner that each trial can take only result in one of two outcomes. Such trials are called Bernoulli Trials. The coin toss is an easy way to think about it since the outcomes can only be either Heads or Tails. But one can generalize it to fit their needs for any variable. For instance, if a dice is tossed and one is interested in the outcome of "5" on the face, one can mark each observation as being either "5" or "not 5." If data on household incomes is collected, one can classify each household as "poor" or "not poor" based on a threshold value such as earning $18,000 per year or less (poor) and earning more than $18,000 per year (not poor). Similarly, businesses could be classified as "large" or "not large" based upon the number of employees or total output. Thus, a *RV* that follows a Binomial Distribution can only have a "success" value or a "failure" value. The assumptions that comprise the Binomial Distribution are as follows:

1. The *RV* consists of the observations obtained from the outcomes of a fixed number of independent trials, *n*.

2. The outcomes are discrete and cannot overlap (if one gets Heads on a coin toss, one cannot get a Tails in the same observation)

3. The outcomes are "binary" and have either a "success" value or a "failure" value

4. The probability of success, defined as *p*, remains the same for each trial.

5. The probability of failure, defined as $q = 1 - p$, also remains the same for each trial.

6. Binomial Distribution for a random variable *X* is written as $X \sim B(n, p)$ where *n* and *p* are considered to be the parameters indicating the distribution of *X*.

7. The formula for identifying the probability of getting *x* successes in *n* trials is given as follows:

$$P(X = x) = \binom{n}{x} p^x q^{(n-x)}$$

8. The Mean (or the expected number of successes) for the Binomial Probability Distribution $= \mu = n.p$ and the standard deviation $= \sigma = \sqrt{n.p.q}$

9. If the $p = q = 0.5$, the Binomial Distribution of *X* is symmetrical, otherwise it is not.

Example 4:2. Tossing a Dice 8 times

Suppose a dice is tossed 8 times and one defines getting either a 5 or a 6 on the face as a success. Answer the following questions:
1. Obtain the probability of getting 4 successes.
2. Obtain the probability of getting less than 4 successes, more than 4 successes, and getting at least one success
3. Obtain the Mean E(*X*), Variance Var(*X*), and standard deviation of *X* for this distribution

Solution: Replicating the process used in *Example 4.1* it is possible to create the table of outcomes for the 8 dice tosses as shown below or one can use formulas directly in Excel to obtain the desired solutions by using the Binomial Distribution formula "=BINOM.DIST(number_s, trials, probability_s, cumulative)".

Table 4.2. Tossing a dice 8 times – Manual calculations & Excel formulas

Tossing 8 dice

n =	8		
x =	0, 1, 2, 3, 4, 5, 6, 7, 8		
p =	0.33	=1/3	
q =	0.67	=1-B5	

Number of Successes X	$\binom{n}{x} = \dfrac{n!}{x!\,(n-x)!}$ Combinations of x out of n	p^x	q^(n-x)	$P(X = x) = \binom{n}{x} p^x q^{(n-x)}$ P(X = x)
0	1	1.000	0.0390	0.0390
1	8	0.333	0.0585	0.1561
2	28	0.111	0.0878	0.2731
3	56	0.037	0.1317	0.2731
4	70	0.012	0.1975	0.1707
5	56	0.004	0.2963	0.0683
6	28	0.001	0.4444	0.0171
7	8	0.000	0.6667	0.0024
8	1	0.000	1.0000	0.0002

Mean = Mu =	n*p	2.667
Var. =	n*p*q	1.778
Std. dev. =	Sqrt of var =	1.333
P(X = 4)=	refer to the P(X = x) cell for x=4	0.1707
P(X < 4) =	P(X=0)+P(X=1)+P(X=2)+P(X=3)	0.7414
P(X > 4)=	P(X=5)+P(X=6)+P(X=7)+P(X=8)	0.0879
P(X > 1) =	1 - P(X=0) - P(X=1)	0.8049

Probability Distribution Function

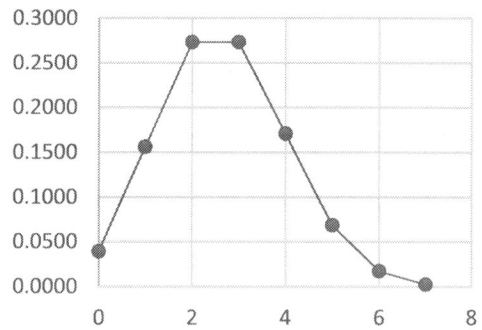

NOTE: This Excel sheet can be used for upto 20 trials by simply changing the numbers in the Gray-shaded cells to reflect the problem at hand.

Binomial Distribution: Tossing dice 8 times

n =	8		success defined as getting either 5 or 6 on the face	
p =	0.33	=1/3	Thus, probability of success is 2/6 or 1/3 for any dice toss	
q =	0.67	=1-I4		

Mean =	2.667	=I3*I4	
Var. =	1.778	=I3*I4*I5	
Std. Dev.=	1.333	=SQRT(I8)	

Probability Distribution Function

Cumulative Density Function

X	P(X)	CDF
0	0.0390	0.0390
1	0.1561	0.1951
2	0.2731	0.4682
3	0.2731	0.7414
4	0.1707	0.9121
5	0.0683	0.9803
6	0.0171	0.9974
7	0.0024	0.9998
8	0.0002	1.0000
9	#NUM!	#NUM!
10	#NUM!	#NUM!
11	#NUM!	#NUM!
12	#NUM!	#NUM!
13	#NUM!	#NUM!
14	#NUM!	#NUM!
15	#NUM!	#NUM!

Answers Using Table to the left:

x =	4	=I19
P(X =4) =	0.1707	=J19
P(X < 4) =	0.7414	=K18
P(X > 4) =	0.0879	=1-K19
P(X >1) =	0.8049	=1-K16

Answers Using direct Binomial formula

x =	4	
P(X =4) =	0.1707	=BINOM.DIST(N19,I3,I4,FALSE)
P(X < 4) =	0.7414	=BINOM.DIST((N19-1),I3,I4,TRUE)
P(X > 4) =	0.0879	=1 - BINOM.DIST(N26,I3,I4,TRUE)
P(X >1) =	0.8049	=1-BINOM.DIST(1,I3,I4,TRUE)

4.1.2. Poisson Distribution

Poisson Distribution was discovered by S.D. Poisson in 1837 and is a limiting form of the Binomial Distribution. Suppose that in a Binomial Distribution, the probability of success, p is very small, and the number of trials n is so large that the value of the expected mean, $\mu = n.p$ is almost constant. Note that like the Binomial Distribution, there are still only two outcomes – "success" or "failure." Thus, the characteristics of the Poisson Distribution as follows:

1. Poisson Distribution gives the probability of a number of discrete (whole numbers) events occurring during a fixed interval of time or space at a fixed rate.

2. The RV consists of the successes obtained from the outcomes of a large number of independent trials, n within a given interval of interest.

3. The probability of success, defined as p, is very small and remains the same for each trial.

4. Poisson Distribution for a random variable X is written as $X \sim \rho(\mu)$ where the expected arrival rate μ is the parameter indicating the distribution of X.

5. The formula for identifying the probability of getting x successes in n trials is given as follows:

$$P(X = x) = \frac{\mu^x e^{-\mu}}{x!}$$

Note that e = Euler's number (an irrational number with an approximate value of 2.718, which was discussed in Chapter 1 Section 1.1.2.)

6. The Mean (or the expected number of successes) for the Poisson Probability Distribution = μ = np = number of occurrences expected within a given time interval and the standard deviation = σ = $\sqrt{\mu}$

A couple of examples will help to understand the Poisson Distribution and how it is different from Binomial Distribution better. The first one is a simple example of Arrival Rates, since the Poisson Distribution is often used for measuring Arrival rates in higher level courses of statistics to calculate models in Queuing Theory.

Example 4:3. Poisson Distribution - Arrival Rates of Customers

Assume that a gas station is trying to determine whether to remain open between the hours of 10 PM and 11 PM every night, since the number of customers coming in during that time frame is uncertain. After observing the patterns of customers for a few weeks, the owner determines that on an average 6 customers enter the store in any given hour. He wants to see what the probabilities of arrivals are between 10 and 11 PM. Help him to answer the following questions:
1. What is the probability that exactly 3 customers arrive in the store during 10 and 11 PM?
2. What is the probability that less than 5 customers arrive in the store in that hour?
3. What is the probability that exactly 10 customers arrive in the store in that hour?
4. What is the probability that 12 or more customers arrive in the store in that hour?
5. What is the mean and the standard deviation of this Poisson Distribution?

Solution: Here, the mean arrival rate or μ = 6. Based on this one can create a table of outcomes for the Poisson Values with various outcomes as shown in Table 4.3 or one can use Poisson Distribution formulas directly in Excel to obtain the desired solutions by using the Poisson Distribution formula "=POISSON.DIST(x, mean, cumulative)".

Table 4.3. Poisson Distribution for Arrival Rate of 6 per hour

Poisson Distribution: Arrival Rate of 6 customers per hour

Mean = E(X) =	6	
Std. Dev. =	2.449	=SQRT(B3)
e^-µ =	0.0025	=EXP(-B3)

Answers with Manual Calculation:

X	µ^x	x!	$P(X = x) = \dfrac{\mu^x e^{-\mu}}{x!}$
0	1	1	0.0025
1	6	1	0.0149
2	36	2	0.0446
3	216	6	0.0892
4	1296	24	0.1339
5	7776	120	0.1606
6	46656	720	0.1606
7	279936	5040	0.1377
8	1679616	40320	0.1033
9	10077696	362880	0.0688
10	60466176	3628800	0.0413
11	362797056	39916800	0.0225
12	2176782336	479001600	0.0113
13	13060694016	6227020800	0.0052
14	78364164096	87178291200	0.0022

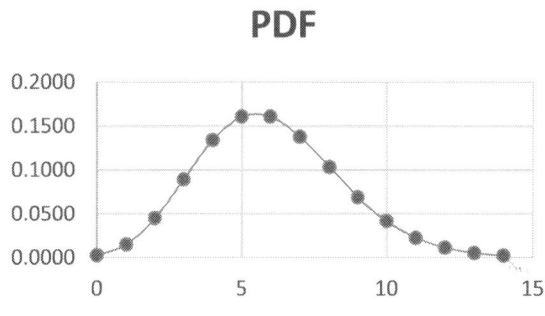

PDF

P(X = 3) =	refer to cell for X=3	0.0892
P(X < 5) =	P(X=0) + P(X=1) + P(X=2) + P(X=3) + P(X=4)	0.2851
P(X = 10) =	refer to cell for X=10	0.0413
P(X >= 12) =	1 - P(X=0) - P(X=2)... - P(X=11)	0.0201

NOTE: This Excel sheet can be used for upto mean=20 by simply changing the numbers in the Gray-shaded cells to reflect the problem at hand.

Poisson Distribution: 6 customers per hour

mean = 6

X	P(X)	CDF
0	0.0025	0.0025
1	0.0149	0.0174
2	0.0446	0.0620
3	0.0892	0.1512
4	0.1339	0.2851
5	0.1606	0.4457
6	0.1606	0.6063
7	0.1377	0.7440
8	0.1033	0.8472
9	0.0688	0.9161
10	0.0413	0.9574
11	0.0225	0.9799
12	0.0113	0.9912
13	0.0052	0.9964
14	0.0022	0.9986
15	0.0009	0.9995
16	0.0003	0.9998
17	0.0001	0.9999
18	0.0000	1.0000
19	0.0000	1.0000
20	0.0000	1.0000

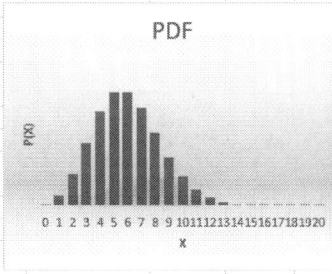

PDF

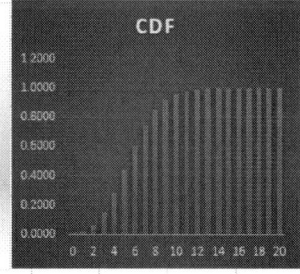

CDF

Answers Using Table to the left:

P(X = 3) =	0.0892	=H9
P(X < 5) =	0.2851	=I10
P(X = 10) =	0.0413	=H16
P(X >= 12) =	0.0201	=1-I17

Answers Using direct Poisson Formula:

P(X = 3) =	0.0892	=POISSON.DIST(3,H3,FALSE)
P(X < 5) =	0.2851	=POISSON.DIST(5-1,H3,TRUE)
P(X = 10) =	0.0413	=POISSON.DIST(10,H3,FALSE)
P(X >= 12) =	0.0201	=1-POISSON.DIST(12-1,H3,TRUE)

Sometimes, instead of being given the actual mean (or expected value) for a Poisson Distribution, one is given a probability p which is very low and a large number of trials n. One would need to derive the mean or expected value by using the formula $\mu = np$ in order to proceed. See Example 4.4 for an illustration of how this would work.

Example 4:4. Poisson Distribution for a Bad Reaction to Medicine

The probability that an individual suffers a bad reaction from a certain medicine is 0.001. Determine the probability that out of 2000 individuals:
(a.) Exactly 3 will suffer a bad reaction
(b.) more than 2 people will suffer a bad reaction.

Solution: In this example, one can see that the $p = 0.001$ (which is very low) and the $n = 2000$ (large number). Thus, one would start by calculating the expected value or mean μ by finding the product of the n and the p. One can create the table of outcomes as shown in Table 4.4 for the Poisson Values with various outcomes as shown below or one can use Poisson Distribution formulas directly in Excel to obtain the desired solutions by using the Poisson Distribution formula "=POISSON.DIST(x, mean, cumulative)".

Table 4.4. Poisson Distribution for a Bad Reaction to Medicine

Poisson Distribution: Probability of Bad Reaction

n =	2000	
p =	0.001	
Mean = E(X) =	2	=B3*B4
Std. Dev. =	1.414	=SQRT(B5)
e^-μ =	0.1353	=EXP(-B5)

Answers with Manual Calculation:

X	μ^x	x!	$P(X = x) = \dfrac{\mu^x e^{-\mu}}{x!}$
0	1	1	0.1353
1	2	1	0.2707
2	4	2	0.2707
3	8	6	0.1804
4	16	24	0.0902
5	32	120	0.0361
6	64	720	0.0120
7	128	5040	0.0034
8	256	40320	0.0009
9	512	362880	0.0002
10	1024	3628800	0.0000
11	2048	39916800	0.0000
12	4096	479001600	0.0000
13	8192	6227020800	0.0000
14	16384	87178291200	0.0000

P(X = 3) =	refer to cell for X=3	0.1804	=D14
P(X> 2) =	1 - P(X=0) - P(X=1) - P(X=2)	0.3233	=1 - D11-D12-D13

Poisson Distribution: Probability of Bad Reaction

n =	2000	
p =	0.001	
mean =	2	=H3*H4

X	P(X)	CDF
0	0.1353	0.1353
1	0.2707	0.4060
2	0.2707	0.6767
3	0.1804	0.8571
4	0.0902	0.9473
5	0.0361	0.9834
6	0.0120	0.9955
7	0.0034	0.9989
8	0.0009	0.9998
9	0.0002	1.0000
10	0.0000	1.0000
11	0.0000	1.0000
12	0.0000	1.0000
13	0.0000	1.0000
14	0.0000	1.0000
15	0.0000	1.0000
16	0.0000	1.0000
17	0.0000	1.0000
18	0.0000	1.0000
19	0.0000	1.0000
20	0.0000	1.0000

Answers Using Table to the left:

P(X = 3) = 0.1804 =H11

P(X > 2) = 0.3233 =1-I10

Answers Using direct Poisson Formula:

P(X = 3) = 0.1804 =POISSON.DIST(3,H5,FALSE)

P(X > 2) = 0.3233 =1-POISSON.DIST(2,H5,TRUE)

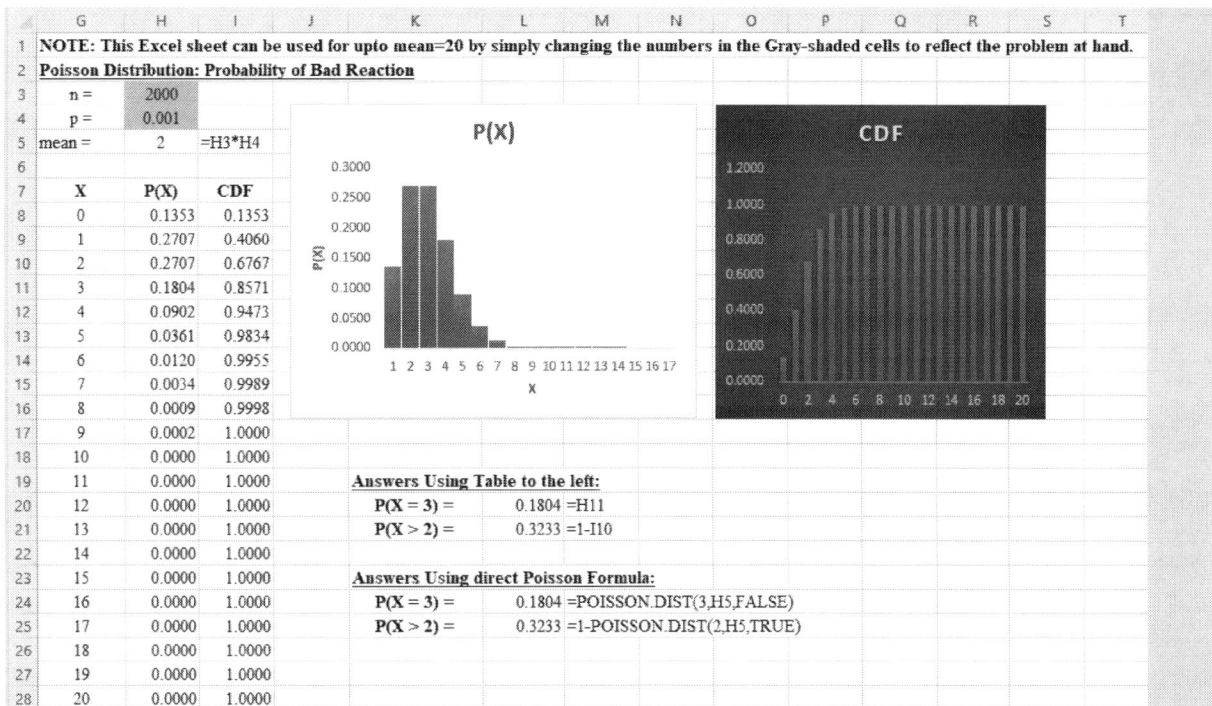

4.2. Continuous Probability Distributions

The definitions of "continuous" Random Variables (*RV*) can often be very ambiguous, so specification of events helps identify these variables more clearly. Unlike the Discrete probability distributions that have specific outcomes that are distinct from each other, the continuous distributions have an infinite number of possibilities, which results in the probability of any specific outcome as being equal to 0. (NOTE: if the possibilities are infinite, the probability of a specific outcome would be equal to $1/\infty = 0$.) Thus, the Probability Density Function (*PDF*) or the Probability Distribution Function is also going to be continuous for continuous *RVs*, unlike the graphs for the Discrete *PDFs* (refer to Examples 4.2-4.4), which had "bars" separating the various discrete outcomes. Similarly, the Cumulative Density Functions (*CDF*) will also be continuous.

This section starts by defining the general characteristics of the Continuous Probability Density Functions and then proceeds to discuss the Uniform and Exponential Distributions in as sub-sections. The Normal Distribution is also a Continuous Probability Distribution so the following characteristics and assumptions are also applicable to the Normal Distribution, which will be covered in subsequent chapters.

1. The graph of the Probability Density Function (*PDF*) is a curve defined as the probability *p* being a function f(*x*) of infinite continuous outcomes, *x* of a random variable *X*.

2. The outcomes of continuous random variable *X* are not "counted" but are measured.

3. The area under the curve is defined as the Cumulative Density Function (*CDF*) and is obtained by getting the integral of f(*x*), given by $\int f(x).dx$. The total area under the curve is always unity or equal to 1.

4. The Probability of any one specific value of X is always equal to 0. So, $P(X = x) = 0$ because all calculations require measurement of an "area."

5. Probability calculations in continuous distributions are always a measure of the relative percentage of certainty between any 2 given or specified outcomes of the variable X. Thus, probability is found for intervals of x values and not for any specific x-value.

    i. $P(c \leq X \leq d)$ = probability that RV X lies between values of $X = c$ and $X = d$.

    ii. $P(c < X < d) = P(c \leq X \leq d)$ = area under the curve between $X = c$ and $X = d$.

4.2.1. Uniform Distribution

The Uniform Distribution is a continuous probability distribution between values a and b of the random variable X, that consists of all outcomes between a and b occurring with the same probability. The *PDF* of a Uniform Distribution, $f(x)$ is defined as the reciprocal of the difference between the highest and lowest values of X and the expected value (or mean) μ is the average of the highest and lowest values of X. It is possible to represent a random variable X that is distributed with a Uniform Distribution in the form X~U(a, b) where a is the smallest value and b is the highest value of X. The formulas for the f(x), μ, and the standard deviation σ are given as follows:

$$f(x) = \frac{1}{(b-a)} \; for \; a \leq x \leq b; \; a \; is \; lowest \; value \; \& \; b \; is \; highest \; value$$

$$Mean \; \mu = \frac{(a+b)}{2}; \; Std.Dev. \sigma = \sqrt{\frac{(b-a)^2}{12}}$$

Figure 4.1 shows how the values of a and b are placed in the Uniform Distribution and how to calculate the probability between any two values of interest, c and d within the (a, b) range of the variable X, since the probability of outcomes is consistent at f(x) = 1/($b - a$)

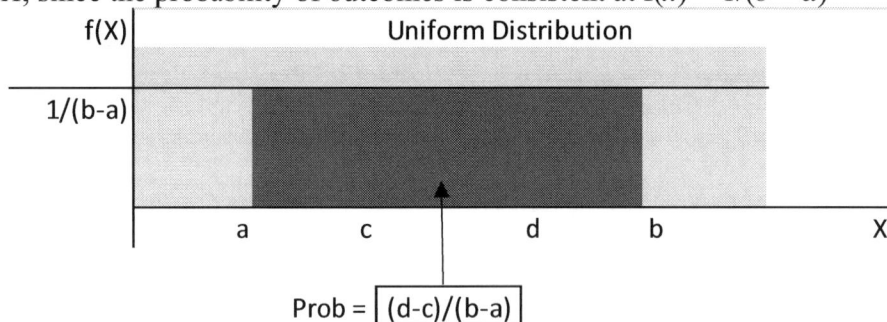

Figure 4.1. Uniform Distribution of X~U(a, b)

    Remember that the probability of B falling between any two values of interest such as c and d is determined by the area of the curve between the two values. Since the Uniform Distribution is a rectangular-shaped distribution, it is equivalent to getting the area of a rectangle, which is defined as the length x height of the rectangle. In the case of the brown-shaded rectangle above, one can see that the length = ($d - c$) and the height = 1/($b - a$) = f(x). Thus, the $P(c < X < d)$ can be written as:

$$P(c < X < d) = (d - c) \times f(x) = (d - c) \times \frac{1}{(b-a)} = \frac{(d-c)}{(b-a)}$$

An example of the Uniform Distribution will help to understand how to use the Uniform Distribution in various ways to estimate probabilities of desired outcomes. The main use of Uniform Distribution is to help with decision-making in businesses where demand forecasting for products or resources is essential to identify how much to purchase or produce or hire in order to meet the customer needs satisfactorily, while maximizing the revenues and minimizing the costs of production and other investment.

Example 4:5. Uniform Distribution of Demand for Boots

Suppose a business selling snow boots is preparing for the upcoming year. They know that the demand for snow boots is follows a Uniform Distribution each year and ranges from 400 to 800 pairs of boots sold each year during the season. A new manager is trying to determine exactly how many shoes to hold in inventory and needs to calculate the probability of selling between 450 and 680 shoes. She would also like to calculate the probability of selling more than 680 shoes. Help her to answer the following questions:
1. Identify the highest and lowest values of this distribution and write the mathematical formulation to represent the distribution of B or the demand for snow boots in a given year. Draw the graph of the distribution.
2. Calculate the Mean and the Standard Deviation of this distribution.
3. What is the actual uniform probability function value?
4. Find P(450 < B < 680)
5. Find P(B > 680)

Solution It is given that the demand for snow boots, B is a Uniform Distribution so one can proceed to answer the questions manually. Excel does not provide a significant improvement over manual calculation for Uniform Distributions since it does not have inbuilt functions to address Uniform Distributions.

a. *Identify the highest and lowest values of this distribution and write the mathematical formulation to represent the distribution of B or the demand for snow boots in a given year. Draw the graph of the distribution.*

The highest value, $b = 800$ and the lowest value, $a = 400$. Thus, one can write $B \sim U(400, 800)$ to represent the Uniform Distribution of B. The graph is as follows:

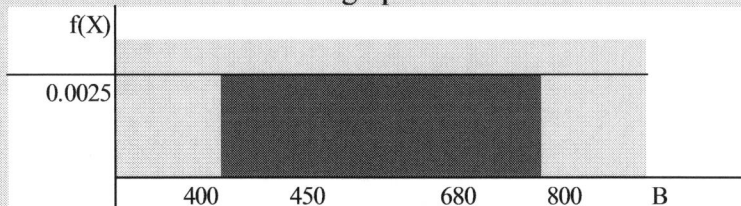

Figure 4.2. Uniform Distribution for Snow Boots

b. *Calculate the Mean and the Standard Deviation of this distribution.*

$$Mean\ \mu = \frac{(a + b)}{2} = \frac{400 + 800}{2} = 600$$

$$Std.Dev.\ \sigma = \sqrt{\frac{(b - a)^2}{12}} = \sqrt{\frac{(800 - 400)^2}{12}} = \sqrt{13333} = 115.47$$

c. What is the actual uniform probability function value?

$$f(x) = \frac{1}{(b-a)} = \frac{1}{(800-400)} = \frac{1}{400} = 0.0025$$

d. Find P(450 < B < 680)

Here, $c = 450$ and $d = 680$. So, the calculation would be:

$$P(c < B < d) = \frac{(d-c)}{(b-a)} = \frac{(680-450)}{(800-400)} = 0.575$$

e. Find P(B > 680)

Note that the highest value possible in this distribution is 800, so if one wants to find the probability of B having a value higher than 680, one can look at the graph in Figure 4.2 at the rectangle shaded in red between the B values of 680 and 800.

$$P(680 < B < 800) = \frac{(800-680)}{(800-400)} = 0.30$$

The Excel method of solving this problem is shown in Figure 4.3 below. The sheet corresponding to example 4.5 can be used by changing the values in the gray cells to reflect the values of a, b, c, d, etc. in order to obtain the probability answers, as relevant. Note that the rectangular area of Uniform distribution is not an output of any Excel functions so, the sheet has the numbers manually created for the graph and for the formula outputs.

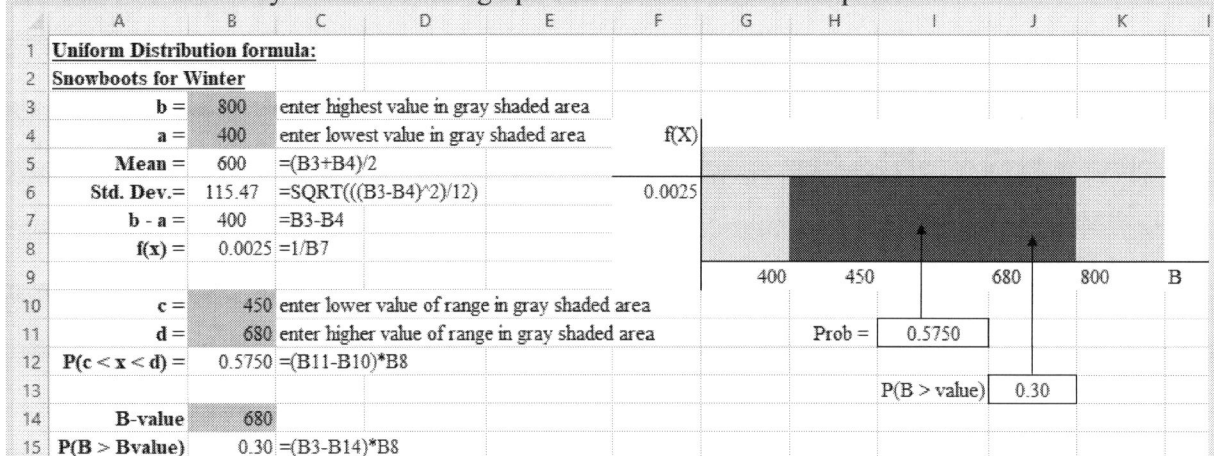

	A	B	C	D	E	F	G	H	I	J	K	l
1	**Uniform Distribution formula:**											
2	**Snowboots for Winter**											
3	b =	800	enter highest value in gray shaded area									
4	a =	400	enter lowest value in gray shaded area		f(X)							
5	**Mean =**	600	=(B3+B4)/2									
6	**Std. Dev.=**	115.47	=SQRT(((B3-B4)^2)/12)		0.0025							
7	b - a =	400	=B3-B4									
8	f(x) =	0.0025	=1/B7									
9							400	450		680	800	B
10	c =	450	enter lower value of range in gray shaded area									
11	d =	680	enter higher value of range in gray shaded area					Prob =	0.5750			
12	P(c < x < d) =	0.5750	=(B11-B10)*B8									
13									P(B > value)	0.30		
14	**B-value**	680										
15	P(B > Bvalue)	0.30	=(B3-B14)*B8									

Figure 4.3. Solution for Example 4.5 using Excel

4.2.2. Exponential Distribution

The Exponential Distribution is also a continuous probability distribution that depends on the "countdown" until a specific event occurs. Any event that is measured over a length of time, in seconds, minutes, hours, days, weeks, months, or even years can be represented using an Exponential Distribution. The key concept behind Exponential distribution is that for a random variable X, there are a large number of smaller values but few large values. These distributions are often used for calculations of how dependable or long-lasting a product is or to calculate what the rate of service is in businesses such as restaurants or call-centers. Questions such as "what is the probability that some event will occur in the next t time period" or "what is the probability that some event will occur between t_1 and t_2 time periods" or "what is the probability that the event would take more than t time periods to finish" are commonly answered by using the Exponential Distribution[1].

If one defines m as the historical value of a given random variable X, then the expected value (mean rate) and the standard deviation of X are both represented by $\mu = 1/m$. The Probability Density Function for Exponential Distribution of X, defined as $X \sim E(\mu)$ is given by:

$$f(x) = \frac{1}{m}e^{-\frac{1}{m}x} = \mu.e^{-\mu x}$$

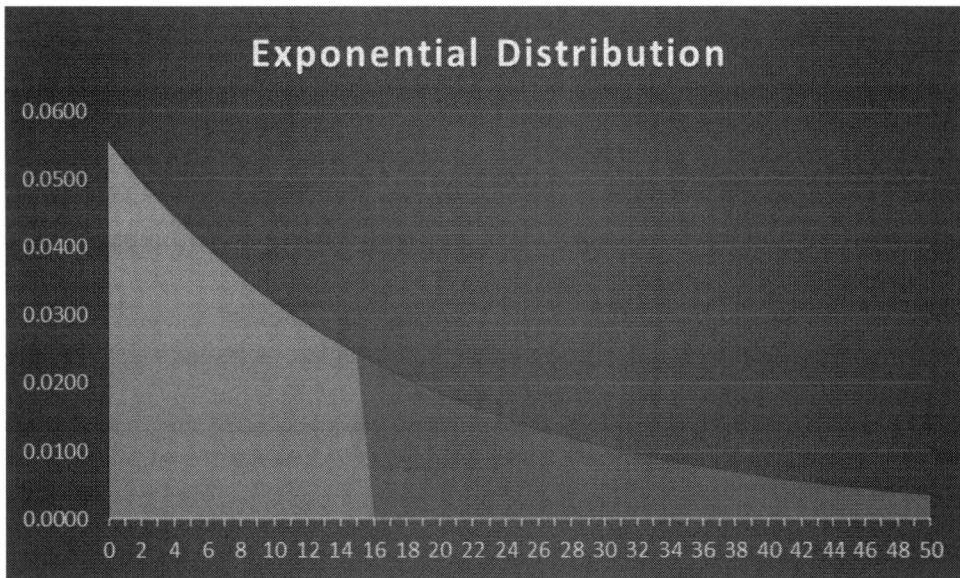

Figure 4.4. General Graph of Exponential Distribution

The Cumulative Density Function (CDF) for Exponential distribution gives the area under the curve below a given value of X and is obtained by finding the integral of the PDF resulting in the following formula:

$$P(X \leq x) = 1 - e^{-\mu x}$$
$$P(X > x) = e^{-\mu x}$$

Figure 4.4 gives the general Exponential Distribution graph, where the orange area shows the probability of taking less time than a certain value of X and the blue area shows the probability of taking more time than a certain value of X.

Example 4:6. Exponential Distribution of Lifespan of a Toy

A new parent is told by their peers that toys purchased for toddlers historically last about 8 months before they break or tear. Given that it is a question of a "countdown" or Exponential Distribution before the child's toy breaks, the parent is wondering how to plan to purchase toys in the future and needs help with answering the following questions:

---

[1] The descriptions of the decay or historical rate m and μ given here are often differently explained in various sources. The way I have defined them here are to ensure that there is consistency between this book and the book used in the next MSC 3371 class

1. What is the expected number of toys that would need to be replaced each month (also known as the "mean rate")? What is the standard deviation value in months of toys breaking? Write the mathematical formulation to represent the distribution of T
2. What is the probability that a given toy lasts more than 12 months?
3. What is the probability that a given toy lasts less than 10 months?
4. Suppose there is a particular toy that the child is attached to, and the parent wants to purchase 3 units of that toy to be able to quickly replace broken toys, how many months would all the units last in total?
5. Estimate how long do 67% (two-thirds of the toys) last in months.

Solution: Since it is known that the distribution for toys, T is an Exponential Distribution one can proceed to answer the questions manually or one can use the Excel or other software.

1. *What is the expected number of toys that would need to be replaced each month (also known as the "mean rate")? What is the standard deviation value in months of toys breaking? Write the mathematical formulation to represent the distribution of T.*
   Historical Average = m = 8 months
   Mean rate = μ = $1/m$ = $1/8$ = 0.125
   Std. Dev. = σ = $1/m$ = $1/8$ = 0.125
   Mathematical Formulation: $T \sim E(0.125)$
2. *What is the probability that a given toy lasts more than 12 months?*
   Calculate the $P(T > 12)$
   $$P(T > 12) = e^{-\mu t} = e^{-0.125 \times 12} = 0.2231$$
3. *What is the probability that a given toy lasts less than 10 months?*
   Calculate the $P(T < 10)$
   $$P(T \leq 10) = 1 - e^{-\mu t} = 1 - e^{-0.125*10} = 1 - 0.2865 = 0.7135$$
4. *Suppose there is a particular toy that the child is attached to, and the parent wants to purchase 3 units of that toy to be able to quickly replace broken toys, how many months would all the units last in total?*
   Since 1 toy is expected to last for 8 months, one can calculate the total expected time of 3 toys given one after the other to last for 8 x 3 = 24 months
5. *Estimate how long do 67% (two-thirds of the toys) last in months.*
   One needs to find the value of t, given that $P(T < t) = 0.67$
   $$P(T \leq t) = 1 - e^{-\mu t} = 0.67$$
   $$\therefore 0.67 = 1 - e^{-0.125t}$$
   $$\therefore e^{-0.125t} = 1 - 0.67 = 0.33$$
   $$\therefore -0.125t = ln(0.33) = -1.109$$
   $$\therefore t = \frac{-1.109}{-0.125} = 8.872 \; months$$

The Excel method of solving this problem is shown in Figure 4.5 below. The sheet corresponding to example 4.6 can be used by changing the values in the gray cells to reflect the values of m, t, etc. in order to obtain the corresponding answers, as relevant. the Excel function "=EXPON.DIST(x, lambda, cumulative)" can also be used to find the solutions.

	A	B	C	D	E
1	**Exponential Distribution for Toys**				
2				Units	Formulatext
3	Historical average, m =		8	mths	
4	Mean, μ =		0.1250		=1/C3
5	Std. Dev. Of distribution, σ =		0.1250		=C4
6	t =		12		
7	PDF: f(T = t) =		0.0279		=EXPON.DIST(C6,C4,FALSE)
8	CDF: P(T < t) =		0.7769		=EXPON.DIST(C6,C4,TRUE)
9	CDF: P(T > t) =		0.2231		=1-C8
10					
11	P(T < 10) =	10	0.7135		=EXPON.DIST(B11,C4,TRUE)
12					
13	How long do 3 toys last =	3	24	mths	=B13* C3
14					
15	How long do 67% toys last?	67%	8.87	mths	=-LN(1-B15)/C4

Figure 4.5. Exponential Distribution Solutions Using Excel Formulas

Chapter 5. Normal Distribution and Curve

The Normal Distribution is the most commonly used Theoretical Probability Distribution of a continuous Random Variable (*RV*) that is attributed to the statisticians Demoivre, Gauss, and Laplace who discussed and enhanced it in the late eighteenth and beginning of the nineteenth century. There are some characteristics that are unique to the Normal Distribution, which makes it a popular choice among researchers and practical experts in various fields that utilize data to make predictions and decisions in business, economics, society, and public policy, among others. This chapter starts by discussing the characteristics of the Normal Distribution Curve followed by the application of the Central Limit Theorem. Thereafter, comparisons of sampling and sampling distributions with the population characteristics by identifying standard errors, creating margins of error, and evaluating confidence intervals in sample distributions in order to accurately predict the probabilities for the population characteristics, are discussed. This chapter concludes by discussing how to apply the Normal Distribution features to binomial distributions (binomial approximations) and to the estimates of proportions instead of the simple mean and standard deviation values.

5.1. Characteristics of Normal Distribution

The fundamental characteristics of the Theoretical Normal Distribution are:
1. There are a large number of observations (infinite) that are included in the distribution of a *Random Variable* of interest and the curve is smooth, symmetrical around the mean, and has a singular mode.

2. The values of the mean, median, and mode are equal to each other, and the curve stretches to infinity in both directions from the mean.

3. The mean (and therefore the median and the mode) of the population distribution is μ and the standard deviation is σ, and both the mean and the standard deviation are called the "parameters" of the Normal Distribution.

4. Since the Normal Distribution is a probability distribution, the total area under the curve is 1 or 100%.

5. A normally distributed Random Variable (*RV*) defined as *X* with a mean of μ and a standard deviation of σ is written as $X \sim N(\mu, \sigma)$ and its Probability Distribution Function (*PDF*) is given by the following formula:

$$f(X) = \frac{1}{\sigma\sqrt{2\pi}}e^{-\frac{1}{2}\left(\frac{x-\mu}{\sigma}\right)^2} = \frac{1}{\sigma\sqrt{2\pi}}e^{-\frac{1}{2}z^2}$$

Here the μ helps to identify where on the number line the distribution is located and the σ indicates how thick the tails or how far the spread of the distribution is. If one needs to find the probability of an event occurring between two *x*-values, one can find the value by calculating the integral of the *PDF* between those two values. Luckily, one does not need to learn how to do the integration, because one can use the standardized *Z*-values to find this probability. In Chapter 2, the value of *Z* was first defined as the distance of a number from the mean of the dataset in terms of number of standard deviations. Notice that the formula above also uses the value of *Z*, which is given as:

$$Z = \frac{x - \mu}{\sigma}$$

6. The Graph of $X \sim N(\mu, \sigma)$ is shown in Figure 5.1. The center of the graph that splits the curve into two parts is given by the mean μ. Each part, orange and black, represents 50% of the probability under the curve.

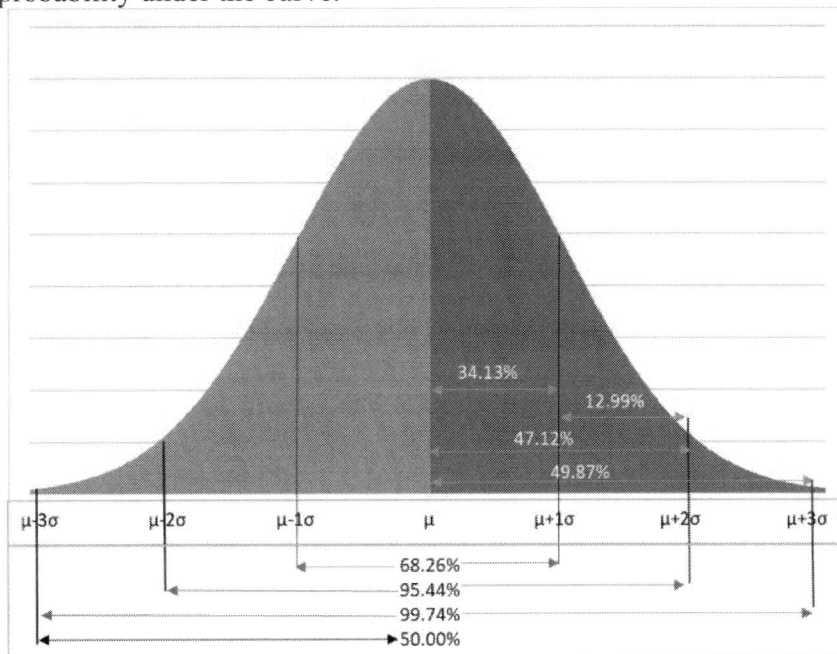

Figure 5.1. Graph of the Distribution of $X \sim N(\mu, \sigma)$

7. <u>The Empirical Rule</u>: If a random variable *X* can be represented as a normal distribution, $X \sim N(\mu, \sigma)$, the probability that a specific value of *x* lies within one standard deviation interval from the mean is 0.6826 or 68.26%, the probability that a specific value of *x* lies within two standard deviation interval from the mean is 0.9544 or 95.44% and the probability that a specific value of *x* lies within three standard deviation interval from the mean is 0.9974 or 99.74%. This was first covered in Chapter 2 in the section <u>2.3.2 Empirical Rule.</u> Since the normal distribution is symmetrical around the mean, one can

find that the probability (or area of the curve) between the mean and one standard deviation is 0.3413 or 34.13%, the probability between the mean and two standard deviations is 0.4712 or 47.12%, and the probability between the mean and three standard deviations is 0.4987 or 49.87%. Similarly, the probability (or area under the curve) between the x-value at one standard deviation from mean and the x-value at two standard deviations from the mean is 0.1299 or 12%.

8. Standard Normal Distribution: If the mean of a RV is 0 and the standard deviation is 1, one obtains a special case of the Normal Distribution called the Standard Normal Distribution, where the RV is "Z." This is also called a Z-distribution and is represented as $Z \sim N(0, 1)$. The Z-score is obtained by the formula shown above and represents the distance of a particular score (x) from the mean (μ) in terms of the number of standard deviations (σ). Thus, if the value of a Z-score for a particular x is 1.2, it implies that the value of that specific x is 1.2 standard deviations away from the mean of the random variable X. Figure 5.2 shows the curve for the Standard Normal Distribution $Z \sim N(0, 1)$.

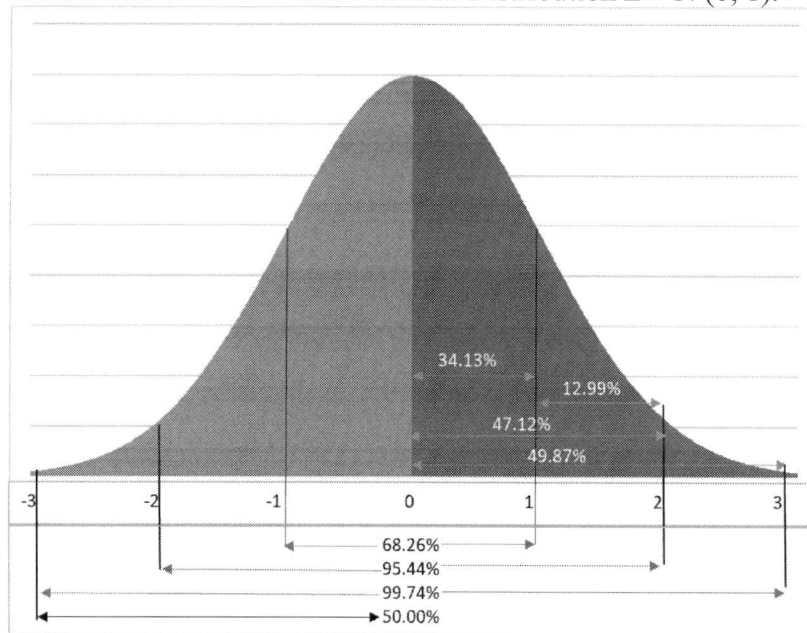

Figure 5.2. Standard Normal Distribution Graph

Standard Normal Distribution is used to compare an observed or empirical distribution to a theoretical Normal Distribution by "standardizing" it and calculating the Z-scores for any specific value x of the empirical distribution. If the value of $x > \mu$, the corresponding Z-score will be positive, if the value of $x < \mu$, the corresponding Z-score will be negative, and if the value of $x = \mu$, the corresponding Z-score will be zero. The Table for Z-scores is given as Table A in the Appendix for this book.

Example 5:1. High Efficiency LED Bulbs Example for Normal Distribution

The life (X) of the new efficient LED bulbs is expected to be normally distributed with a mean of 155 days and a standard deviation of 19 days. What is the probability that the life of the bulb will be:
1. less than 117 days
2. more than 193 days
3. between 117 and 193 days?
Also, find the life expectancy of the LED bulbs at the third quartile (75th percentile)

Solution: It is most advisable to take a stepwise approach to finding the solution to this problem. There are certain steps in which one can use Excel to find the respective values more easily than manual calculations, and those will be clearly identified after the manual steps are completed.
STEP 1: Identify mean and standard deviations.
    Here, $\mu = 155$ and $\sigma = 19$ days.
STEP 2: Identify the problems to be solved, one at a time.
    The first one, "less than 117 days". So, one needs to find $P(X < 117)$.
STEP 3: Calculate the Z-value for x.
    Here $x = 117$

$$Z = \frac{x - \mu}{\sigma} = \frac{117 - 155}{19} = -2$$

STEP 4: Draw the curve(s) and identify the area to be found for the probability.

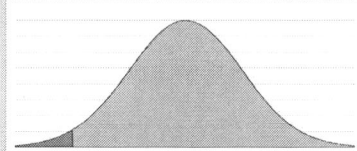 Find area in orange

STEP 5: Find Probabilities of each area identified using Z-tables (or Excel formulas).
    Note that the Table A in the Appendix only gives probabilities for the positive values of Z, but remember that the normal distribution curve is symmetrical, which allows one to calculate the orange region for the value of $Z = -2$ with some manipulation. First, find the value of $Z = 2$, as shown below as 0.9772. Thus, the area below the value of $Z = 2$ is 0.9772. This implies that the area above $Z = 2$ is $(1 - 0.9772 =) 0.0228$. Due to the symmetry of the distribution, one can say that the area below $Z = -2$ is the same as the area above $Z = 2$.

Z-value	0.00	0.01	0.02	0.03	0.04	0.05	0.06	0.07	0.08	0.09
					Standard Normal Distribution Z-Table showing P(x < Z)					
0.0	0.5000	0.5040	0.5080	0.5120	0.5160	0.5199	0.5239	0.5279	0.5319	0.5359
0.1	0.5398	0.5438	0.5478	0.5517	0.5557	0.5596	0.5636	0.5675	0.5714	0.5753
0.2	0.5793	0.5832	0.5871	0.5910	0.5948	0.5987	0.6026	0.6064	0.6103	0.6141
0.3	0.6179	0.6217	0.6255	0.6293	0.6331	0.6368	0.6406	0.6443	0.6480	0.6517
0.4	0.6554	0.6591	0.6628	0.6664	0.6700	0.6736	0.6772	0.6808	0.6844	0.6879
0.5	0.6915	0.6950	0.6985	0.7019	0.7054	0.7088	0.7123	0.7157	0.7190	0.7224
0.6	0.7257	0.7291	0.7324	0.7357	0.7389	0.7422	0.7454	0.7486	0.7517	0.7549
0.7	0.7580	0.7611	0.7642	0.7673	0.7704	0.7734	0.7764	0.7794	0.7823	0.7852
0.8	0.7881	0.7910	0.7939	0.7967	0.7995	0.8023	0.8051	0.8078	0.8106	0.8133
0.9	0.8159	0.8186	0.8212	0.8238	0.8264	0.8289	0.8315	0.8340	0.8365	0.8389
1.0	0.8413	0.8438	0.8461	0.8485	0.8508	0.8531	0.8554	0.8577	0.8599	0.8621
1.1	0.8643	0.8665	0.8686	0.8708	0.8729	0.8749	0.8770	0.8790	0.8810	0.8830
1.2	0.8849	0.8869	0.8888	0.8907	0.8925	0.8944	0.8962	0.8980	0.8997	0.9015
1.3	0.9032	0.9049	0.9066	0.9082	0.9099	0.9115	0.9131	0.9147	0.9162	0.9177
1.4	0.9192	0.9207	0.9222	0.9236	0.9251	0.9265	0.9279	0.9292	0.9306	0.9319
1.5	0.9332	0.9345	0.9357	0.9370	0.9382	0.9394	0.9406	0.9418	0.9429	0.9441
1.6	0.9452	0.9463	0.9474	0.9484	0.9495	0.9505	0.9515	0.9525	0.9535	0.9545
1.7	0.9554	0.9564	0.9573	0.9582	0.9591	0.9599	0.9608	0.9616	0.9625	0.9633
1.8	0.9641	0.9649	0.9656	0.9664	0.9671	0.9678	0.9686	0.9693	0.9699	0.9706
1.9	0.9713	0.9719	0.9726	0.9732	0.9738	0.9744	0.9750	0.9756	0.9761	0.9767
2.0	0.9772	0.9778	0.9783	0.9788	0.9793	0.9798	0.9803	0.9808	0.9812	0.9817
2.1	0.9821	0.9826	0.9830	0.9834	0.9838	0.9842	0.9846	0.9850	0.9854	0.9857

STEP 6: Calculate the answer to the question identified in STEP 2.

Therefore, P $(x < 117) = 0.0228$

Now, one can solve the section (2):

STEP 1: Identify mean and standard deviations.

Here, $\mu = 155$ and $\sigma = 19$ days.

STEP 2: Identify the problems to be solved, one at a time.

One needs to find the probability that a bulb lasts "more than 193 days". So, find P($X >$ 193).

STEP 3: Calculate the Z-value for x.

Here $x = 193$

$$Z = \frac{x - \mu}{\sigma} = \frac{193 - 155}{19} = 2$$

STEP 4: Draw the curve(s) and identify the area to be found for the probability.

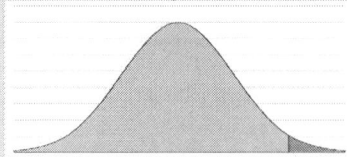
Find area in orange

STEP 5: Find Probabilities of each area identified using Z-tables (or Excel formulas).

Note that the Table A in the Appendix only gives probabilities for the positive values of Z. First, find the value of $Z = 2$, as shown below as 0.9772. Thus, the area below the value of $Z = 2$ is 0.9772. This implies that the area above $Z = 2$ is $(1 - 0.9772 =) 0.0228$.

Standard Normal Distribution Z-Table showing P(x < Z)										
Z-value	0.00	0.01	0.02	0.03	0.04	0.05	0.06	0.07	0.08	0.09
0.0	0.5000	0.5040	0.5080	0.5120	0.5160	0.5199	0.5239	0.5279	0.5319	0.5359
0.1	0.5398	0.5438	0.5478	0.5517	0.5557	0.5596	0.5636	0.5675	0.5714	0.5753
0.2	0.5793	0.5832	0.5871	0.5910	0.5948	0.5987	0.6026	0.6064	0.6103	0.6141
0.3	0.6179	0.6217	0.6255	0.6293	0.6331	0.6368	0.6406	0.6443	0.6480	0.6517
0.4	0.6554	0.6591	0.6628	0.6664	0.6700	0.6736	0.6772	0.6808	0.6844	0.6879
0.5	0.6915	0.6950	0.6985	0.7019	0.7054	0.7088	0.7123	0.7157	0.7190	0.7224
0.6	0.7257	0.7291	0.7324	0.7357	0.7389	0.7422	0.7454	0.7486	0.7517	0.7549
0.7	0.7580	0.7611	0.7642	0.7673	0.7704	0.7734	0.7764	0.7794	0.7823	0.7852
0.8	0.7881	0.7910	0.7939	0.7967	0.7995	0.8023	0.8051	0.8078	0.8106	0.8133
0.9	0.8159	0.8186	0.8212	0.8238	0.8264	0.8289	0.8315	0.8340	0.8365	0.8389
1.0	0.8413	0.8438	0.8461	0.8485	0.8508	0.8531	0.8554	0.8577	0.8599	0.8621
1.1	0.8643	0.8665	0.8686	0.8708	0.8729	0.8749	0.8770	0.8790	0.8810	0.8830
1.2	0.8849	0.8869	0.8888	0.8907	0.8925	0.8944	0.8962	0.8980	0.8997	0.9015
1.3	0.9032	0.9049	0.9066	0.9082	0.9099	0.9115	0.9131	0.9147	0.9162	0.9177
1.4	0.9192	0.9207	0.9222	0.9236	0.9251	0.9265	0.9279	0.9292	0.9306	0.9319
1.5	0.9332	0.9345	0.9357	0.9370	0.9382	0.9394	0.9406	0.9418	0.9429	0.9441
1.6	0.9452	0.9463	0.9474	0.9484	0.9495	0.9505	0.9515	0.9525	0.9535	0.9545
1.7	0.9554	0.9564	0.9573	0.9582	0.9591	0.9599	0.9608	0.9616	0.9625	0.9633
1.8	0.9641	0.9649	0.9656	0.9664	0.9671	0.9678	0.9686	0.9693	0.9699	0.9706
1.9	0.9713	0.9719	0.9726	0.9732	0.9738	0.9744	0.9750	0.9756	0.9761	0.9767
2.0	0.9772	0.9778	0.9783	0.9788	0.9793	0.9798	0.9803	0.9808	0.9812	0.9817
2.1	0.9821	0.9826	0.9830	0.9834	0.9838	0.9842	0.9846	0.9850	0.9854	0.9857

STEP 6: Calculate the answer to the question identified in STEP 2.

Therefore, P $(x > 193) = 0.0228$

Now, one can solve the section (3):

STEP 1: Identify mean and standard deviations.

Here, $\mu = 155$ and $\sigma = 19$ days.

STEP 2: Identify the problems to be solved, one at a time.

One needs to find the probability that a bulb lasts "between 117 and 193 days". So, find $P(117 < X < 193)$.

STEP 3: Calculate the Z-values for x-values.

Here x_1 (the smaller value) is 117 and x_2 (the larger value) is 193. Look at calculated the respective Z-values for each as -2 and 2, respectively in sections (1) and (2) earlier.

STEP 4: Draw the curve(s) and identify the area to be found for the probability.

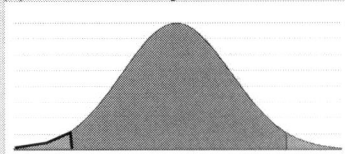 Find area in orange

STEP 5: Find Probabilities of each area identified using Z-tables (or Excel formulas).

Notice that the $P(X < 117) = 0.0228$ was found in part (1) and $P(X > 193) = 0.0228$ was found in part (2). Those are now the gray-shaded areas in the graph. Thus, one can find the orange area by subtracting the gray-shaded areas from 1.

STEP 6: Calculate the answer to the question identified in STEP 2.

Therefore, $P(117 < X < 193) = 1 - 0.0228 - 0.0228 = 0.9544$

In order to find the third quartile (also called the 75th percentile), one would need to learn how to do a reverse look up in the Z-table given in Table A in the Appendix. So, first present the problem at hand in the form of Find x: $P(x < X) = 0.75$

$$\therefore P\left(\frac{x - \mu}{\sigma} < \frac{X - \mu}{\sigma}\right) = P\left(\frac{x - 155}{19} < Z\right) = 0.75$$

To find the value of Z one can look at the Z-table given in Table A in the Appendix to find the probability value that is closest to 0.75. Refer to the image below for how to find the value. One can see that there is no direct 0.75 but there are 0.7486 and 0.7517 highlighted in brown. The corresponding Z-score would be between 0.67 and 0.68, as a result. For convenience one can round 0.675 or either 0.67 or 0.68. To find the value of x in the given problem, one can consider the $Z = 0.67$

Standard Normal Distribution Z-Table										
Z-value	0.00	0.01	0.02	0.03	0.04	0.05	0.06	0.07	0.08	0.09
0.0	0.5000	0.5040	0.5080	0.5120	0.5160	0.5199	0.5239	0.5279	0.5319	0.5359
0.1	0.5398	0.5438	0.5478	0.5517	0.5557	0.5596	0.5636	0.5675	0.5714	0.5753
0.2	0.5793	0.5832	0.5871	0.5910	0.5948	0.5987	0.6026	0.6064	0.6103	0.6141
0.3	0.6179	0.6217	0.6255	0.6293	0.6331	0.6368	0.6406	0.6443	0.6480	0.6517
0.4	0.6554	0.6591	0.6628	0.6664	0.6700	0.6736	0.6772	0.6808	0.6844	0.6879
0.5	0.6915	0.6950	0.6985	0.7019	0.7054	0.7088	0.7123	0.7157	0.7190	0.7224
0.6	0.7257	0.7291	0.7324	0.7357	0.7389	0.7422	0.7454	0.7486	0.7517	0.7549

$$\therefore \frac{x - 155}{19} = 0.67$$
$$\therefore x = 155 + 0.67 \times 19 = 167.73$$

Thus, the third quartile life expectancy of an LED bulb is about 168 days.

The Excel method for solving this problem is shown in Figure 5.3 below. Note that the graphs significantly add to the visualization of the problem being solved, but Excel does not provide them by itself. They were constructed manually. There is a slight difference in the probability calculations done manually and in Excel (manually, the answer obtained 0.9544 whereas the answer is 0.9545 in Excel) due to rounding differences; these are considered to be insignificant.

	A	B	C
1	**High Efficiency LED Bulbs**		
2			
3	mean =	155	
4	std. dev. =	19	
5			
6	**Less Than Probability**		
7	x =	117	
8	P(X < x)	0.0228	=NORM.DIST(B7,$B$3,$B$4, TRUE)
9			
10	**Greater Than Probability**		
11	x =	193	
12	P(X > x)	0.0228	=1-NORM.DIST(B11,$B$3,$B$4, TRUE)
13			
14	**Area between 2 x-values**		
15	smaller number x1 =	117	
16	larger number x2 =	193	
17	P(x1 < X < x2) =		
18	= P(X < x2) - P(X < x1)	0.9545	=NORM.DIST(B16,$B$3,$B$4,TRUE) - NORM.DIST(B15,$B$3,$B$4,TRUE)
19			
20	**Third Quartile Value**		
21	Desired Percentile =	75%	
22	X-value =	167.8	=NORM.INV(B21,B3,B4)

Figure 5.3. Excel Method for Solving Example 5.1

5.1.1. Comparing Two Populations

Since the Standard Normal Distribution (Z-distribution) allows one to "shrink" any Normal Distribution regardless of its mean and standard deviation to the same standardized measurement of Z, it becomes possible to compare expectations of different populations using the Z-distribution. Using an example will help to understand how to apply this in the real world. Some similar examples were discussed in Chapter 2 in the section 2.3.3. However, it is possible to also find the corresponding probabilities using the normal distribution and Z-tables for specific values in order to compare them. Note that the probabilities obtained by using Z-tables (given in Table A in the Appendix) also refer to the percentile rank of the observation within the distribution by rounding up or down, as appropriate.

Example 5:2. Comparing Men vs. Women using IQ scores
Suppose that a researcher finds that the Intelligence Quotient (IQ) scores of men have a mean of 100 with a standard deviation of 15, whereas the IQ scores of women have a mean value of 110 with a standard deviation of 10. Identify the appropriate intervals based on the Empirical Rule for both men and women. If a randomly chosen man and randomly chosen woman, both have an IQ score of 125, identify their respective Z-scores within their groups and conclude which one is scoring higher as compared to their groups. Calculate the probability of a random male scoring less than 125 and the probability of a random female scoring less than 125 on the IQ test and identify their respective percentile ranks.

Solution: First identify the variables for this analysis clearly.
$$\mu_m = 100; \; \mu_f = 105$$
$$\sigma_m = 15; \; \sigma_f = 12$$
Calculate intervals and corresponding probability for boys:
1) $68.26\%\; population\; belongs\; to\; interval\; (\mu \pm \sigma) = (100 \pm 15) = (85, 115)$
2) $96.44\%\; population\; belongs\; to\; interval\; (\mu \pm 2\sigma) = (100 \pm 30) = (70, 130)$
3) $99.74\%\; population\; belongs\; to\; interval\; (\mu \pm 3\sigma) = (100 \pm 45) = (55, 145)$
Calculate intervals and corresponding probability for girls:
1) $68.26\%\; population\; belongs\; to\; interval\; (\mu \pm \sigma) = (110 \pm 10) = (100, 120)$
2) $96.44\%\; population\; belongs\; to\; interval\; (\mu \pm 2\sigma) = (110 \pm 20) = (90, 130)$
3) $99.74\%\; population\; belongs\; to\; interval\; (\mu \pm 3\sigma) = (110 \pm 30) = (80, 140)$

Given that $x = 125$, calculate the Z-values for the man and the woman as follows:
$$Z_m = \frac{x - \mu_m}{\sigma_m} = \frac{125 - 100}{15} = 1.67$$
$$Z_f = \frac{x - \mu_f}{\sigma_f} = \frac{125 - 110}{10} = 1.5$$

Since the Z_m is 1.67, one can say that the individual is 1.67 standard deviations away from the mean of the IQ scores of all men. The Z_f is 1.5 so one can say that the individual is 1.5 standard deviations away from the average IQ score of all women. Thus, the man with an IQ of 125 is doing much better than the rest of his group as compared to a woman with an IQ of 125 in her group.

Calculating Probabilities:

$P(m < 125) = P(Z_m < 1.67) = 0.9525$ based on the Z-tables given in Table A in the Appendix. Thus, the probability that a male has an IQ score less than 125 is 95.25%. Thus, the percentile rank of a male with 125 IQ score is 95th percentile.

$P(f < 125) = P(Z_f < 1.5) = 0.9332$ based on the Z-tables given in Table A in the Appendix. Thus, the probability that a female has an IQ score less than 125 is 93.32%. The percentile rank of a female with 125 IQ is 93rd percentile.

Standard Normal Distribution Z-Table showing P(x < Z)

Z-value	0.00	0.01	0.02	0.03	0.04	0.05	0.06	0.07	0.08	0.09
0.0	0.5000	0.5040	0.5080	0.5120	0.5160	0.5199	0.5239	0.5279	0.5319	0.5359
0.1	0.5398	0.5438	0.5478	0.5517	0.5557	0.5596	0.5636	0.5675	0.5714	0.5753
0.2	0.5793	0.5832	0.5871	0.5910	0.5948	0.5987	0.6026	0.6064	0.6103	0.6141
0.3	0.6179	0.6217	0.6255	0.6293	0.6331	0.6368	0.6406	0.6443	0.6480	0.6517
0.4	0.6554	0.6591	0.6628	0.6664	0.6700	0.6736	0.6772	0.6808	0.6844	0.6879
0.5	0.6915	0.6950	0.6985	0.7019	0.7054	0.7088	0.7123	0.7157	0.7190	0.7224
0.6	0.7257	0.7291	0.7324	0.7357	0.7389	0.7422	0.7454	0.7486	0.7517	0.7549
0.7	0.7580	0.7611	0.7642	0.7673	0.7704	0.7734	0.7764	0.7794	0.7823	0.7852
0.8	0.7881	0.7910	0.7939	0.7967	0.7995	0.8023	0.8051	0.8078	0.8106	0.8133
0.9	0.8159	0.8186	0.8212	0.8238	0.8264	0.8289	0.8315	0.8340	0.8365	0.8389
1.0	0.8413	0.8438	0.8461	0.8485	0.8508	0.8531	0.8554	0.8577	0.8599	0.8621
1.1	0.8643	0.8665	0.8686	0.8708	0.8729	0.8749	0.8770	0.8790	0.8810	0.8830
1.2	0.8849	0.8869	0.8888	0.8907	0.8925	0.8944	0.8962	0.8980	0.8997	0.9015
1.3	0.9032	0.9049	0.9066	0.9082	0.9099	0.9115	0.9131	0.9147	0.9162	0.9177
1.4	0.9192	0.9207	0.9222	0.9236	0.9251	0.9265	0.9279	0.9292	0.9306	0.9319
1.5	0.9332	0.9345	0.9357	0.9370	0.9382	0.9394	0.9406	0.9418	0.9429	0.9441
1.6	0.9452	0.9463	0.9474	0.9484	0.9495	0.9505	0.9515	0.9525	0.9535	0.9545
1.7	0.9554	0.9564	0.9573	0.9582	0.9591	0.9599	0.9608	0.9616	0.9625	0.9633

The Excel solution for this problem is given in Figure 5.4 below

	A	B	C	D	E	F	G
1	**Comparing IQs for Men and Women**						
2							
3	**Male Mean**		100				
4	**Male Std. Dev.**		15				
5		std.dev. dist.	lower	upper			
6	**68.26% interval $\mu\pm\sigma$**	1	85	115			
7	**96.44% interval $\mu\pm2\sigma$**	2	70	130			
8	**99.74% interval $\mu\pm3\sigma$**	3	55	145			
9							
10	**Less Than Probability**						
11	x =		125				
12	Z=		1.67	=(C11-C3)/C4			
13	P(X < x)		0.9522	=NORM.DIST(C11,$C$3,$C$4, TRUE)			
14	Percentile Rank =		95%	=ROUND(C13,2)			
15							
16	**Female Mean**		110				
17	**Female Std. Dev.**		10				
18		std.dev. dist.	lower	upper			
19	**68.26% interval $\mu\pm\sigma$**	1	100	120			
20	**96.44% interval $\mu\pm2\sigma$**	2	90	130			
21	**99.74% interval $\mu\pm3\sigma$**	3	80	140			
22	**Less Than Probability**						
23	x =		125				
24	Z=		1.50	=(C23-C16)/C17			
25	P(X < x)		0.9332	=NORM.DIST(C23,$C$16,$C$17, TRUE)			
26	Percentile Rank =		93%	=ROUND(C25,2)			

Figure 5.4. Excel Solution for Example 5:2

5.1.2. Finding Raw Score based on Z-value

If one wanted to find the value of normally distributed random variable $X \sim N(\mu, \sigma)$ at a specific distance measured in standard deviations from the mean, one can use the Z-distribution and Z-score formula to do find the value of X. This principle is especially useful when finding confidence intervals to find the possible range of values of the population based on sample observations, which will be covered later in this chapter.

$$X = \mu + Z\sigma$$

Example 5:3. Finding Raw Score based on Z-value

Suppose a random variable age A is distributed normally in Sophomore year of XYZ College with a mean of 20 and a variance of 4.78. Find the ages of the following individuals:
1. An individual who falls 1.34 standard deviations above the mean
2. An individual who falls 1.56 standard deviations below the mean

Solution: In this example, the $\mu = 20$ and $\sigma^2 = 4.78$ so the standard deviation $\sigma = \sqrt{4.78} = 2.19$. Thus, the distribution of age can be represented as $A \sim N(20, 2.19)$.
1. The Z-score for individual who falls 1.34 std.devs. above the mean is Z = 1.34
$$A = \mu + Z\sigma = 20 + 1.34(2.19) = 20 + 2.93 = 22.93 \text{ years old}$$
2. The Z-score for individual who falls 1.56 std.devs. below the mean is Z = -1.56
$$A = \mu + Z\sigma = 20 - 1.56(2.19) = 20 - 3.42 = 16.58 \text{ years old}$$
Figure 5.5 shows the Excel method of solving this problem without doing manual calculations.

	A	B	C
1	**Raw Age Value Based on Z-scores**		
2			
3	**Mean =**	20	
4	**Std. Dev. =**	2.19	=SQRT(4.78)
5			
6	**Z-score =**	1.34	
7	**X-value =**	22.93	=$B$3+B6*$B$4
8			
9	**Z-score =**	-1.56	
10	**X-value =**	16.59	=$B$3+B9*$B$4

Figure 5.5. Raw Age Value Based on Z-Scores

5.2. Sampling and Sample Distributions

In the real world, one often does not know what the exact extent of the population of interest might be or even if one knows that, one might not necessarily know what the characteristics of interest within that population might be. For instance, if one is trying to estimate the average household size in the United States, one might not be able to collect data on all households within the United States since even the Census Data collection efforts have errors. In cases like this, one can draw "inferences" regarding the population characteristics based upon the samples that one is able to collect and measure. These sample-based characteristic values allow one to infer what the population characteristics might be. Until now, the primary reliance has been on descriptive statistics for any given dataset for analysis. However, now it is possible to continue by working on inferential statistics, where one uses observed values by taking samples of a random variable to make or draw inferences about general behaviors or characteristics of the population pertaining to that random variable.

As discussed in Chapter 1 in Section 1.1.5, the purpose of drawing samples is to make predictions about the characteristics of the population from which the sample is obtained. However, the size of the sample that is chosen can impact the determination and decision regarding the population. While the characteristics of the population are called "parameters" and denoted by Greek symbols like μ for mean, σ for standard deviation, and ρ for proportion, the corresponding characteristics of the sample are called "statistics" and denoted using English letters like $\bar{X}$, s, and p. The population parameters or characteristics are always fixed, but one might not always know what those values are, which is why one uses sample statistics, which are measurable, in order to *estimate* or infer what the corresponding values of the population might be.

In order to get more accuracy in the predictions, one would draw multiple samples and test for how "representative" they are of the population distribution. If one were to create a distribution using the means and the standard deviations that one obtained from each sample, one would get a distribution of all those means whose standard deviation from each other is called the standard error.

Think of it more practically – what if one took a sample of 10 students from the population of students at a university and found that the average age in that sample was 22 years? Now, if one took another sample of 12 students and found that the average age in that sample was 24 years, what conclusions can be drawn regarding the population of students at that university? So, one can take another sample of 15 students and find the mean of that sample to be 23. In order to make a prediction about the mean of the population of all students, the easy option would be to take the average of all the sample means that one found by adjusting for the sample sizes. For the sake of understanding, it is better to omit the sample standard deviations for now. Thus, in the 3-sample example a good prediction of the population mean age could be obtained by the following formula, which is the same as the Weighted Mean formula discussed in Chapter 2:

$$Mean\ Age = \frac{22 \times 10 + 24 \times 12 + 23 \times 15}{10 + 12 + 15} = \frac{220 + 288 + 345}{37} = 23.05\ years$$

Now, instead of just 3 samples, what if one were to collect more samples? One could now have a distribution of all the sample means and their own standard deviations from each other's mean values. This type of distribution obtained from taking a theoretical unlimited number of samples is called a sampling distribution. The standard deviation of a sampling distribution is smaller than the standard deviation of the population and therefore, one can focus on the probability associated with obtaining a sample mean $\bar{X}$ that is different from the population mean μ. One could expect that the mean of this sampling distribution of means is equal to the true population mean and therefore the normal distribution curve in this case refers to the probability of the sampling mean being different from the true population mean, as explained by the Central Limit Theorem and the Law of Large Numbers.

5.2.1. Central Limit Theorem

The Central Limit Theorem pertains to the generalizability of the Normal Distribution and says that if one draws finite samples of size n (must be greater than 30) from a given population with a known mean, μ and standard deviation, σ, the distribution of the sample means always follow a Normal Distribution, regardless of the actual distribution of the population. Figure 5.6 shows how the sampling distribution of means of samples drawn from a population with any distribution, are distributed normally. The Law of Large Numbers states that as the sample size n increases, the mean of the distribution of means becomes closer to the population mean μ and the standard error decreases.

The mean of this sampling distribution has the theoretical expected value of μ and the standard deviation of this sampling distribution is given by $\sigma_{\bar{X}}$ and is called the "standard error." In this case, the variable of interest is $\bar{X}$, which represents the sample mean of a specific sample. If the population standard deviation of σ is known, then the standard error of this distribution is denoted by $\sigma_{\bar{X}}$. The value of the standard error depends upon the sample size, n and is given by the following formula:

$$\sigma_{\bar{X}} = \frac{\sigma}{\sqrt{n}}$$

The Z-values for the sampling distribution are calculated using the following formula, which is similar to the Z-value that was calculated for the general Normal Distribution but is adapted to fit the sampling distribution of $\bar{X} \sim N(\mu, \sigma_{\bar{X}})$.

$$Z = \frac{\bar{X} - \mu}{\sigma_{\bar{X}}}$$

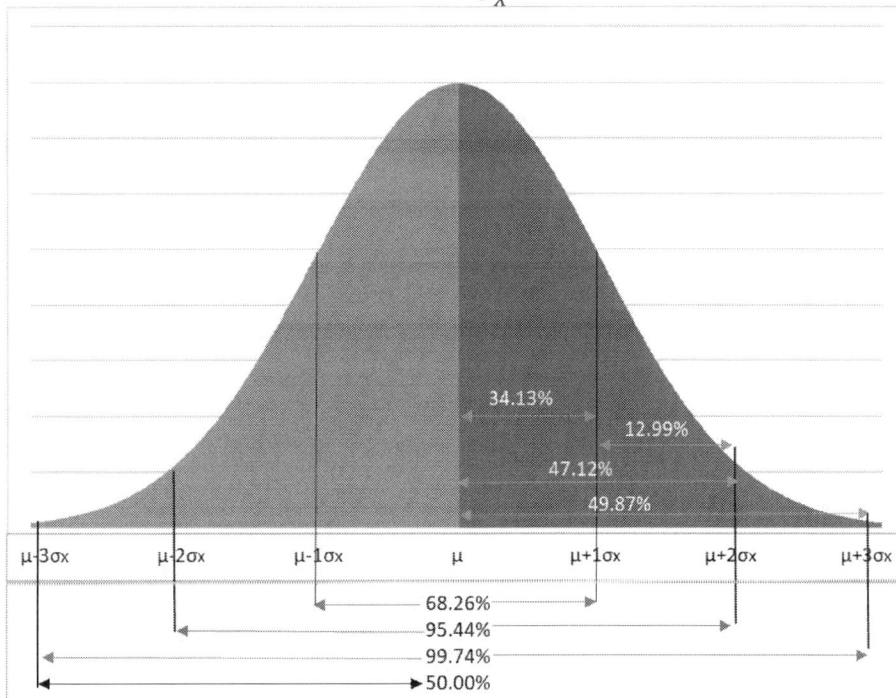

Figure 5.6. Sampling Distribution of Means

In the real world, the standard deviation (σ) of the population is often unknown, so one can approximate the standard deviation of a given sample to represent the standard error and denote it as $s_{\bar{x}}$, which will be discussed in more detail in the section on *t-distributions* later in this chapter for small sample sizes n. If the sample size is larger than 30, the $s_{\bar{x}}$ can directly represent the Standard Error given by the formula:

$$s_{\bar{X}} = \frac{\sigma}{\sqrt{n-1}}$$

Table 5.1 shows the symbols and various formulas for representing different characteristics of interest in descriptive and inferential statistics. Note that the standard deviation for the sampling distribution is called "standard error" and is adjusted for sample size n.

Table 5.1. Characteristics and Formulas

Characteristic	Population Parameter	Sample Statistic	Sampling Distribution of Means
Mean (Average)	$E(X) = \mu$	$E(X) = \bar{X}$	$E(\bar{X}) = \mu_{\bar{x}} = \mu$
Standard Deviation or Standard Error	$STDEV(X) = \sigma$	$STDEV(X) = s$	$SE(\bar{X}) = \sigma_{\bar{x}} = \frac{\sigma}{\sqrt{n}}$
Z-score for Means	$Z = \frac{X-\mu}{\sigma}$	$Z = \frac{X-\bar{X}}{s}$	$Z = \frac{\bar{X}-\mu}{\sigma_{\bar{x}}}$
Proportion Mean	$\rho = np$	$p' = \frac{x}{n}$	$p' = E(p') = \rho$
Proportion Standard Deviation	$\sigma_\rho = \sqrt{npq}$	Treat sample like population	$\sigma_{p'} = \sqrt{\frac{p(1-p)}{n}}$
Z-score for Proportions	$Z = \frac{p-\rho}{\sigma_\rho}$	Treat sample like population	$Z = \frac{p'-\rho}{\sigma_{p'}}$

Example 5:4. Finding Probabilities for a Sampling Distribution

A researcher is interested in IQ scores of people living in a particular city. The researcher knows that the standard deviation of IQ scores is consistent with a value of 15 points for a given population. She takes a sample of 20 people and measures their IQ scores to find that the average IQ score is 95. Help the researcher find the probability that the IQ score of the population lies between 90 and 102 points. Find the value of IQ that would be 2 standard errors above the mean. What is the value of the first quartile in this sample distribution?

Solution: In this example, one can see that the population standard deviation is steady at 15 points. However, the researcher is taking a sample of only 20 people from the city, so one would need to first adjust for the standard error SE by using the formula:

$$\sigma_{\bar{X}} = \frac{\sigma}{\sqrt{n}} = \frac{15}{\sqrt{20}} = 3.35$$

Thus, one can say that the sampling distribution of IQs in the city can be represented as N(15, 3.35). For finding the probability that the true mean of the population IQ lies between 90 and 102 points, one needs to find $P(90 < \bar{X} < 102)$. One can follow the same steps as Example 5.1 in order to solve this problem, but a more condensed version of those steps is used here for efficiency. For sampling distributions, the Z-score is given by the formula for Z-score for means given in Table A in Appendix. One can convert this normal distribution into Z-scores as follows:

$$P(90 < \bar{X} < 102) = P\left(\frac{90-95}{3.35} < \frac{\bar{X}-\mu}{\sigma_{\bar{X}}} < \frac{102-95}{3.35}\right) = P(-1.49 < Z < 2.09)$$

As seen in Figure 5.7, a graph can be drawn in order to shade the area that one is interested in finding and the probabilities of the blue shaded regions can be obtained from the Z-tables. One finds that the $P(Z < -1.49) = 0.0680$ and the $P(Z < 2.09) = 0.9816$. Thus, the area in orange can be found by taking the difference of these two probabilities $= 0.9135$ or one can say that there is a 91.35% probability that the true population mean lies between 90 and 102 for IQ scores.

To find the IQ score that lies 2 Standard Errors above the mean, one would simply add 2 x 3.35 = 6.7 to the mean 95 to get a value of 101.7.

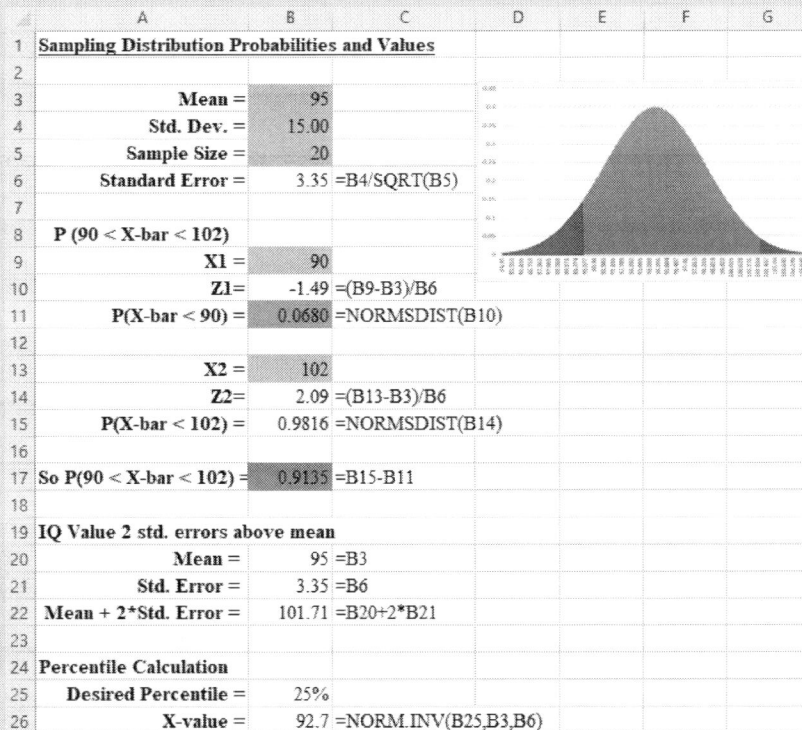

	A	B	C	D	E	F	G
1	Sampling Distribution Probabilities and Values						
2							
3	Mean =	95					
4	Std. Dev. =	15.00					
5	Sample Size =	20					
6	Standard Error =	3.35 =B4/SQRT(B5)					
7							
8	P (90 < X-bar < 102)						
9	X1 =	90					
10	Z1=	-1.49 =(B9-B3)/B6					
11	P(X-bar < 90) =	0.0680 =NORMSDIST(B10)					
12							
13	X2 =	102					
14	Z2=	2.09 =(B13-B3)/B6					
15	P(X-bar < 102) =	0.9816 =NORMSDIST(B14)					
16							
17	So P(90 < X-bar < 102) =	0.9135 =B15-B11					
18							
19	IQ Value 2 std. errors above mean						
20	Mean =	95 =B3					
21	Std. Error =	3.35 =B6					
22	Mean + 2*Std. Error =	101.71 =B20+2*B21					
23							
24	Percentile Calculation						
25	Desired Percentile =	25%					
26	X-value =	92.7 =NORM.INV(B25,B3,B6)					

Figure 5.7. Solution to Example 5.4 Using Excel Formulas

To find the 25th percentile (or the first quartile) value:

$$P(x < \bar{X}) = 0.25$$

$$\therefore P\left(\frac{x-95}{3.35} < \frac{\bar{X}-\mu}{\sigma_{\bar{X}}}\right) = 0.25$$

$$\therefore P\left(\frac{x-95}{3.35} < Z\right) = 0.25$$

The value of Z corresponding to 0.25 probability can be found by reverse lookup using the Z-table Table A in Appendix to obtain the value of $Z = -0.67$.

$$\therefore \frac{x - 95}{3.35} = -0.67$$
$$\therefore x = 95 - 0.67 \times 3.35 = 92.7$$

5.2.2. Confidence Intervals and Margin of Error

Inferential statistics focuses on using sample data and characteristics to generalize characteristics of an unknown population. A confidence interval is a range of values that one can find around the mean of the sample to demonstrate confidence in the estimate of the mean (or any population parameter) when using sampling distributions. If one defines Significance Level as alpha (α) as the probability that the confidence interval does NOT contain the population mean, then $(1 - \alpha)$ refers to the probability that the confidence interval contains the true population mean or parameter. Thus, the general formula for Confidence Intervals can be written as:

$$(1-\alpha)\% \; CI = \bar{X} \pm Z_{\alpha/2} \cdot \sigma_{\bar{X}}$$

In words, one can say that with a confidence level of $(1 - \alpha)$%, the value of the true mean of the population lies within a certain margin from the sample mean. This margin is also called the Margin of Error (*ME*) and is defined as the product of the Z-value corresponding to the significance level $\alpha/2$ for a two-tailed distribution ($Z_{\alpha/2}$) and the Standard Error of the sampling distribution ($\sigma_{\bar{X}}$). Thus, the *ME* can be calculated using the following formula, if the population standard deviation σ is known:

$$(1-\alpha)\% \; ME = Z_{\alpha/2} \cdot \sigma_{\bar{X}} = Z_{\alpha/2} \cdot \frac{\sigma}{\sqrt{n}}$$

This allows for the confidence interval formula to be further generalized as follows and is interpreted as the range of feasible values of the possible population parameter that are on either side of the sampling mean:

$$(1-\alpha)\% \; CI = \bar{X} \pm ME$$

Since the standard error and therefore the margin of error is inversely related to the sample size n, it is important to note that the higher the value of n, the smaller is the value of *ME*, allowing for more close estimates of the population means. In cases where the population standard deviation σ is not known and the sample size n is small, one typically does not use the Z-distribution so the corresponding formulas for the ME and the CI will be discussed in the Section on *t-distribution* later in this chapter. In cases where the Confidence Interval needs to be calculated for population proportions, the basic formula for Margin of Error remains the same, but the standard error is defined differently. This will be covered in the last section of this chapter.

The general steps on how to find Confidence Intervals for means are discussed below but should help with any type of distribution problems to find the corresponding confidence intervals for any sampling distribution estimate of a population parameter:

> **Calculating Confidence Intervals for μ when σ is known or n is large:**
>
> Step 1. Identify the values of sample size (n), mean of sample ($\bar{X}$), and Standard Error SE ($\sigma/\sqrt{n}$).
> Step 2. Find the correct significance level. The most commonly used ones are 0.01, 0.02, 0.05, and 0.10 that correspond to confidence levels of 99%, 98%, 95% and 90%, respectively.
> Step 3. Identify the value of $\alpha/2$ and find the corresponding Z-score of $Z_{\alpha/2}$ by using reverse look-up using the Z-table Table A in Appendix, or refer to Table 5.2 given in this chapter.
> Step 4. Calculate the Margin of Error (ME) $= Z_{\alpha/2} \cdot \sigma_{\bar{X}} = Z_{\frac{\alpha}{2}}. SE$
> Step 5. Calculate the Confidence Interval (CI) $= \bar{X} \pm ME$ written as $(\bar{X} - ME, \bar{X} + ME)$

Four of the most commonly used values of $Z_{\alpha/2}$ are shown in Table 5.2 and are worth remembering in order to avoid constantly referring to the Z-table. Moreover, these values are helpful when checking for significance for hypothesis testing, which will be covered in the next chapter. The graph of the confidence interval is also placed above the Table to identify where the $Z_{\alpha/2}$ values fall in the normal distribution. The orange shaded area shows the range or interval under which, one is confident that the population parameter value falls. The value of α represents the total of the blue shaded areas, where the value of the population parameter is not likely to fall.

Table 5.2. Common Values for Key Significance Levels

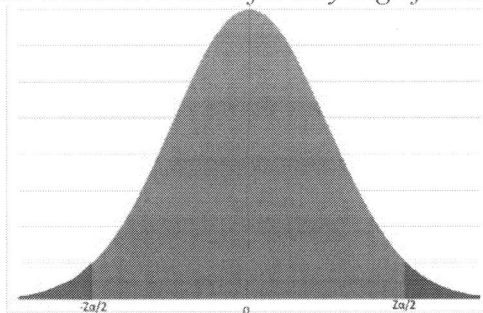

Significance Level α	Confidence Coefficient $(1 - \alpha)$	Confidence Level	$\alpha/2$	$Z_{\alpha/2}$	Confidence Interval
0.1	0.9	90%	0.05	1.645	$\bar{X} \pm 1.645\sigma_{\bar{x}}$
0.05	0.95	95%	0.025	1.96	$\bar{X} \pm 1.96\sigma_{\bar{x}}$
0.02	0.98	98%	0.01	2.33	$\bar{X} \pm 2.33\sigma_{\bar{x}}$
0.01	0.99	99%	0.005	2.575	$\bar{X} \pm 2.575\sigma_{\bar{x}}$

Example 5:5. Finding Confidence Intervals for Z-distribution

A City Council is interested in identifying the average age of Senior Citizens in their city to determine the total demand for assisted living conditions. Based on past experience, they know that the standard deviation of ages is around 5 years but are uncertain about the population average in the year 2022. They hire a researcher, who decides to take a sample of 36 Senior Citizens from a Assisted Living Facility to identify the range of mean age of Senior Citizens in the population who require assisted living facilities at a 0.10 significance level. She finds that the average age of the residents in the Facility she chose is 73 years. Find the corresponding confidence interval and write in words what the researcher's findings are.

Solution: One can follow the steps to create the confidence interval since value of $\sigma = 5$ is known:

Step 1. Identify the values of sample size (n), mean of sample ($\bar{X}$), and Standard Error SE ($\sigma/\sqrt{n}$).

Here, the $n = 36$, $\bar{X} = 73$, and the $SE = \sigma/\sqrt{n} = \frac{5}{\sqrt{36}} = 0.83$

Step 2. Find the correct significance level.

The $\alpha = 0.10$ for this problem

Step 3. Identify the value of $\alpha/2$ and find the corresponding Z-score of $Z_{\alpha/2}$ by using reverse look-up using the Z-table.

$\alpha/2 = 0.10/2 = 0.05$

Based on Table 5.2, this means that the $Z_{\alpha/2} = 1.645$

Step 4. Calculate the Margin of Error (ME) $= Z_{\alpha/2} \cdot \sigma_{\bar{X}} = Z_{\alpha/2}.SE$

$$ME = Z_{\alpha/2}.SE = 1.645 \times 0.83 = 1.37$$

Step 5. Calculate the Confidence Interval (CI) $= \bar{X} \pm ME$ written as $(\bar{X} - ME, \bar{X} + ME)$

$$90\% \; CI = \bar{X} \pm ME = 73 \pm 1.37$$
$$90\% \; CI = (73 - 1.37, 73 + 1.37) = (71.63, 74.37)$$

Answer in words: The researcher can say with 90% confidence that the average age of the population of Senior Citizens in the city who require assisted living facilities is between 71.63 and 74.37 years old. Figure 5.8 shows the Excel formulas and methods to solve this problem

	A	B	C	D	E
1	**Calculating Confidence intervals if std.dev. σ is known or if n is large**				
2					
3	**Mean of sample X-bar =**	73			
4	**Std. Dev. of Population σ =**	5.00			
5	**Sample Size n =**	36			
6	**Standard Error SE =**	0.83	=B4/SQRT(B5)		
7					
8	**Significance Level α =**	0.10			
9	**Two-tails α/2 =**	0.05	=B8/2		
10	**Z-value Z_a/2 =**	1.645	=ABS(NORM.S.INV(B9))		
11	**Margin of Error ME =**	1.37	=B10*B6		
12	**(Direct ME formula)**	1.37	=CONFIDENCE.NORM(B8,B4,B5)		
13	**Confidence Interval =**	**Lower**			
14		71.63	=B3-B11		
15		**Upper**			
16		74.37	=B3+B11		
17	We can say with 90% confidence that average age of the population				
18	lies between 71.63 and 74.37 years.				

Figure 5.8. Confidence Interval Calculation Using Excel

5.2.3. Reverse Calculations Given Confidence Intervals or Margin of Error

The fascinating thing about confidence intervals derived based on a sample is that one can do a reverse calculation to find the mean and standard error of the sample that was used to create the confidence interval in the first place and if one knows the sample size, it can be used to estimate the standard deviation of the population of interest. Note that in some data that is shared, the Margin of Error is reported instead of a Confidence Interval and the mean of the sample is reported as the statistic. This is more common in proportions (e.g., results of polls, etc.) and it will be covered towards the end of the chapter in Section 5.5. An example would help to see how the reverse calculation would work.

Example 5:6. Reverse Calculations based on a Confidence Interval

An organization that is trying to influence policy on drunk driving claims with a 95% confidence that between 43 and 48 people are killed by drunk drivers every month. Find the sample mean, standard error, and the assumed standard deviation of the population if the sample size used by the organization is 15 months of drunk driving incidents.

Solution: Here, the confidence level is 95%, which implies that the significance level (α) is 0.05. Thus, the corresponding $Z_{\alpha/2}$ value (from Table 5.2) would be 1.96. The reported sample size $n = 15$. The 95% confidence interval is (43, 48).

Thus, the sample mean can be calculated using the following formula:

$$\bar{X} = \frac{(lower\ CI + Upper\ CI)}{2} = \frac{43 + 48}{2} = 45.5$$

The Margin of Error $ME = Upper\ CI - \bar{X} = 48 - 45.5 = 2.5$

$ME = Z_{\alpha/2}.SE$ which implies that $SE = \frac{ME}{Z_{\alpha/2}} = \frac{2.5}{1.96} = 1.28$

$SE = \frac{\sigma}{\sqrt{n}}$ which implies that $\sigma = SE \times \sqrt{n} = 1.28 \times \sqrt{15} = 4.96$

Thus, one can conclude that the sample mean (and therefore the population mean) was estimated to be 45.5 deaths per month with a standard error of 1.28, whereas the standard deviation of the population is 4.96 deaths per month. Figure 5.9 shows the Excel version of solving this problem.

	A	B	C	D
1	**Reverse Calculation for Mean and Standard Deviations**			
2	**Sample size n =**		15	
3		**Lower**	**Upper**	
4	**Confidence Interval CI =**	43	48	
5	**Confidence Level =**		95%	
6	**Significance level α =**		0.05	=1-C5
7	**α/2 =**		0.025	=C6/2
8	**Z-value Z_α/2 =**		1.96	=ABS(NORM.S.INV(C7))
9	**Mean of Sample =**		45.5	=(B4+C4)/2
10	**Margin of Error =**		2.5	=C4-C9
11	**Standard Error =**		1.28	=C10/C8
12	**Standard Deviation σ =**		4.94	=C11*SQRT(C2)

Figure 5.9. Reverse Calculation for Mean and Std. Dev. using Excel

One can also use reverse calculations to identify what sample size one would need if one wanted to meet a certain requirement for the Margin of Error when designing or planning to conduct any research by using the sampling methodology. In situations like these, the goal is to have a desired Margin of Error in order to maintain consistency in results and their interpretations. For instance, a producer might be interested in making sure that the estimate of the population mean of manufacturing defects in their product lies within a 3% Margin of Error (*ME*) and wants to have a confidence level of 95% to ensure that there are no significant complaints from the consumers later on as a result of defective goods. This implies that for every batch of the product a certain amount of the product needs to be selected for sampling. Typically, the producer would start with a preliminary small sample to identify the range of the values and then use that estimate to identify what a proper sample size should be in order to ensure a fixed Margin of Error. Since the *ME* is defined as a product of the Z-value ($Z_{\alpha/2}$) and the SE ($\sigma/\sqrt{n}$), one can see that if the sample size *n* increases, the value of the *SE* and the *ME* would decrease. The formula for sample size *n* can be derived from the formula of *ME* as follows:

$$ME = Z_{\frac{\alpha}{2}} \times \frac{\sigma}{\sqrt{n}}$$

$$\therefore \sqrt{n} = Z_{\frac{\alpha}{2}} \times \frac{\sigma}{ME}$$

$$\therefore n = \left(Z_{\frac{\alpha}{2}} \times \frac{\sigma}{ME}\right)^2$$

An example would help to understand this more clearly. Note that when using t-distributions or if the standard deviation of population is unknown and sample size is small, there is a modified version of this formula that will be implemented. This will be covered in the Section 5.3 on t-distributions. In order to calculate the sample size *n* for proportions, one would use a slightly different formula as well, which will be covered in Section 5.5 on Proportions.

Example 5:7. Calculate the Sample Size n if σ is known

The owner of a bread factory is interested in identifying how long the average loaf of bread produced in his factory is and knows that a fluctuation of around 0.8 cm is common due to factors such as humidity and temperature levels in the factory. For a preliminary sample using 5 loafs, he finds that the mean length is 32 cm. Find the sample size that he should test from each batch of loaves to ensure that the Margin of Error is 0.5 cm at a 95% confidence level.

Solution: In this case the population standard deviation σ is 0.8 cm. It is also known that the confidence level is 95%, implying that the corresponding $Z_{\alpha/2}$ value is 1.96 (from Table 5.2). The desired *ME* is 0.5 cm. Thus, one can insert this information in the formula for the required sample size *n*

$$n = \left(Z_{\frac{\alpha}{2}} \times \frac{\sigma}{ME}\right)^2 = \left(1.96 \times \frac{0.8}{0.5}\right)^2 = 9.83$$

One can round this up to say that if samples of a minimum of 10 loaves were drawn from each batch of bread produced, the owner will be able to ensure with a 95% level of confidence that there is no more than 0.5cm error in measurement from the expected mean value of 32 cm in each batch.

5.3. t-distributions

Sections 5.1 and 5.2 have considered the general characteristics of the Normal Distribution and how the Normal Distribution can be applied to sampling distributions if either the standard deviation of the population (σ) is known or if the sample size n is larger than 30 observations. However, in the real world, the likelihood of knowing the population standard deviation (σ) is rather low. The easiest way to combat this lack of information would be to use a sample size n that is greater than 30 but even that might be difficult to achieve in many situations such as the one discussed in Example 5:7 for the owner of the bread factory. In cases like these, one has to use the standard deviation (s) of the sample as an approximation for the population standard deviation by adjusting the variance by the sample size n as shown below:

$$\hat{\sigma} = s\sqrt{\frac{n}{n-1}}$$

Standard Error calculation for a sample of size n when the population standard deviation (σ) is known is given by $\sigma/\sqrt{n}$. Thus, when one is using the approximation given above by using the value of sample standard deviation (s), the Standard Error of the mean is given as:

$$s_{\bar{X}} = \frac{s}{\sqrt{n-1}}$$

As a result of this adjustment, one can no longer say that the standardized deviation score is distributed as a standard normal or Z-distribution due to the approximation and small sample size concerns. This is why the "Student's t distribution" is used for calculations and estimates of the population parameters. The value of *t-statistic* (also called t-value or t-ratio) is given by the following formula and is distributed with degrees of freedom ($n-1$):

$$t = \frac{\bar{X} - \mu}{s_{\bar{X}}}$$

Remember that the true population parameter μ is still unknown, and the goal is to estimate the interval within which the mean can fall with some level of confidence. If the sample size n is large, the *t*-distribution is closer to the Z-distribution. Moreover, *t*-tables are used instead of the Z-tables when one is faced with small samples derived from populations whose standard deviations are unknown. For smaller sample sizes, the *t*-distribution has thicker tails as compared to the standard normal distribution, Z. As can be seen in Figure 5.10, at larger values of n, the *t*-distribution resembles the Z-distribution more closely. At smaller values of n, the *t*-distribution has different thickness in the tails.

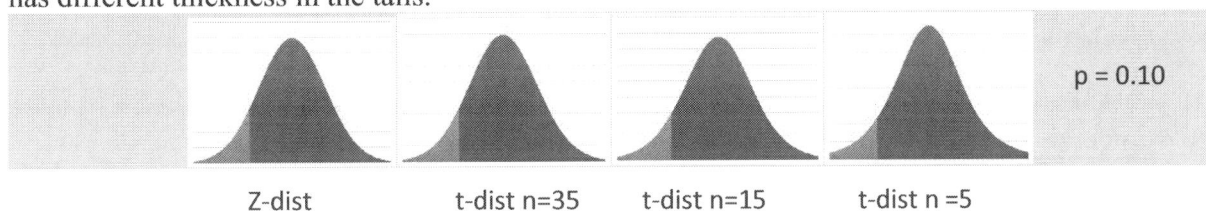

Z-dist   t-dist n=35   t-dist n=15   t-dist n =5   p = 0.10

Figure 5.10. Differences in the Z and t-distributions with different n values

The Table B for *t*-distribution is given in the Appendix at the end of the book. There is a big difference in using the Z-table (Table A) as compared to the *t*-table (Table B). In the Z-tables the contents of the table comprise of the probability of the population parameter being less than the chosen level of significance (α if one-tailed and $\alpha/2$ if two-tailed). However, in the t-tables, the level of significance (α if one-tailed and $\alpha/2$ if two-tailed) is chosen first, then the sample size n and the resultant degrees of freedom, df given by $(n-1)$ are considered and used to calculate the corresponding value of the critical t from the contents of the table. Note that the table only gives the absolute value of the t-ratio, implying that just like the symmetrical Z-distribution, one will consider the negative value for t if it lies below the mean and a positive value if it lies above the mean of 0. Thus, if one wants to find the t-value corresponding to a sample of $n = 15$ observations with a significance level (α) of 0.10 one can find the $df = n - 1 = 14$ and look up the corresponding t-value of 1.345 as shown in Figure 5.11.

cumu. Prob.	t (0.50)	t(0.75)	t(0.80)	t(0.85)	t(0.90)	t(0.95)	t(0.975)	t(0.99)	9(0.995)	t(0.999)	t(0.9995)
α (or α/2)	0.50	0.25	0.20	0.15	0.10	0.05	0.025	0.01	0.005	0.001	0.0005
df											
1	0.000	1.000	1.376	1.963	3.078	6.314	12.706	31.821	63.657	318.309	636.619
2	0.000	0.816	1.061	1.386	1.886	2.920	4.303	6.965	9.925	22.327	31.599
3	0.000	0.765	0.978	1.250	1.638	2.353	3.182	4.541	5.841	10.215	12.924
4	0.000	0.741	0.941	1.190	1.533	2.132	2.776	3.747	4.604	7.173	8.610
5	0.000	0.727	0.920	1.156	1.476	2.015	2.571	3.365	4.032	5.893	6.869
6	0.000	0.718	0.906	1.134	1.440	1.943	2.447	3.143	3.707	5.208	5.959
7	0.000	0.711	0.896	1.119	1.415	1.895	2.365	2.998	3.499	4.785	5.408
8	0.000	0.706	0.889	1.108	1.397	1.860	2.306	2.896	3.355	4.501	5.041
9	0.000	0.703	0.883	1.100	1.383	1.833	2.262	2.821	3.250	4.297	4.781
10	0.000	0.700	0.879	1.093	1.372	1.812	2.228	2.764	3.169	4.144	4.587
11	0.000	0.697	0.876	1.088	1.363	1.796	2.201	2.718	3.106	4.025	4.437
12	0.000	0.695	0.873	1.083	1.356	1.782	2.179	2.681	3.055	3.930	4.318
13	0.000	0.694	0.870	1.079	1.350	1.771	2.160	2.650	3.012	3.852	4.221
14	0.000	0.692	0.868	1.076	1.345	1.761	2.145	2.624	2.977	3.787	4.140
15	0.000	0.691	0.866	1.074	1.341	1.753	2.131	2.602	2.947	3.733	4.073

t-values corresponding to α and n

Figure 5.11. Using t-tables based on df and α values.

Note that in many textbooks, the Standard Error SE calculation for t-distribution is often given as $s/\sqrt{n}$ instead of $s/\sqrt{n-1}$. From a statistical perspective, this should not make a significant difference in the outcomes or estimates but when n is really small, this difference can matter. The formula for calculating Confidence Intervals of the mean of the population using t-distribution is given as:

$$(1-\alpha)\% \; CI = \bar{X} \pm t_{\alpha/2} \cdot s_{\bar{X}}$$

The steps for calculating a Confidence Interval using a t-distribution are as follows. Remember that if one does not know what the population standard deviation is and the sample size is less than 30, one should always use the t-distribution instead of the Z-distribution for these estimates.

Calculating Confidence Intervals for μ when σ is unknown and n is small:

Step 1. Identify the values of sample size (n), degrees of freedom ($n-1$), mean of sample ($\bar{X}$), and Standard Error of sample SE ($s/\sqrt{n-1}$).

Step 2. Find the correct significance level. The most commonly used ones are 0.01, 0.02, 0.05, and 0.10 that correspond to confidence levels of 99%, 98%, 95% and 90%, respectively.

Step 3. Identify the value of $\alpha/2$ and find the corresponding t-ratio of $t_{\alpha/2}$ by using the t-table Table B in Appendix for the appropriate degrees of freedom.

Step 4. Calculate the Margin of Error $(ME) = t_{\alpha/2} \cdot s_{\bar{X}} = t_{\frac{\alpha}{2}}. SE$

Step 5. Calculate the Confidence Interval $(CI) = \bar{X} \pm ME$ written as $(\bar{X} - ME, \bar{X} + ME)$

Example 5:8. Finding Confidence Intervals for t-distribution

A City Council is interested in identifying the average age of Senior Citizens in their city to determine the total demand for assisted living conditions. They have no available estimates of either the mean or the standard deviation of the population of Senior Citizens that require assisted living in their city. They hire a researcher, who decides to take a sample of 20 Senior Citizens from a Assisted Living Facility to identify the range of mean age of Senior Citizens in the population who require assisted living facilities at a 0.10 significance level. She finds that the sample mean is 73 years, and the sample standard deviation is 3 years. Find the corresponding confidence interval using a t-distribution and write in words what the researcher's findings are.

Solution: Follow the steps to create the confidence interval using t-distribution since the value σ is unknown and the sample size is small (< 30 observations)

Step 1. Identify the values of sample size (n), degrees of freedom ($n-1$), mean of sample ($\bar{X}$), and Standard Error of sample SE ($s/\sqrt{n-1}$).

    Here, the $n = 20$, $df = 19$, $\bar{X} = 73$, and the $SE = s/\sqrt{n-1} = \frac{3}{\sqrt{20-1}} = 0.69$

Step 2. Find the correct significance level.

    The $\alpha = 0.10$ for this problem

Step 3. Identify the value of $\alpha/2$ and find the corresponding t-score of $t_{\alpha/2}$ by using t-tables Table B in Appendix, for the appropriate degrees of freedom.

    $\alpha/2 = 0.10/2 = 0.05$ and $df = 19$

    Based on Table B, this means that the $t_{\alpha/2} = 1.729$

Step 4. Calculate the Margin of Error $(ME) = t_{\alpha/2} \cdot s_{\bar{X}} = t_{\alpha/2}. SE$

    $ME = t_{\alpha/2}. SE = 1.729 \times 0.69 = 1.19$

Step 5. Calculate the Confidence Interval $(CI) = \bar{X} \pm ME$ written as $(\bar{X} - ME, \bar{X} + ME)$

$$90\% \, CI = \bar{X} \pm ME = 73 \pm 1.19$$
$$90\% \, CI = (73 - 1.19, 73 + 1.19) = (71.81, 74.19)$$

	A	B	C	D
1	**Calculating Confidence intervals if std.dev. σ is unknown and if n is small**			
2				
3	Mean of sample X-bar =	73		
4	Std. Dev. of Sample s =	3.00		
5	Sample Size n =	20		
6	Degrees of Freedom =	19		
7	Standard Error SE =	0.69	=B4/SQRT(B6)	
8				
9	Significance Level α =	0.10		
10	Two-tails α/2 =	0.05	=B9/2	
11	t-value t$_{α/2}$ =	1.729	=ABS(T.INV(B10,B6))	
12	Margin of Error ME =	1.19	=B11*B7	
13	(Direct ME formula)	1.19	=CONFIDENCE.T(B9,B4,B6)	
14	Confidence Interval =	Lower		
15		71.81	=B3-B12	
16		Upper		
17		74.19	=B3+B12	
18	We can say with 90% confidence that average age of the population			
19	lies between 71.81 and 74.19 years.			

Figure 5.12. Confidence Interval Calculation Using Excel

Answer in words: The researcher can say with 90% confidence that the average age of the population of Senior Citizens in the city who require assisted living facilities is between 71.81 and 74.19 years old.

Note that if one compares this example with Example 5.5 where the population standard deviation was known, and the sample size was larger, there is a slight difference between the obtained confidence intervals. The interval is narrower for the *t*-distribution as compared to the *Z*-distribution. Figure 5.12 shows the Excel formulas and methods to solve this problem

For reverse calculations, the minimum sample size formula for n when a desired Margin of Error (also known as the Error-Bound of the Mean) is given as follows:

$$n = \left(t_{\frac{\alpha}{2}} \times \frac{s}{ME} \right)^2 + 1$$

Example 5:9. Calculate the Sample Size n if σ is unknown

The owner of a bread factory is interested in identifying how long the average loaf of bread produced in his factory is and needs to identify the minimum sample size for each batch of bread baked. For a preliminary sample using 5 loafs, he finds that the mean length is 32 cm and the sample standard deviation is 0.6 cm. Find the sample size that he should test from each batch of loaves to ensure that the Margin of Error is 0.5 cm at a 95% confidence level.

Solution: In this case the population standard deviation is unknown, but the sample standard deviation $s = 0.6$. It is also known that the confidence level is 95%, indicating that the $\alpha = 0.05$ and the $\alpha/2 = 0.025$ and the degrees of freedom are $(5 - 1 = 4)$ implying that the corresponding t$_{α/2}$

value is 2.776 (from Table B in Appendix). The desired *ME* is 0.5 cm. Thus, the formula for the required minimum sample size n would be:

$$n = \left(t_{\frac{\alpha}{2}} \times \frac{s}{ME}\right)^2 + 1 = \left(2.776 \times \frac{0.6}{0.5}\right)^2 + 1 = 11.10 + 1 = 12.10$$

One can round this up to say that if samples of a minimum of 13 loaves were drawn from each batch of bread produced, the owner will be able to ensure with a 95% level of confidence that there is no more than 0.5cm error in measurement from the expected mean value of 32 cm in each batch. Compare this estimate of 13 loaves with the estimate of 10 loaves in Example 5.7, where the standard deviation of the population was known to see how *t*-distributions result in different values.

5.4. Estimating Binomial with Normal Distribution

Refer to the Section 4.1.1. from Chapter 4 which discusses the Discrete Binomial Distribution to revisit that the mean of the Binomial Distribution μ is obtained by finding the product of the number of trials n and the probability of success p. Similarly, the standard deviation σ of a Binomial distribution is given by the formula $\sqrt{npq}$. Now, if n is greater than 30, one can apply the Central Limit Theorem to the Binomial Distribution and obtain the probabilities of interest using the normal approximation. An example will help to understand how a normal approximation of the Binomial Distribution can be useful in finding probabilities of success in a given distribution.

Example 5:10. Normal Approximation of Binomial Distribution

Suppose a dice is thrown 200 times. The Event of interest is obtaining a 4 value on its face. What is the probability that one obtains between 25 and 40 successes in this experiment?

Solution: Here, the event of interest is getting a 4 on the face value. Thus, the probability of success in each throw of the dice is p = 1/6. The probability of failure q = 5/6. The dice is tossed 200 times so the value of n = 200. Finding the value of P(25 < X < 40) is the question on hand.

This is a binomial distribution but with a large number of trials, so one can use the Normal Approximation to solve this problem. The mean of this Normal distribution is given by $\mu = np$ and the standard deviation is given by $\sqrt{npq}$.

$$\mu = np = 200 \times \frac{1}{6} = 33.33$$
$$s.d. = \sqrt{npq} = \sqrt{200 \times 1/6 \times 5/6} = 5.27$$
$$P(25 \leq X \leq 40) = P\left(\frac{25 - 33.33}{5.27} \leq \frac{X - \mu}{\sigma} \leq \frac{40 - 33.33}{5.27}\right) = P(-1.58 \leq Z \leq 1.26)$$

One can find the probabilities by using the Z-tables (Table A in Appendix):
$$P(Z \leq -1.58) = 0.0571 \text{ and } P(Z \leq 1.26) = 0.8962$$
$$P(-1.58 \leq Z \leq 1.26) = 0.8962 - 0.0571 = 0.84$$

Thus, one can say that there is an 84% probability that one will have between 25 and 40 successes in this experiment. The graph and the Excel method for solving this problem are shown in Figure 5.13. Note that since Excel formulas do not round off (unlike manual calculations) so there might be slight differences in the answers between manually calculated answers and Excel answers.

	A	B	C	D	E	F	G	H	I
1	**Normal Approximation for Binomial Distribution with large n**								
2									
3	Number of observations n =	200							
4	Probability of success p =	0.167	=1/6						
5	Probability of failure q =	0.833	=1-B4						
6	**mean =**	33.33	=B3*B4						
7	**std. dev. =**	5.27	=SQRT(B3*B4*B5)						
8									
9	**Area between 2 x-values**								
10	smaller number x1 =	25							
11	larger number x2 =	40							
12	P(x1 < X < x2) =								
13	= P(X < x2) - P(X < x1)	0.84	=NORM.DIST(B11,$B$6,$B$7,TRUE) - NORM.DIST(B10,$B$6,$B$7,TRUE)						

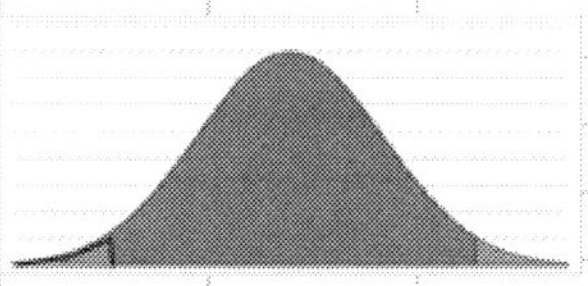

Figure 5.13. Normal Approximation for Binomial Distribution

5.5. Estimating Proportions with Normal Distribution

If one is interested in the proportions of a particular outcome in a large number of trials, similar to the probabilities of success that were covered in the Binomial Distribution, one can find the proportion of the particular outcome of interest as a ratio of the number of desired outcomes (X) and the total number of trials (n). Thus, $p' = X/n$ for the sample. If the expected proportion of success in the population is given by the Greek letter Rho (ρ), one can apply the normal distribution to the proportion distribution in the form $P' \sim N(p', \sigma_{p'})$, where the mean is given by p' and the standard error of the proportions $\sigma_{p'}$ is given by the following formula (also given in Table 5.1):

$$\sigma_{p'} = \sqrt{\frac{p(1-p)}{n}}$$

A key thing to remember about proportions is that regardless of the distribution or sample size, one always uses the Z-distribution to estimate probabilities or calculate the confidence intervals. The t-distribution is not used for proportions or comparisons of proportions in two populations. The Z-score to identify the probabilities of the true population proportion as compared to the sample proportion is obtained using the following formula:

$$Z = \frac{p' - \rho}{\sigma_{\rho'}}$$

The confidence intervals for proportion are calculated using the following formula and the steps below the formula are used when finding *CI* for proportions:

$$(1 - \alpha)\% \ C.I. \ for \ \rho = p' \pm ME = p' \pm Z_{\alpha/2}\sigma_{p'}$$

Calculating Confidence Intervals of ρ for proportions:

Step 1. Identify the values of sample size (n), observed proportion of sample ($p' = X/n$), and Standard Error SE ($\sigma_{p\prime}$).
Step 2. Find the correct significance level. The most commonly used ones are $0.01, 0.02, 0.05$, and 0.10 that correspond to confidence levels of 99%, 98%, 95% and 90%, respectively.
Step 3. Identify the value of $\alpha/2$ and find the corresponding Z-score of $Z_{\alpha/2}$ by using reverse look-up using the Z-table Table A in Appendix or refer to Table 5.2 given in this chapter.
Step 4. Calculate the Margin of Error (ME) $= Z_{\alpha/2} \cdot \sigma_{p\prime} = Z_{\frac{\alpha}{2}}.SE$
Step 5. Calculate the Confidence Interval (CI) $= p' \pm ME$ written as ($p' - ME, p' + ME$)

Example 5:11. Confidence Intervals for Proportion

The number of students who sign up for an AP course in 9th grade at a local school is 58 out of a total of 130 students enrolled at the school. Find the 98% confidence interval for the population proportion of 9th grade students in the school district based on the sample.

Solution: Follow the steps for finding the confidence interval for proportions
Step 1. Identify the values of sample size (n), observed proportion of sample ($p' = X/n$), and Standard Error SE ($\sigma_{p\prime}$).
     Here the sample size $n = 130$, observed proportion $p' = 58/130 = 0.45$ and *SE* is calculated as follows:

$$SE = \sigma_{p\prime} = \sqrt{\frac{p(1-p)}{n}} = \sqrt{\frac{0.45 \times 0.55}{130}} = 0.044$$

Step 2. Find the correct significance level.
     Here the confidence level is 98% so the significance level $\alpha = 0.02$
Step 3. Identify the value of $\alpha/2$ and find the corresponding Z-score of $Z_{\alpha/2}$ by using reverse look-up using the Z-table Table A in Appendix or refer to Table 5.2 given in this chapter.
     Here the $\alpha/2 = 0.01$, so the value of $Z_{\alpha/2} = 2.33$ (from Table 5.2 or Table A in Appendix Z-tables)
Step 4. Calculate the Margin of Error (ME) $= Z_{\alpha/2} \cdot \sigma_{p\prime} = Z_{\frac{\alpha}{2}}.SE$
$$ME = Z_{\alpha/2} \cdot \sigma_{p\prime} = 2.33 \times 0.044 = 0.10$$
Step 5. Calculate the Confidence Interval (CI) $= p' \pm ME$ written as ($p' - ME, p' + ME$)
$$98\% \; CI \; for \; \rho = p' \pm ME = 0.45 \pm 0.10 = (0.35, 0.55)$$

     Thus, one can say with 98% confidence that between 35% and 55% of 9th grade students in the school district sign up for an AP course. Figure 5.14 shows the Excel method to find this confidence interval. Note that when using proportions, the direct formula for finding *ME* using CONFIDENCE.NORM is avoided. Also, notice that using proportions based on one school to generalize about 9th graders enrolling in AP courses in the school district is a good instance of overgeneralizing in non-homogenous (all kids have different interests and inclinations) populations, implying that proportion-based confidence intervals should be carefully checked to confirm that the population of interest is truly homogenous or not.

	A	B	C	D
1	**Calculating Confidence intervals for Proportions**			
2				
3	Sample Size n =	130		
4	Number of successes X =	58		
5	Sample proportion p' =	0.45	=B4/B3	
6	Standard Error SE =	0.04	=SQRT(B5*(1-B5)/B3)	
7	Confidence Level =	98%		
8	Significance Level α =	0.02		
9	Two-tails α/2 =	0:01	=B8/2	
10	Z-value $Z_{\alpha/2}$ =	2.326	=ABS(NORM.S.INV(B9))	
11	Margin of Error ME =	0.101	=B10*B6	
12	Confidence Interval =	Lower		
13		0.3447	=B5-B11	
14		Upper		
15		0.5476	=B5+B11	
16	We can say with 98% confidence that between 35% and 55%			
17	of 9th graders choose an AP class in the district.			

Figure 5.14. Confidence Intervals for Proportion

The formula for calculating the minimum sample size *n* for an expected value of ME, also known as the Level of Tolerance in reference to proportions, is given as follows and below that Table 5.3 shows the typical sample sizes recommended based on the Level of Tolerance (*ME*) for a 90% and a 95% confidence level:

$$n = p(1-p)\left(\frac{Z_{\alpha/2}}{ME}\right)^2$$

Table 5.3. Typical Sample Sizes for Various Levels of Tolerance

Level of Tolerance	Sample Size for Confidence Level of 90%	Sample Size for Confidence Level of 95%
2% = 0.02	1691	2401
3% = 0.03	752	1067
5% = 0.05	271	384
10% = 0.10	68	96

An interesting thing to observe from Table 5.3 is that when the margin of error is increased from 2% to 3%, the minimum sample size drops to almost half of the original value. Think about the various polls that are conducted for political or economic conditions and feedback from residents in countries to identify approval (or disapproval) of a particular individual or policy. Statistically speaking, the poll can be conducted by questioning only between 750 to 1100 people with a 3% margin of error to draw large-scale conclusions about the success or failure of a policy or individual! This is why polls and samples of proportions that represent a significantly larger and diverse population should be believed with caution. Proportions, and related conclusions about the population, from a statistical standpoint are <u>only valid if the population is homogenous.</u>

List of Formulas from Chapters 4 and 5

I. Binomial Distribution

    a. If RV $X \sim B(n, p)$, where n = limited number of trials, p = probability of success and q = 1 – p (probability of failure) for each trial:

$$\mu = np$$
$$\sigma = \sqrt{npq}$$
$$P(X = x) = \binom{n}{x} p^x q^{(n-x)}$$

Excel formula for finding probability:
BINOM.DIST(number_s, trials, probability_s,cumulative)
    number_s = x
    trials = n
    probability_s = p
    cumulative = *TRUE* for cumulative and *FALSE* for probability function

    b. If RV $X \sim B(n, p)$, where n = large number of trials, p = probability of success and q = 1 – p (probability of failure) for each trial, one can use the normal approximation where $X \sim N(\mu, \sigma)$ and the rest of the formulations are similar to #V. Normal Distribution (given toward the end of this list).

$$\mu = np$$
$$\sigma = \sqrt{npq}$$

II. Poisson Distribution

If RV $X \sim P(\mu)$ where μ = expected value with infinite trials n:

$$\mu = np$$
$$\sigma = \sqrt{\mu}$$
$$P(X = x) = \frac{\mu^x e^{-\mu}}{x!}$$

Excel Formula for finding probability:
POISSON.DIST(X, Mean, Cumulative)
    X = x
    Mean = μ
    cumulative = *TRUE* for cumulative and *FALSE* for probability function

III. Uniform Distribution

If RV $X \sim U(a, b)$ where a is the smallest value and b is the largest value

$$\mu = \frac{a + b}{2}$$

$$\sigma = \sqrt{\frac{(b-a)^2}{12}}$$

$$f(x) = \frac{1}{b-a}$$

$$P(X < x) = \frac{(x-a)}{(b-a)}; P(X > x) = \frac{(b-x)}{(b-a)}; P(c < X < d) = \frac{(d-c)}{(b-a)}$$

Excel does not have an inbuilt formula for Uniform Distribution

IV. **Exponential Distribution**

If a RV $X \sim E(\mu)$, and m is the historical expected value of X. The mean is also referred to as lambda for exponential distribution.

$$\mu = \sigma = \frac{1}{m} = \lambda$$

$$P(X \leq x) = 1 - e^{-\mu x}; P(X > x) = e^{-\mu x}; P(c < X < d) = e^{-\mu d} - e^{-\mu c}$$

Excel Formula for finding probability:
EXPON.DIST(x, lambda, cumulative)
   x = x
   lambda = mean μ
   cumulative = *TRUE* for cumulative and *FALSE* for probability function

V. **Normal Distribution**

a. If RV $X \sim N(\mu, \sigma)$, and the population values of μ and σ are known:

$$Z = \frac{x - \mu}{\sigma}; Z \sim N(0,1)$$

$$P(x < X) = P\left(\frac{x - \mu}{\sigma} < Z\right); P(X < x) = P\left(Z < \frac{x - \mu}{\sigma}\right);$$

$$P(c < X < d) = P\left(\frac{c - \mu}{\sigma} < Z < \frac{d - \mu}{\sigma}\right)$$

Excel Formula 1 for finding probability without knowing Z:
NORM.DIST(X, Mean, Standard_dev, Cumulative)
   X = x
   Mean = μ
   Standard_dev = σ
   cumulative = *TRUE* for cumulative and *FALSE* for probability function

Excel Formula 2 for finding probability if Z is known:
NORM.S.DIST (z, cumulative)
   z = Z (if known)
   cumulative = *TRUE* for cumulative and *FALSE* for probability function

Excel Formula 3 for using known probability to find X:
NORM.INV(probability, mean, standard_dev)
   probability = value of known probability
   mean = μ

Standard_dev = σ

Excel Formula 4 for finding value of Z based on probability:
NORM.S.INV(probability)
  probability = value of known probability

b. If RV defined as a particular population parameter (population mean in first case), is assumed to have a normal sampling distribution of the type $X \sim N(\bar{X}, \sigma_{\bar{X}})$, and one has the population value of σ or a large sample size n:

$$\mu = \bar{X}; \; \sigma_{\bar{X}} = \frac{\sigma}{\sqrt{n}}$$

$$Z = \frac{x - \mu}{\sigma_{\bar{X}}}; Z \sim N(0,1)$$

$$P(x < X) = P\left(\frac{x - \mu}{\sigma_{\bar{X}}} < Z\right); P(X < x) = P\left(Z < \frac{x - \mu}{\sigma_{\bar{X}}}\right);$$

$$P(c < X < d) = P\left(\frac{c - \mu}{\sigma_{\bar{X}}} < Z < \frac{d - \mu}{\sigma_{\bar{X}}}\right)$$

The Confidence Interval for a specific significance level α is given by:
$$(1 - \alpha)\% \; CI = \bar{X} \pm ME = \bar{X} \pm Z_{\alpha/2} \cdot \sigma_{\bar{X}}$$

Excel Formula 1 for finding probability without knowing Z:
NORM.DIST(X, Mean, Standard_dev, Cumulative)
  X = x
  Mean = μ
  Standard_dev = $\sigma_{\bar{X}}$
  cumulative = *TRUE* for cumulative and *FALSE* for probability function

Excel Formula 2 for finding probability if Z is known:
NORM.S.DIST (z, cumulative)
  z = Z (if known)
  cumulative = *TRUE* for cumulative and *FALSE* for probability function

Excel Formula 3 using known probability to find X:
NORM.INV(probability, mean, standard_dev)
  probability = value of known probability
  mean = μ
  Standard_dev = $\sigma_{\bar{X}}$

Excel Formula 4 for finding value of Z based on probability:
NORM.S.INV(probability)
  probability = value of known probability

Excel Formula 5 for finding Margin of Error:
CONFIDENCE.NORM(alpha, standard_dev, size)
  Alpha = α
  Standard_dev = $\sigma_{\bar{X}}$
  Size = n

c. If RV defined as a particular population parameter (population proportion in this case), is assumed to have a normal sampling distribution of the type $P' \sim N(p', \sigma_{p'})$, with sample size n and X successes:

$$\rho = p' = X/n; \; \sigma_{p'} = \sqrt{\frac{p'(1-p')}{n}}$$

$$Z = \frac{p' - \rho}{\sigma_{p'}}; Z \sim N(0,1)$$

$$P(p_1' < P') = P\left(\frac{p_1' - \rho}{\sigma_{p'}} < Z\right); P(P' < p_1') = P\left(Z < \frac{p_1' - \rho}{\sigma_{p'}}\right);$$

$$P(p_1' < P' < p_2') = P\left(\frac{p_1' - \rho}{\sigma_{p'}} < Z < \frac{p_2' - \rho}{\sigma_{p'}}\right)$$

The Confidence Interval for a specific significance level α is given by:
$$(1 - \alpha)\% \; C.I. \; for \; \rho = p' \pm ME = p' \pm Z_{\alpha/2}\sigma_{p'}$$

Avoid using inbuilt Normal Distribution formulas for Proportions for the most part but if the Z-related formulas can be used correctly:

Excel Formula 1 for finding probability if Z is known:
NORM.S.DIST (z, cumulative)
   z = Z (if known)
   cumulative = *TRUE* for cumulative and *FALSE* for probability function

Excel Formula 2 for finding value of Z based on probability:
NORM.S.INV(probability)
   probability = value of known probability

d. If RV defined as a particular population parameter (population mean in first case), is assumed to have a normal sampling distribution of the type $X \sim N(\bar{X}, s_{\bar{X}})$, and one does not know the population value of σ and has a small sample size n:

$$\mu = \bar{X}; \; s_{\bar{X}} = \frac{s}{\sqrt{n-1}}; df = n - 1$$

$$t = \frac{x - \mu}{s_{\bar{X}}}$$

$$P(x < X) = P\left(\frac{x - \mu}{s_{\bar{X}}} < t\right); P(X < x) = P\left(t < \frac{x - \mu}{s_{\bar{X}}}\right);$$

$$P(c < X < d) = P\left(\frac{c - \mu}{s_{\bar{X}}} < t < \frac{d - \mu}{s_{\bar{X}}}\right)$$

The Confidence Interval for a specific significance level α is given by:
$$(1 - \alpha)\% \; CI = \bar{X} \pm ME = \bar{X} \pm t_{\alpha/2} \cdot s_{\bar{X}}$$

Excel Formula 1 for finding left-tailed probability:
T.DIST(X, deg_freedom, Cumulative)
   X = x

Deg_freedom = df

cumulative = *TRUE* for cumulative and *FALSE* for probability function

Excel Formula 2 for finding 2 tailed probability:
T.DIST.2T (X, deg_freedom)

    X = x

    Deg_freedom = df

Excel Formula 3 using known probability to find t:
T.INV(probability, deg_freedom)

    probability = value of known probability

    Deg_freedom = df

Excel Formula 4 for finding Margin of Error:
CONFIDENCE.T(alpha, standard_dev, size)

    Alpha = α

    Standard_dev = s

    Size = n

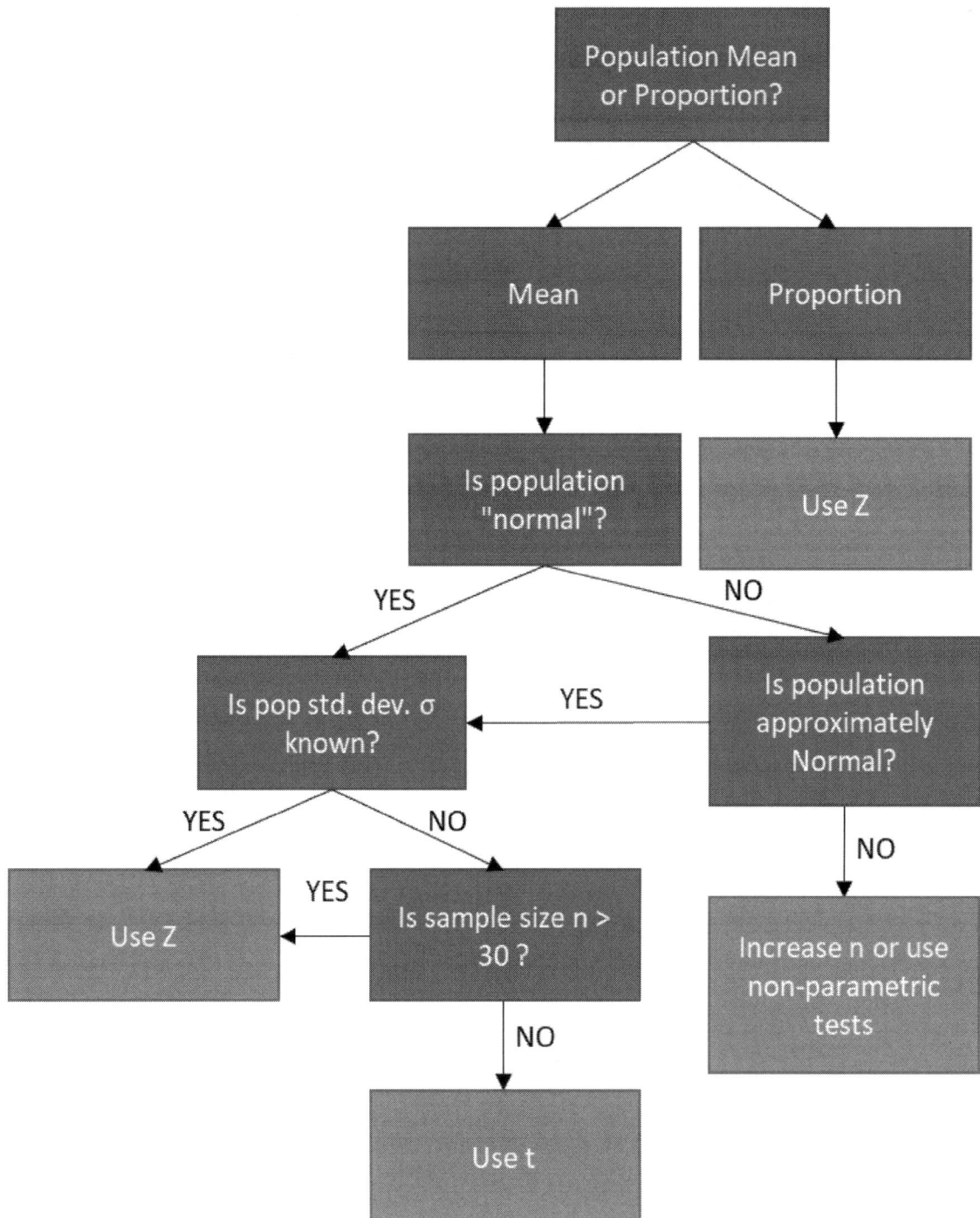

Figure 5.15. Identifying when to use Z-distribution or t-distribution

Chapter 6. Hypotheses Testing and ANOVA

One of the key features of any scientific method is the presentation and testing of a hypothesis, which is a prediction regarding a particular event or outcome based upon available information. By testing a hypothesis, the goal of the scientific method is to obtain reliable information and draw conclusions about a particular phenomenon that occurs in either natural or controlled conditions. The formation of a hypothesis hinges upon identifying two contradictory statements regarding the particular event or outcome of interest. One of them is called the "**Null Hypothesis**" and refers to a "no difference" or "zero difference" statement which negates any predictability of a particular event or outcome. The other statement is called the "**Alternative Hypothesis**" and directly contradicts the Null in terms of assigning a level of significance to the predictability of a particular event or outcome. These two statements together refer to the action of hypotheses testing (hypothesis – with an "i" refers to singular and hypotheses with an "e" refers to the plural) in statistics.

Most of the time, the term "testing a hypothesis" is assumed to refer to the Alternative Hypothesis because it clearly states the relationship that one is trying to prove to be statistically significant. However, it is important to note that typically one is testing both the statements comprising of the "hypotheses" together. The goal is to either "reject" or "fail to reject" the null hypothesis in favor of the alternative hypothesis.

Some modern books have been notorious for using the term "accept" for hypotheses testing. This is WRONG. One cannot "accept" a hypothesis because once something is "accepted," it is no longer subject to any scientific method for retesting and refers to the fallacy of "the science is settled." By its very definition, science is the pursuit of an inquiry and therefore cannot be "settled" – it is always subject to revision as more information about any phenomenon is obtained. Some books also use the term "retain" or "fail to retain," which is an acceptable alternative to the corresponding "fail to reject" or "reject" hypothesis.

Why would one want to do hypotheses testing in statistics? For one, one does not always have information about the entire population of interest and is relying on sample statistics to make predictions about the population. The chapters 1 to 5 of this book discuss how to visualize, describe, and make inferences about the population using samples. This current toolkit gives one the means to understand the information gathered from samples and to identify the potential distributions of the sample statistics as compared to the population parameters. These tools can be used to analyze available data and to determine whether the null hypothesis in a hypotheses testing scenario can be rejected or not from a statistical point of view in favor of the alternative hypothesis. This enables one to derive conclusions about the population parameter behaviors even if only the sample data is available as opposed to the population data. This chapter starts by discussing the logistics of hypotheses testing and the importance of statistical significance, followed by one-sample hypotheses testing, two-sample hypothesis testing, and a multi-sample Analysis of Variance (ANOVA) hypotheses testing methodology.

6.1. Hypotheses and Types of Errors

The most commonly used null: alternative hypotheses combinations with their corresponding types of tests, are shown in Table 6.1. One would test these hypotheses at a particular level of statistical significance α, that was discussed in earlier chapters. The tests of these hypotheses typically use normally distributed or normally approximated distributions such as Z or t-test if one knows that the population is normally distributed (or close to normally distributed). In many cases, the population is not normally distributed, and the tests used for hypotheses testing for those populations are called non-parametric tests such as the F-test, Chi-Squared test, etc. The later part of this chapter discusses the F-test in the context of the ANOVA whereas the general F-test and Chi-squared (χ^2) tests are covered in Chapter 8.

Table 6.1. Common Null: Alternative Hypothesis Pairs

Null Hypothesis (H₀)	Alternative Hypothesis (Hₐ)	Type of Test using α
Two things are "equal to" each other (=)	The two things are "not equal to" each other ($\neq$)	Two-tailed test
One thing is "greater than or equal" to the other ($\geq$)	The one thing is "less than" the other ($<$)	One-tailed test
One thing is "less than or equal" to the other ($\leq$)	The one thing is "greater than" the other ($>$)	One-tailed test

6.1.1. Type I versus Type II Errors

What exactly is being represented by the statistical significance α? In order to understand this, one should take a little detour into understanding what the most important errors are with respect to hypotheses testing. *Type I Error* refers to the probability of rejecting the null hypothesis, when it is actually true, and *Type II Error* refers to the probability of failing to reject the null hypothesis when it is actually false. When decisions are made in the real world, they are based upon the expectations of a certain behavior in the population of interest or a given state of nature. This is within the control of the decision-maker. However, the behavior of the population of interest or the state of nature is beyond the control of the decision-maker, so there is no way to know until after a particular event, whether the decision was a correct one or not.

An illustration will clarify how decision-making is always a trade-off between two types of errors. Assume that one has to decide on whether or not to take an umbrella when they are going for a walk. If the weather is sunny, one would expect that there will not be any rain and would decide to not take an umbrella with them. Similarly, if the weather is cloudy, one would expect that there will be rain and would decide to take an umbrella with them. Only after their walk is over would one know if the decision to take the umbrella or not was the right decision to make. For instance, if one decided not to take an umbrella because it was sunny but if there was a sudden downpour, they would get wet. Alternatively, if one chose to take an umbrella because it was cloudy, but it did not rain, they just carried an umbrella on their walk for no reason. Creating a little matrix to understand the correct decision versus the incorrect decision, as shown in Figure 6.1 is helpful in visualizing these scenarios. In both cases there is a bit of "risk" that one is taking when making a decision of what to do.

Decision to be made	State of Nature	
	Rain	No Rain
No Umbrella	Got wet	GOOD decision
Take Umbrella	GOOD decision	Lugged umbrella

Decision to be made	State of Nature	
	Ho True	Ho False
Reject Ho	TYPE I Error	No Error
Fail to Reject Ho	No Error	Type II Error

Figure 6.1. Type I versus Type II Errors

In the top half of the figure, one can see how the example of deciding to take the umbrella (or not) versus the state of nature (rain or no rain) can result in getting two good or error-free decisions or two decisions with errors. Of the two error-filled decisions, one is more harmful (the individual got wet!) as compared to the other (the individual lugged an umbrella for their walk despite not using it). The first one is a result of omitting sufficient caution on the walk and the second one is a result of being over-cautious when going for a walk.

For the first decision, one rejected the probability of it raining because it was not raining when they left from home. In other words, they rejected the null hypothesis of "it can rain anytime" based on their observation of a sunny sky and decided to take a risk. This risk is called the statistical significance α, because one can reject a valid null hypothesis based on the observed data. This type of risk-taking is called the level of significance or how much does one trust their observations before deciding a course of action. In the second portion of Figure 6.1, one can see the corresponding statistical table for *Type I* or *Type II* errors. So, the α refers to the probability of making a Type I error, rejecting the null hypothesis when it is in fact, true! The corresponding value of $(1 - \alpha)$ is called the Confidence Level and represents how confident one is in the decision that they are making based on the assumption of what the State of Nature is likely to be.

For the second (alternative) decision, the individual was concerned with the probability of it raining because it was cloudy when they left from home. In other words, they failed to reject the null hypothesis of "it can rain anytime" based on their observation of a cloudy sky and decided to protect themselves with an umbrella, just in case! This type of cautious behavior leads to the Type

II error, defined as the failure to reject the null hypothesis even when it is false. It is represented by β and the corresponding value of $(1 - \beta)$ is called the Power of the Test, which indicates how much caution is being wielded in making a particular decision. In fields that require great care and precision (e.g., medicines, vehicles, or speed limits on roads) the decisions often involve a higher level of β because precaution is always advisable.

6.1.2. How to Test Hypotheses in Statistics

Steps of Hypotheses Testing

Step 1. Clearly identify and state the Null Hypothesis (H_0) and Alternative Hypothesis (H_a)

Step 2. Specify the level of significance α (also called the acceptable risk of making a Type I error). If the null hypothesis is of the form "two things are equal to each other," make sure to use the two-tailed $\alpha/2$ levels in Step 4 below.

Step 3. Select and calculate the appropriate value of the Test Statistic (Z-score, t-value, F-score, χ^2, etc.)

Step 4. Determine the Critical Value (CV) of the appropriate distribution based on the level of α. If the H_0 is the form of "two things are equal to each other," use the two-tailed distribution to find critical value, otherwise use the one-tailed distribution to find critical value using the Tables given in the Appendix. Clearly demarcate the Rejection Region (RR)

Step 5. Compare the Test Statistic to the Critical Value to identify whether the null hypothesis is rejected or not at the level of significance α. If the Test Statistic falls in the Rejection Region, reject the null hypothesis, otherwise fail to reject the null.

Step 6. Write a clear conclusion based on the determination made in Step 5.

It is easiest to use Z-distribution in order to visualize these steps more clearly in the illustration given below on how to follow these steps, but the concept remains the same for other distributions and their corresponding graphs as well. The test-statistics for different types will be covered in the appropriate sections and sub-sections in this chapter.

Step 1. Let the H_0 be that a particular sample is representative of the population from which it was drawn or in simpler words it is assumed that the mean of the sample ($\bar{X}$) is the same as the mean of the population (μ). The alternative hypothesis would be that the mean of the sample is DIFFERENT from the mean of the population. Thus, one can write the mathematical formulations as follows:

$$H_0 : \bar{X} = \mu$$
$$H_a : \bar{X} \neq \mu$$

Step 2. Let the level of significance be represented by α. Since the H_0 has the "=" sign, one can know that the distribution chosen will be a two-tailed distribution.

Step 3. Since one is choosing the differences in the mean values of the sample and the population, and assuming that the standard deviation of the population (σ) is known, the Test Statistic Z_T is calculated using the following formula:

$$Z_T = \frac{\bar{X} - \mu}{\sigma_{\bar{X}}}$$

Step 4. If the significance level is α, the Critical Value $= Z_\alpha$ for one-tailed tests and Critical Value $= Z_{\alpha/2}$ for two-tailed tests. The blue regions in Figure 6.2 show the identified Rejection Regions for each type of Null Hypothesis. Since in this illustration, a two-tailed distribution is being discussed, the image to the far right will be considered for reference. Note, that in the first two images, the blue area (Rejection Region) shows the probability of Type I error or the significance level α. In the last image, the Rejection Region is split into two parts, each equal to half the probability of Type I error (α) for a total value of the significance remaining the same as α. The orange regions in all three images refer to the probability of not making an error.

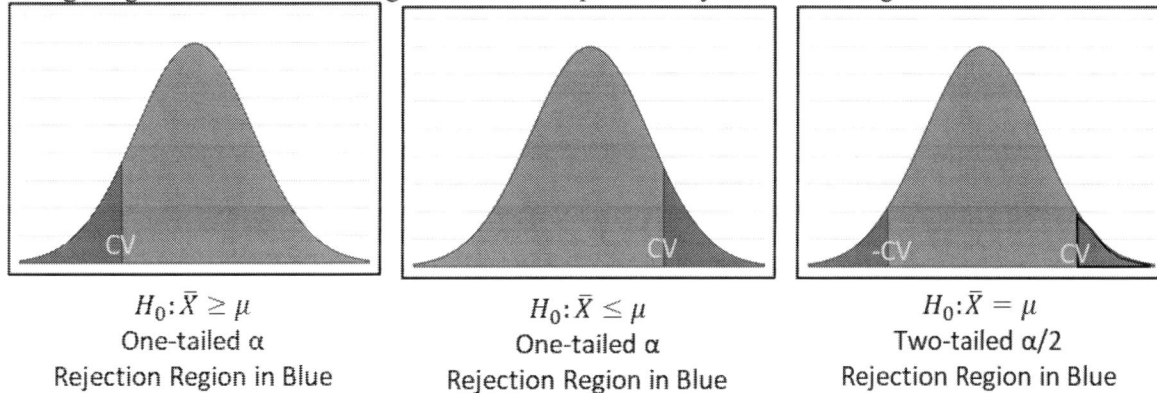

$H_0: \bar{X} \geq \mu$
One-tailed α
Rejection Region in Blue

$H_0: \bar{X} \leq \mu$
One-tailed α
Rejection Region in Blue

$H_0: \bar{X} = \mu$
Two-tailed $\alpha/2$
Rejection Region in Blue

Figure 6.2. Location of the Critical Value (CV) and Rejection Region (RR)

In this illustration, one would identify the appropriate value of $Z_{\alpha/2}$ as the Critical Values for each side of the distribution. Table 6.2 given below is the same as the Table 5.2 that was presented in the previous chapter but has been reproduced for the ease of reference. Thus, if the significance level was chosen as 0.05, one would use the corresponding value of 1.96 for the Critical Value of $Z_{\alpha/2}$. Also, notice that the orange shaded area in the third image in Figure 6.2 (above) is the same as the confidence interval area.

Table 6.2. Common Values for Key Significance Levels

Significance Level α	Confidence Coefficient $(1 - \alpha)$	Confidence Level	$\alpha/2$	$Z_{\alpha/2}$	Confidence Interval
0.1	0.9	90%	0.05	1.645	$\bar{X} \pm 1.645\sigma_{\bar{x}}$
0.05	0.95	95%	0.025	1.96	$\bar{X} \pm 1.96\sigma_{\bar{x}}$
0.02	0.98	98%	0.01	2.33	$\bar{X} \pm 2.33\sigma_{\bar{x}}$
0.01	0.99	99%	0.005	2.575	$\bar{X} \pm 2.575\sigma_{\bar{x}}$

Step 5. Here is where one can compare the Test Statistic Z_T that was calculated in Step 3 with the Critical Value of $Z_{\alpha/2}$. If the location of the Z_T is within the orange shaded region of Figure 2.6, then it does not belong to the blue-shaded Rejection Region. This implies that one would FAIL TO REJECT the null hypothesis. However, if the location of the Z_T is in either of the blue-shaded Rejection Region(s), one can REJECT the null hypothesis. The probability given as $P(X < Z_T)$ is also known as the p-value. This p-value can be compared with the α directly as well. Note that one can avoid drawing any graphs at all, once there is a familiarity with the visualization by simply

noting that the rejection regions lie to the left of the negative value of *CV* and to the right of the positive value of the *CV* in two-tailed distributions and either to the left or to the right in one-tailed distributions. Thus, if $|Z_T| > CV$, one can reject the null hypothesis, otherwise one fails to reject it.

Step 6. If one Fails to Reject the Null Hypothesis in Step 5, one can conclude that there is no statistical difference between the sample mean and the population mean at the chosen significance level, implying that the sample is indeed representative of the population. If one Rejects the Null Hypothesis in Step 5, one can conclude that there is a statistically significant difference between the sample mean and the population, implying that the sample is NOT representative of the population.

The following sections demonstrate various types of examples to understand how to test various types of hypotheses using the basic steps of hypotheses-testing and by simply changing how one defines the Test Statistic and Critical Values for each type.

6.2. One-sample Hypotheses Testing

One-sample hypotheses testing typically consists of comparing the means or proportions that exist in a chosen sample to the corresponding population parameters to identify whether the sample is representative of the population or not. The variation comes in based upon what one knows about the population and how big the sample size is. For instance, if one is testing for difference in proportions, one always uses the Z-distribution, as discussed in Chapter 5. However, when one is testing for difference in means, one can only use the Z-distribution if the population standard deviation (σ) is known oor if the sample size is large ($n > 30$). If the population standard deviation (σ) is unknown and if the sample size is small ($n < 30$), one must use the *t*-distribution based on the estimates of the standard deviation (s) of the sample. The following sub-sections discuss various examples of each type. Table 6.3 shows the most commonly used Test Statistics for testing hypotheses

Table 6.3. Test Statistics for Testing Hypotheses

Type	Population Information	Sample Size	Standard Error	Test Statistic
Means:	σ is known	doesn't matter	$\dfrac{\sigma}{\sqrt{n}}$	$Z_T = \dfrac{\bar{X} - \mu}{\sigma_{\bar{X}}}$
	σ is unknown	n > 30	$\dfrac{s}{\sqrt{n}}$	$Z_T = \dfrac{\bar{X} - \mu}{\sigma_{\bar{X}}}$
	σ is unknown	n < 30	$\dfrac{s}{\sqrt{n-1}}$	$t_T = \dfrac{\bar{X} - \mu}{s_{\bar{X}}}$
Proportions:	ρ is known	doesn't matter	$\sqrt{\dfrac{\rho(1-\rho)}{n}}$	$Z_T = \dfrac{p' - \rho}{\sigma_{p'}}$
	ρ is not known	doesn't matter	$\sqrt{\dfrac{p'(1-p')}{n}}$	$Z_T = \dfrac{p - p'}{\sigma_{p'}}$

6.2.1. Difference of Sample versus Population Means when σ is known or n is large

Example 6:1. Difference of Sample vs. Population Mean Two-tailed using Z

A researcher is interested in identifying the characteristics of CEOs of various American Corporations and selects a sample of 100 CEOs from the year 2020. He finds that the average age of these CEOs in his sample is 68 years. If the expected mean age of all CEOs in the population is 70 years with a standard deviation of 11 years, conduct a test of significance at 0.05 level to confirm whether his sample is reliable or not.

Solution: Follow the steps of Hypotheses Testing

Step 1. According to the given information, researcher is trying to compare the mean age in his sample with the mean age of the population, which is 70. Thus, he can write his mathematical formulations as follows:

$$H_0: \bar{X} = 70$$
$$H_a: \bar{X} \neq 70$$

Step 2. The level of significance $\alpha = 0.05$. Since the H_0 has the "=" sign, the distribution will be a two-tailed distribution. So, $\alpha/2 = 0.025$ for each tail.

Step 3. The information given states that the calculated value of $\bar{X} = 68$ and the standard deviation of population $\sigma = 11$ years and sample size $n = 100$. This implies that the Standard Error $\sigma_{\bar{X}} = \frac{11}{\sqrt{100}} = 1.1$ Thus, the Test Statistic Z_T is calculated using the following formula:

$$Z_T = \frac{\bar{X} - \mu}{\sigma_{\bar{X}}} = \frac{68 - 70}{1.1} = -1.82$$

Step 4. The Critical Value of $Z_{\alpha/2} = 1.96$ based on Table 6.2. Thus, one can define the Rejection Region shaded in blue similar to the third image in Figure 6.2.

Step 5. Now plot the Z_T on the graph (see Figure 6.3) and one can see that the value of Z_T lies in the orange region. Thus, one would fail to reject the null hypothesis in this case. Alternatively, here $|-1.82| < 1.96$, implies failure to reject the null hypothesis.

Step 6. Since the decision is that one would Fail to Reject the Null Hypothesis in Step 5, one can conclude that there is no statistical difference between the sample mean of 68 and the population mean of 70 at a 0.05 significance level, implying that the sample of CEOs is indeed representative of the age distribution of the population of CEOs in American Corporations.

	A	B	C	D	E	F	G	H	I
1	**Difference of Sample vs. Population Mean Two-tailed Example using Z**								
2	**Ho:**		X-bar = 70	two-tailed test because "="					
3	**Ha:**		X-bar ≠ 70						
4	**Alpha:**		0.05						
5	**1- alpha:**		0.95	=1-C4					
6	**Tails:**		2						
7	**Test Statistic**								
8		**X-bar =**	68						
9		**σ =**	11						
10		**μ =**	70						
11		**n =**	100						
12		**Z_T =**	-1.82	=(C8-C10)/(C9/SQRT(C11))					
13		**p-value =**	0.03	=NORM.S.DIST(C12, TRUE)					
14	**Critical Value**								
15		**Z critical =**	-1.960	=IF(C6=1, (NORM.S.INV(C4)), (NORM.S.INV(C4/2)))					
16									
17	**Decision:**	Fail to reject Ho		=IF(ABS(C15) > ABS(C12), "Fail to reject Ho", "Reject Ho")					
18	**Conclusion:**	The sample mean is representative of the population mean at 95% confidence level.							

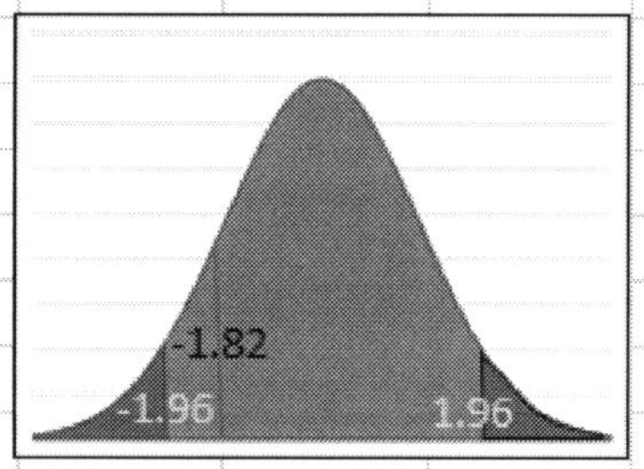

(Chart shown in cells D7:G13 with normal distribution curve labeled -1.82, -1.96, and 1.96)

Figure 6.3. Example 6.1 Two-Tailed Z Solved Using Excel Formulas.

6.2.2. Difference of Sample versus Population Means when σ is unknown and n is small

Example 6:2. Difference of Sample vs. Population Mean One-Tailed using t

A researcher is interested in identifying the characteristics of CEOs of various American Corporations and selects a sample of 10 CEOs from the year 2021. He finds that the average age of these CEOs in his sample is 65 years. The expected mean age of all CEOs in the population based on historical data is 70 years but with all the changes occurring in corporations these days, he is no longer certain of the population standard deviation. The sample standard deviation was found to be 7 years. Help the researcher conduct a test of significance at 0.05 level to confirm if the mean of the new CEOs is less than 70 or not.

Solution: Here, it seems that in the year 2021 there were some changes to the way CEOs were appointed by companies based on the given information. The null hypothesis would be that there is no change, that everything is status quo and the alternative hypothesis (that researcher is interested in) would be that the average CEO ages have actually decreased. Follow the stepwise method to solve this problem.

Step 1. Researcher is trying to compare the mean age in the sample with the mean age of the population, which is 70. Thus, he can write his mathematical formulations as follows:

$$H_0: \bar{X} \geq 70$$
$$H_a: \bar{X} < 70$$

Step 2. The level of significance $\alpha = 0.05$. Since the H_0 has the "≥" sign, the distribution will be a one-tailed distribution. So, $\alpha = 0.05$ for the one-sided tail.

Step 3. The information given states that the calculated value of $\bar{X} = 65$ years, the standard deviation of the sample $s = 7$ years and sample size $n = 10$. Thus, the population standard deviation is unknown and the sample size < 30 observations, so the t-distribution needs to be used to solve this problem. This implies that the Standard Error $s_{\bar{X}} = \frac{7}{\sqrt{10-1}} = 2.33$. Thus, the Test Statistic t_T is calculated using the following formula:

$$t_T = \frac{\bar{X} - \mu}{s_{\bar{X}}} = \frac{65 - 70}{2.33} = -2.15$$

Step 4. The Critical Value of $t_a = 1.833$ based on t-table Table B in the Appendix. Since the Ho has the symbol "$\geq$", one would use the negative value -1.833 for the CV of t. Thus, one can define the Rejection Region shaded in blue similar to the first image in Figure 6.2.

Step 5. Now plot the t_T on the graph (see Figure 6.4) and one can see that the value of t_T lies in the blue Rejection Region. Thus, reject the null hypothesis in this case. Alternatively, one can see that $|-2.15| > 1.833$, so one can reject the null hypothesis.

Step 6. Since the decision is to Reject the Null Hypothesis in Step 5, one can conclude that the mean age of the new group of CEOs in 2021 is not greater than or equal to 70 years anymore at a 0.05 significance level. Thus, the researcher can safely retain the alternative hypothesis that new CEOs are younger than 70 based on the sample data. The Excel solution for this problem is shown in Figure 6.4.

	A	B	C	D	E	F	G	H	I
1	**Difference of Sample vs. Population Mean Two-tailed Example using t**								
2	**Ho:**		X-bar ≥ 70	one-tailed test because "≥"					
3	**Ha:**		X-bar < 70						
4	**Alpha:**		0.05						
5	**1- alpha:**		0.95	=1-C4					
6	**Tails:**		1						
7	**Test Statistic**								
8		**X-bar =**	65			-2.14			
9		**s =**	7						
10		**μ =**	70			-1.83			
11		**n =**	10						
12		**t_T =**	-2.14	=(C8-C10)/(C9/SQRT(C11-1))					
13		**p-value =**	0.03	=T.DIST(C12,C11-1, TRUE)					
14	**Critical Value**								
15		**t critical =**	-1.833	=IF(C6=1, (T.INV(C4,C11-1)), (T.INV(C4/2, C11-1)))					
16									
17	**Decision:**	Reject Ho		=IF(ABS(C15) > ABS(C12), "Fail to reject Ho", "Reject Ho")					
18	**Conclusion:**	The mean age of the new group of CEOs is not greater than or equal to 70							
19		at a 95% confidence level.							

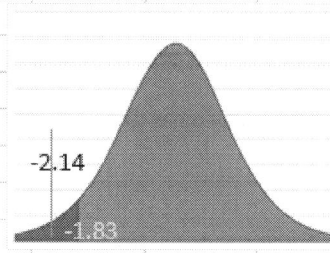

Figure 6.4. Example 6.2 One-Tailed t Solved Using Excel Formulas

6.2.3. Difference of Sample versus Population Proportions

Example 6:3. Difference of Sample vs. Population Proportions One-Tailed Z

A researcher is interested in identifying what is the proportion of female politicians in the United States and selects a sample of 50 politicians from the year 2021. She finds that the of the 50 politicians in State or Federal Governments, 15 are females. In other democracies of the world, female politicians comprise about 20% of all politicians. Help the researcher conduct a test of significance at 0.01 level to confirm if the proportion of female politicians in the USA is higher than that of other countries or not.

Solution: Follow the steps of hypotheses testing for proportions in this example.

Step 1. According to the given information, one is supposed to find out whether the proportion of female politicians in the USA is greater than the proportion of female politicians in the rest of the world or not. The null hypothesis (status quo) would be that the proportion in the USA is less than or equal to the rest of the world and the alternative hypothesis (what one is interested in finding) is that the US proportion is higher than the rest of the world. Thus, one can write the mathematical formulations as follows:

$$H_0: p' \leq 0.20$$
$$H_a: p' > 0.20$$

Step 2. The level of significance $\alpha = 0.01$. Since the H_0 has the "≤" sign, the distribution will be a one-tailed distribution. So, $\alpha = 0.01$ for the right-handed tail.

Step 3. The information given states that the calculated value of the sample proportion $p' = 15/50 = 0.3$, the population proportion $p = 0.20$ and sample size $n = 50$. One can calculate the Standard Error by using the population proportion p in this case, since it is given using the formula $\sigma_{p'} = \sqrt{\frac{p(1-p)}{n}} = \sqrt{\frac{0.8 \times 0.2}{50}} = 0.057$ Thus, the Test Statistic Z_T is calculated using the following formula:

$$Z_T = \frac{p' - \rho}{\sigma_{p'}} = \frac{0.3 - 0.2}{0.057} = 1.75$$

Step 4. The Critical Value of $Z_\alpha = 2.33$ based on Table 6.2. Thus, one can define the Rejection Region shaded in blue similar to the second image in Figure 6.2.

Step 5. Now plot the Z_T on the graph (see Figure 6.5) and one can see that the value of Z_T lies in the orange region. Thus, one would fail to reject the null hypothesis in this case. Alternatively, here $|1.77| < 2.33$, so one would fail to reject the null hypothesis.

Step 6. Since the decision is that one would Fail to Reject the Null Hypothesis in Step 5, one can conclude that there is no statistical support at a 0.01 significance level for the hypothesis that the proportion of female politicians in the USA is greater than the proportion of female populations in the rest of the world, implying that the US female politician proportion is expected to be less than or equal to the female politician proportion in the world. The Excel solution for this problem is shown in Figure 6.5.

	A	B	C	D	E	F	G	H	I
1	**Difference of Sample vs. Population Proportions using Z**								
2	**Ho:**		$p \leq 0.20$	one-tailed test because "≤"					
3	**Ha:**		$p > 0.20$						
4	**Alpha:**		0.01						
5	**1- alpha:**		0.99						
6	**Tails:**		1						
7	**Test Statistic**								
8		**p-hat =**	0.3	=15/50					
9		**p =**	0.2						
10		**n =**	50						
11		**std.error**	0.057	=SQRT(C9*(1-C9)/C10)					
12		**Z =**	1.77	=(C8-C9)/C11					
13		**p-value =**	0.96	=NORM.S.DIST(C12, TRUE)					
14	**Critical Value:**								
15		**Z critical =**	-2.326	=IF(C6=1, NORM.S.INV(C4), NORM.S.INV(C4/2))					
16			Since our Ho has "≤", we would take the positive value of the Z						
17	**Decision:**	Fail to reject Ho		=IF(ABS(C15) > ABS(C12), "Fail to reject Ho", "Reject Ho")					
18	**Conclusion:**	Thus, we fail to confirm that the proportion of female politicians in USA is higher than							
19		that in other countries at a 99% level of confidence.							

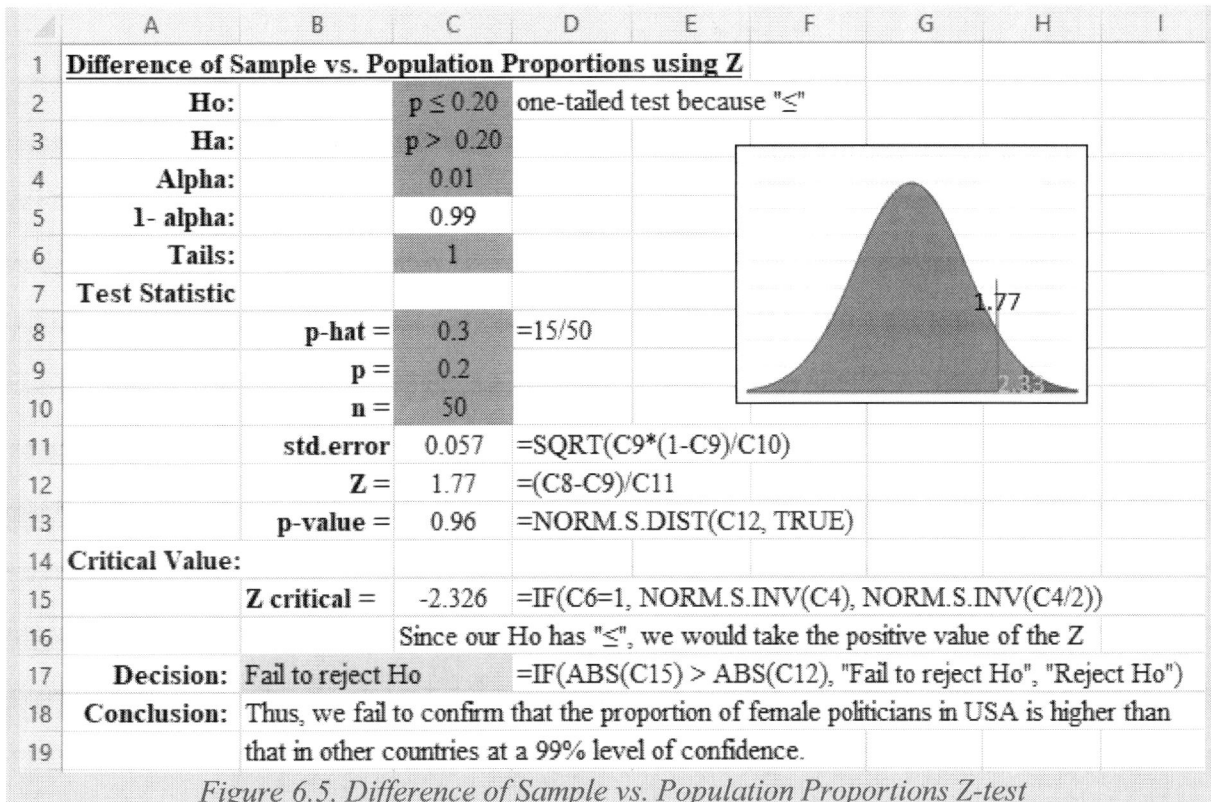

Figure 6.5. Difference of Sample vs. Population Proportions Z-test

6.3. Two-sample Hypotheses Testing

There are many nuances that can be created when one has two independently gathered samples that are being compared with each other, in the context of the means of the random variable of interest or in the context of the proportions represented by each sample. As discussed in Chapter 5, when one is testing proportions, it is a foregone conclusion that the Z-distribution is used. However, when one is testing means, or the difference in means, there are three possibilities.

The first possibility is that the sample is actually the same, but a before-after measurement is taken if the observations are subjected to some sort of a "treatment" to study the impact of the treatment on the values of the random variable of interest. This is also called a "pre-test: post-test" situation, and the t-distribution is typically used to test the hypotheses. This type of test is more common in scientific experiments with limited sample sizes. These types of pre-test post-test difference testing in business are less common since conditions of the tests (assumptions regarding external environment) are not always controllable. The second possibility is that for two independently drawn samples, one knows the corresponding values of the population standard deviations for each, so one can use the Z-distribution. The third possibility is that one does not know the population standard deviations, and therefore the t-distribution is used, regardless of the sizes of the samples.

Type	Sample 1 Information	Sample 2 Information	Standard Error	Test Statistic
Means				
σ known; Same population	$\bar{X}_1 = mean$ $n_1 = sample\ size$	$\bar{X}_2 = mean$ $n_2 = sample\ size$	$\sigma_{\bar{X}_1 - \bar{X}_2} = \dfrac{2\sigma}{\sqrt{n_1 + n_2}}$	$Z_T = \dfrac{\bar{X}_1 - \bar{X}_2}{\sigma_{\bar{X}_1 - \bar{X}_2}}$
σ unknown; Same population	$\bar{X}_1 = mean$ $n_1 = sample\ size$ $s_1 = sample\ s.d$ Pooled std. dev.	$\bar{X}_2 = mean$ $n_2 = sample\ size$ $s_2 = sample\ s.d$	$s_{\bar{X}_1 - \bar{X}_2} = \sqrt{\left(\dfrac{n_1 s_1^2 + n_2 s_2^2}{n_1 + n_2 - 2}\right)\left(\dfrac{1}{n_1} + \dfrac{1}{n_2}\right)}$	$t_T = \dfrac{\bar{X}_1 - \bar{X}_2}{s_{\bar{X}_1 - \bar{X}_2}}$
σ unknown; uncertain population	$\bar{X}_1 = mean$ $n_1 = sample\ size$ $s_1 = sample\ s.d$	$\bar{X}_2 = mean$ $n_2 = sample\ size$ $s_2 = sample\ s.d$	$s_{\bar{X}_1 - \bar{X}_2} = \sqrt{\left(\dfrac{s_1^2}{n_1} + \dfrac{s_2^2}{n_2}\right)}$	$t_T = \dfrac{\bar{X}_1 - \bar{X}_2}{s_{\bar{X}_1 - \bar{X}_2}}$
Before-After sample test	$\bar{X}_1 = mean\ of\ before$ Difference D to measure the differences in each observation before and after; sample size = n	$\bar{X}_2 = mean\ of\ after$	$s_{\bar{D}} = \sqrt{\dfrac{1}{n-1} \times \left(\dfrac{\sum D^2}{n} - (\bar{X}_1 - \bar{X}_2)^2\right)}$	$t_T = \dfrac{\bar{X}_1 - \bar{X}_2}{s_{\bar{D}}}$
Proportion				
Population information treated as a sample itself	$n_1 = sample\ size$ $p_1 = sample\ proportion$ pooled proportion $= p^* = \dfrac{n_1 p_1 + n_2 p_2}{n_1 + n_2}$	$n_2 = sample\ size$ $p_2 = sample\ proportion$	$s_{p_1 - p_2} = \sqrt{p^*(1 - p^*)\left(\dfrac{1}{n_1} + \dfrac{1}{n_2}\right)}$	$Z_T = \dfrac{p_1 - p_2}{s_{p_1 - p_2}}$

The biggest challenge when considering two samples and wanting to do a test of differences between the sample means (or proportions) often arises from the more complex formulas that are used for calculating the Standard Errors and the corresponding Test Statistics. Table 6.4 shows all of these formulas for the reader's knowledge. Using Excel is highly recommended to solve the examples discussed in this section to avoid having to manually calculate the Test Statistics given the complex formulas for the Standard Errors.

6.3.1. Differences in Means of Two Samples from Same Population

Example 6:4. Differences in Means of Two Samples (Same Population) if σ known

The average student scores 500 points on a National Exam with an expected standard deviation of 100 points. Two samples are drawn from this population, with the first sample consisting exclusively of 50 males and the second sample consisting of 50 females. The average of the male sample is found to be 511 points and the average of the female sample is found to be 541 points. Test the hypotheses that there is no difference between male and female scores on the exam at a significance level of 0.05.

Solution: Follow the steps for hypotheses testing:
Step 1. The hypotheses can be written as follows:
$$H_0: \bar{X}_1 = \bar{X}_2$$
$$H_a: \bar{X}_1 \neq \bar{X}_2$$

Step 2. This is a two-tailed test so $\alpha = 0.05$ and $\alpha/2 = 0.025$. Also, it is known that the population from which the samples are drawn is the same, and the standard deviation of the population is also known, so one can use the Z-distribution to test the hypotheses.

Step 3. $\bar{X}_1 = 511$; $\bar{X}_2 = 541$; $n_1 = n_2 = 50$; $\sigma = 100$, so the Standard Error is:

$$\sigma_{\bar{X}_1 - \bar{X}_2} = \frac{2\sigma}{\sqrt{n_1 + n_2}} = \frac{2 \times 100}{\sqrt{50 + 50}} = 20$$

This implies that the Test Statistic is calculated as follows:

$$Z_T = \frac{\bar{X}_1 - \bar{X}_2}{\sigma_{\bar{X}_1 - \bar{X}_2}} = \frac{511 - 541}{20} = -1.5$$

Step 4. The critical value for $Z_{\alpha/2} = 1.96$ for two-tailed Z-distribution (from Table 6.2)

Step 5. Now plot the Z_T on the graph (see Figure 6.6) and one can see that the value of Z_T lies in the orange region. Thus, the decision is "fail to reject the null hypothesis" in this case. Alternatively, here $|1.5| < 1.96$, so decision is: "fail to reject the null hypothesis."

Step 6. Thus, one can conclude that there is no statistical support at a 0.05 significance level for the hypothesis that there is a difference between the performance of males and females on this Exam. The Excel solution for this problem is shown in Figure 6.6.

	A	B	C	D	E	F	G	H	I
1	Difference of Two Samples with Two-tails using Z								
2	Ho:		X1-bar = X-2-bar	two-tailed test because "="					
3	Ha:		X1-bar ≠ X2-bar						
4	Alpha:		0.05						
5	1- alpha:		0.95	=1-C4					
6	Tails:		2						
7	Test Statistic								
8		X1-bar =	511						
9		X2-bar =	541						
10		σ =	100						
11		n1 =	50						
12		n2 =	50						
13		SE =	20	=2*C10/SQRT(C11+C12)					
14		ZT =	-1.50	=(C8-C9)/C13					
15		p-value =	0.07	=NORM.S.DIST(C14, TRUE)					
16	Critical Value								
17		Z critical =	-1.960	=IF(C6=1, (NORM.S.INV(C4)), (NORM.S.INV(C4/2)))					
18									
19	Decision:	Fail to reject Ho		=IF(ABS(C17) > ABS(C14), "Fail to reject Ho", "Reject Ho")					
20	Conclusion:	We cannot say that the mean performance of males is different from females							
21		with a 95% confidence level							

Figure 6.6. Differences of Two Sample Means using Z-Distribution

The next example uses pooled standard errors if the population standard deviation σ is unknown and as discussed earlier, always use the *t*-distribution in such cases consisting of two samples.

Example 6:5. Differences in Means of Two Samples (Same Population) if σ unknown

Suppose that two samples are drawn from the population of all students taking a National Exam, with the first sample consisting exclusively of 50 males and the second sample consisting of 45 females. One can assume that the population is homogenous (males and females are treated equally in terms of preparation for the exam). The average of the male sample is found to be 511 points with a standard deviation of 65 points and the average of the female sample is found to be 541 points with a standard deviation of 75 points. Test the hypotheses that there is no difference between male and female scores on the exam at a significance level of 0.05.

Solution: Follow the steps for hypotheses testing.

Step 1. The hypotheses can be written as follows:
$$H_0: \bar{X}_1 = \bar{X}_2$$
$$H_a: \bar{X}_1 \neq \bar{X}_2$$

Step 2. This is a two-tailed test so $\alpha = 0.05$ and $\alpha/2 = 0.025$. Also, the population from which the samples are drawn is the same, but the standard deviation of the population is unknown, so one would use the t-distribution to test the hypotheses.

Step 3. $\bar{X}_1 = 511$; $\bar{X}_2 = 541$; $n_1 = 50$; $n_2 = 45$; $s_1 = 65$; $s_2 = 75$, and if one assumes that the population is the same or homogenous, the Standard Error is calculated by using the pooled standard deviation using the following formula:

$$s_{\bar{X}_1-\bar{X}_2} = \sqrt{\left(\frac{n_1 s_1^2 + n_2 s_2^2}{n_1 + n_2 - 2}\right)\left(\frac{1}{n_1} + \frac{1}{n_2}\right)} = \sqrt{\left(\frac{50 \times 65^2 + 45 \times 75^2}{50 + 45 - 2}\right)\left(\frac{1}{50} + \frac{1}{45}\right)}$$

$$\therefore s_{\bar{X}_1-\bar{X}_2} = \sqrt{\left(\frac{211250 + 253125}{93}\right)(0.0422)} = 14.52$$

This implies that the Test Statistic is calculated as follows:

$$t_T = \frac{\bar{X}_1 - \bar{X}_2}{s_{\bar{X}_1-\bar{X}_2}} = \frac{511 - 541}{14.52} = -2.07$$

Step 4. The critical value for $t_{\alpha/2} = 1.98$ for two-tailed t-distribution with $df = n_1 + n_2 - 2 = 93$ based on the t-tables (See Table B in Appendix – the degrees of freedom are closest to 100 in last row)

Step 5. Now plot the t_T on the graph (see Figure 6.7) and one can see that the value of t_T lies in the blue Rejection Region. Thus, the decision is to reject the null hypothesis in this case. Moreover, here $|-2.07| > 1.96$, so one can reject the null hypothesis.

Step 6. Since the decision is to Reject the Null Hypothesis in Step 5, one can conclude that there is statistical support at a 0.05 significance level for the hypothesis that there is a difference between the performance of males and females on this Exam. The Excel solution for this problem is shown in Figure 6.7.

	A	B	C	D	E	F	G	H	I	J
1	Difference of Two Samples from Homogenous Population with Two-tails using t									
2	Ho:		X1-bar = X-2-bar	two-tailed test because "="						
3	Ha:		X1-bar ≠ X2-bar							
4	Alpha:		0.05							
5	1- alpha:		0.95	=1-C4						
6	Tails:		2							
7	Test Statistic									
8		X1-bar =	511							
9		X2-bar =	541							
10		s1 =	65							
11		s2 =	75							
12		n1 =	50							
13		n2 =	45							
14		SE =	14.52	=SQRT(((((C12*C10^2)+(C13*C11^2))/(C12+C13-2))*(1/C12+1/C13))						
15		tT =	-2.07	=(C8-C9)/C14						
16		p-value =	0.02	=NORM.S.DIST(C15, TRUE)						
17	Critical Value									
18		d.f. =	93	=C12+C13-2						
19		t critical =	-1.986	=IF(C6=1, (T.INV(C4,C18)), (T.INV(C4/2,C18)))						
20										
21	Decision:	Reject Ho		=IF(ABS(C19) > ABS(C15), "Fail to reject Ho", "Reject Ho")						
22	Conclusion:	We can say that the mean performance of males is different from females								
23		at a 95% confidence level								

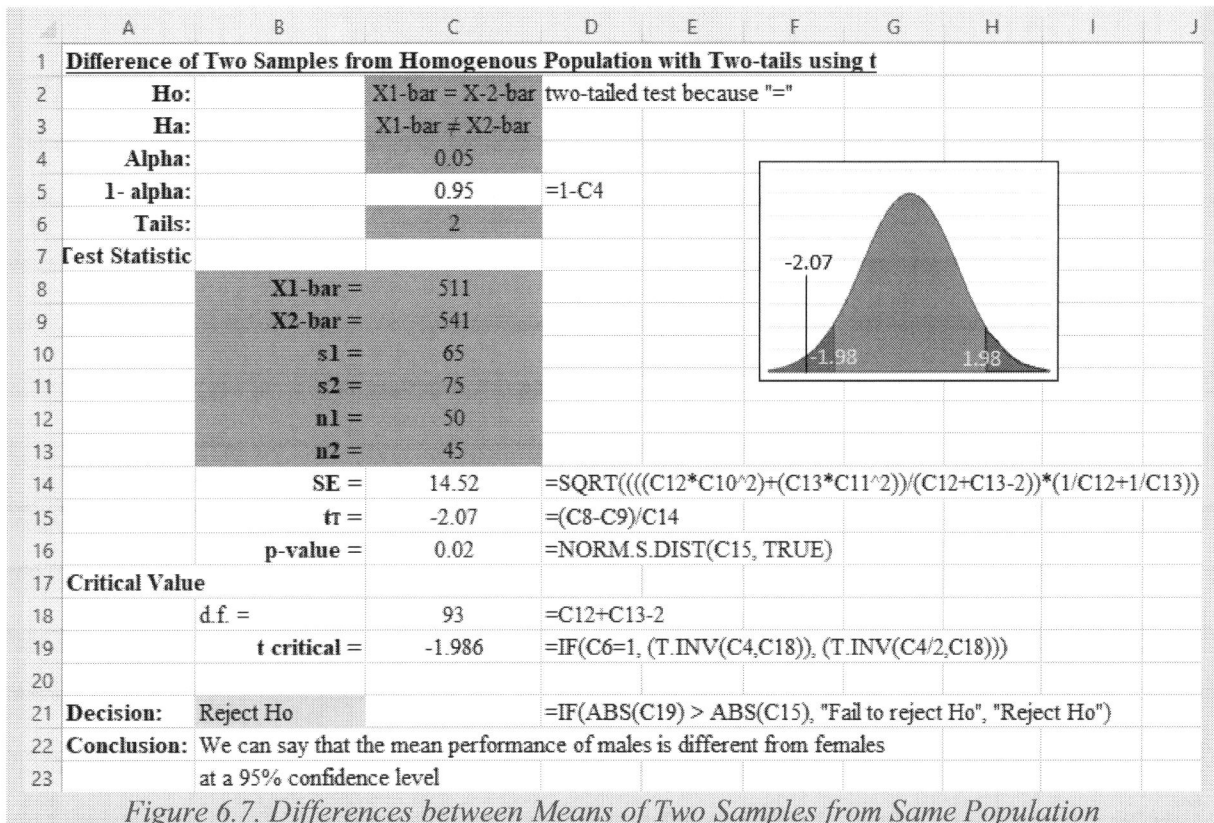

Figure 6.7. Differences between Means of Two Samples from Same Population

6.3.2. Differences in Means for Samples from Uncertain Populations

What if one wanted to see if males and females in the above example were actually from different populations, or in simpler words, if there were differences in their performances on the exam because they were given different tools to prepare for the examination before time. In this case, one can claim that there is "uncertainty" regarding the population homogeneity for the two samples and can test the differences in means a bit differently as shown in Example 6.6.

Example 6:6. Differences in Means of Two Samples from Uncertain Population

Suppose that two samples are drawn from the population of all students taking a National Exam, with the first sample consisting exclusively of 50 males and the second sample consisting of 45 females. There is no information about the population homogeneity, and testing needs to be performed on the differences in the means of performances of males and females. The average of the male sample is found to be 511 points with a standard deviation of 65 points and the average of the female sample is found to be 541 points with a standard deviation of 75 points. Test the hypotheses that there is no difference between male and female scores on the exam at a significance level of 0.05.

Solution: Follow the steps for hypotheses testing.
Step 1. The hypotheses can be written as follows:
$$H_0: \bar{X}_1 = \bar{X}_2; H_a: \bar{X}_1 \neq \bar{X}_2$$

Step 2. This is a two-tailed test so $\alpha = 0.05$ and $\alpha/2 = 0.025$. Also, since there is insufficient information to claim that the population is homogenous so one would use the t-distribution to test the hypotheses.

Step 3. $\bar{X}_1 = 511$; $\bar{X}_2 = 541$; $n_1 = 50$; $n_2 = 45$; $s_1 = 65$; $s_2 = 75$, But population is not necessarily homogenous, so the Standard Error is calculated by using the separate standard deviations using the following formula:

$$s_{\bar{X}_1 - \bar{X}_2} = \sqrt{\frac{s_1^2}{n_1} + \frac{s_2^2}{n_2}} = \sqrt{\frac{65^2}{50} + \frac{75^2}{45}} = \sqrt{84.5 + 125} = 14.47$$

This implies that the Test Statistic is calculated as follows:

$$t_T = \frac{\bar{X}_1 - \bar{X}_2}{s_{\bar{X}_1 - \bar{X}_2}} = \frac{511 - 541}{14.47} = -2.07$$

Step 4. The critical value for $t_{\alpha/2} = 1.98$ for two-tailed t-distribution with $df = n_1 + n_2 - 2 = 93$ based on the t-tables (See Table B in Appendix – degrees of freedom are closest to 100 in last row)

Step 5. Now plot the t_T on the graph (see Figure 6.8) and one can see that the value of t_T lies in the blue Rejection Region. Thus, decision is to reject the null hypothesis in this case. Moreover, here $|-2.07| > 1.96$, so the decision is to reject the null hypothesis.

	A	B	C	D	E	F	G	H	I
1	Difference of Two Samples from Uncertain or different Populations with Two-tails using t								
2	Ho:		X1-bar = X-2-bar	two-tailed test because "="					
3	Ha:		X1-bar ≠ X2-bar						
4	Alpha:		0.05						
5	1- alpha:		0.95	=1-C4					
6	Tails:		2						
7	Test Statistic						-2.07		
8		X1-bar =	511						
9		X2-bar =	541						
10		s1 =	65						
11		s2 =	75						
12		n1 =	50			1.98		1.98	
13		n2 =	45						
14		SE =	14.47	=SQRT((C10^2/C12)+(C11^2/C13))					
15		tт =	-2.07	=(C8-C9)/C14					
16		p-value =	0.02	=NORM.S.DIST(C15, TRUE)					
17	Critical Value								
18		d.f. =	93	=C12+C13-2					
19		t critical =	-1.986	=IF(C6=1, (T.INV(C4,C18)), (T.INV(C4/2,C18)))					
20									
21	Decision:	Reject Ho		=IF(ABS(C19) > ABS(C15), "Fail to reject Ho", "Reject Ho")					
22	Conclusion:	We can say that the mean performance of males is different from females							
23		at a 95% confidence level							

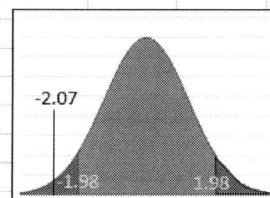

Figure 6.8. Differences in Two Sample Means using t -distribution

Step 6. Since the decision is to Reject the Null Hypothesis in Step 5, one can conclude that there is statistical support at a 0.05 significance level for the hypothesis that there is a difference between the performance of males and females on this Exam. The Excel solution for this problem is shown in Figure 6.8. Also, note that the answers to Examples 6.5 and 6.6 are not different. This similarity can be applied to mean that males and females may not be considered to be from a homogenous population in the context of this test. There might be some underlying differences to begin with which would need to be tested further. Remember that the standard errors were calculated differently in both Example 6.5 and Example 6.6.

6.3.3. Differences in Proportions of two Samples

Sometimes businesses or policy makers need to identify if a particular region is performing at par with the rest of the population in terms of a certain policy outcome or business performance measured as a proportion. One of the common examples in the banking industry is to check if the proportion of loans made by a particular branch to minority populations is in line with the established industry standards (Truth in Lending Act, Home Mortgage Disclosure Act, etc.). The branch's performance in terms of percentage of loans given to minorities is compared with the overall regional percentage of loans given to minorities to identify if the bank is engaging in any biased lending procedures. Similarly, if a particular judge is being examined for biased sentencing towards males in their jurisdiction, the proportions of sentences within that jurisdiction can be compared with the proportions of sentences in the rest of the region to highlight any disproportionate sentencing or actions.

Example 6:7. Testing for Differences in Proportions

A bank claims that out of the 275 loans it makes each month, 125 are made to minority populations. The peer lending rate to minority populations in that region is found to be 1485 out of 2700 total loans. At a 0.05 level of significance, identify if the bank needs to adjust its lending practices or not.

Solution: Remember that for proportion testing, one can use the population as a sample in itself. Follow the steps for hypotheses testing:
Step 1. The hypotheses can be written as follows:
$$H_0: p_1 = p_2$$
$$H_a: p_1 \neq p_2$$

Step 2. This is a two-tailed test so $\alpha = 0.05$ and $\alpha/2 = 0.025$. Tests of proportion always use the Z-distribution.

Step 3. $n_1 = 275; n_2 = 2700; x_1 = 125; x_2 = 1485; p_1 = \frac{125}{275} = 0.45; p_2 = \frac{1485}{2700} = 0.55,$
Find the pooled proportion as follows:
$$p^* = \frac{n_1 p_1 + n_2 p_2}{n_1 + n_2} = \frac{125 + 1485}{275 + 2700} = 0.54$$
Now, the Standard Error is calculated by using the pooled proportion using the following formula:
$$s_{p_1-p_2} = \sqrt{p^*(1-p^*)\left(\frac{1}{n_1}+\frac{1}{n_2}\right)} = \sqrt{0.54 \times 0.46 \times \left(\frac{1}{275}+\frac{1}{2700}\right)} = \sqrt{0.001} = 0.032$$
This implies that the Test Statistic is calculated as follows:
$$Z_T = \frac{p_1 - p_2}{s_{p_1-p_2}} = \frac{0.45 - 0.55}{0.032} = -3.1$$

Step 4. The critical value for $Z_{\alpha/2} = 1.96$ for two-tailed t-distribution from Table 6.2

Step 5. Now plot the Z_T on the graph (see Figure 6.9) and one can see that the value of Z_T lies in the blue Rejection Region. Thus, one can reject the null hypothesis in this case. Moreover, here $|-3.1| > 1.96$, so one can reject the null hypothesis.

Step 6. Since the decision is to Reject the Null Hypothesis in Step 5, one can conclude that there is statistical support at a 0.05 significance level for the hypothesis that there is a difference between the proportions of loans given by the bank to minorities as compared to their peers. Thus, the bank needs to adjust its lending practices to be equivalent to the regional standards. The Excel solution for this problem is shown in Figure 6.9. Note that due to rounding, there are slight differences in the calculated Z_T scores.

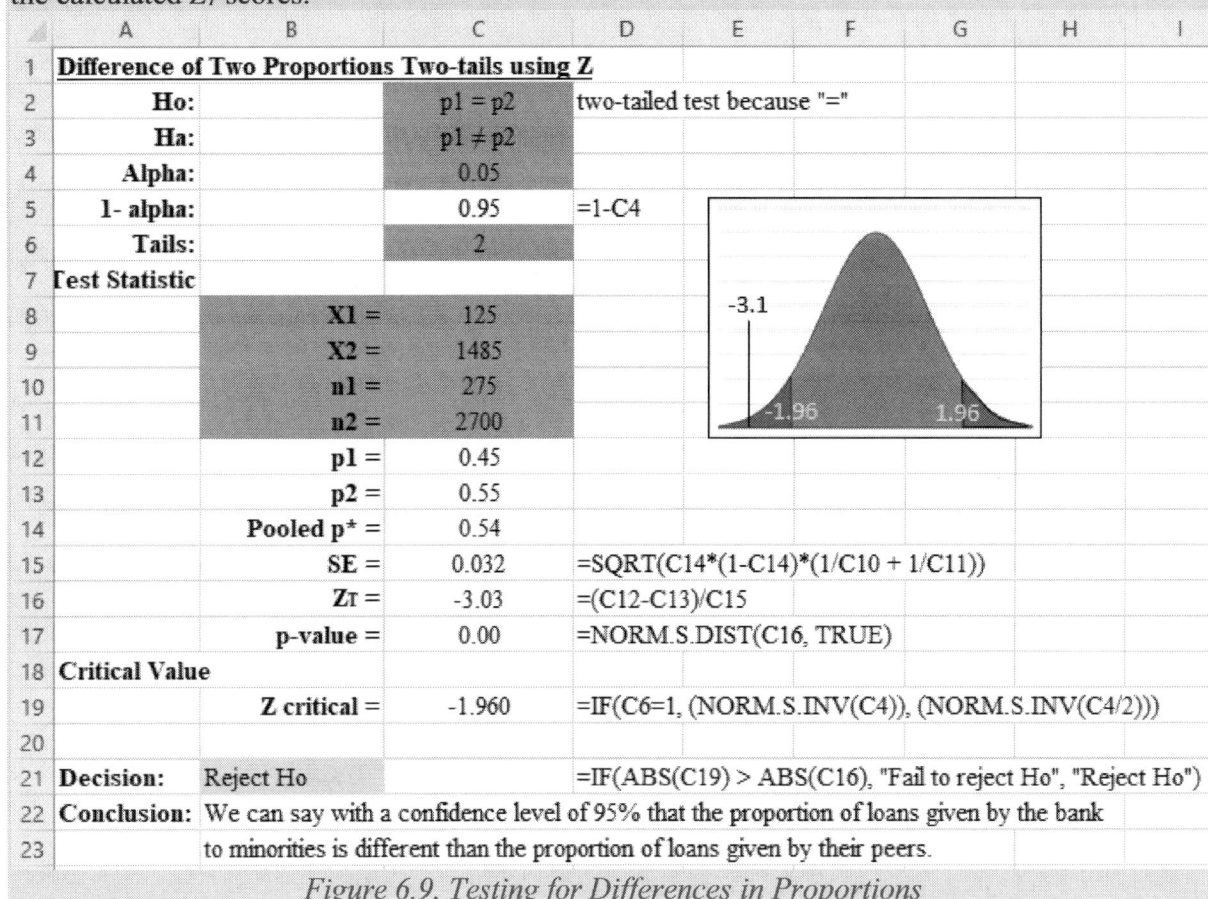

	A	B	C	D	E	F	G	H	I
1	**Difference of Two Proportions Two-tails using Z**								
2		**Ho:**	p1 = p2	two-tailed test because "="					
3		**Ha:**	p1 ≠ p2						
4		**Alpha:**	0.05						
5		**1- alpha:**	0.95	=1-C4					
6		**Tails:**	2						
7	**Test Statistic**								
8		X1 =	125			-3.1			
9		X2 =	1485						
10		n1 =	275						
11		n2 =	2700		-1.96		1.96		
12		p1 =	0.45						
13		p2 =	0.55						
14		Pooled p* =	0.54						
15		SE =	0.032	=SQRT(C14*(1-C14)*(1/C10 + 1/C11))					
16		Z_T =	-3.03	=(C12-C13)/C15					
17		p-value =	0.00	=NORM.S.DIST(C16, TRUE)					
18	**Critical Value**								
19		Z critical =	-1.960	=IF(C6=1, (NORM.S.INV(C4)), (NORM.S.INV(C4/2)))					
20									
21	**Decision:**	Reject Ho		=IF(ABS(C19) > ABS(C16), "Fail to reject Ho", "Reject Ho")					
22	**Conclusion:**	We can say with a confidence level of 95% that the proportion of loans given by the bank							
23		to minorities is different than the proportion of loans given by their peers.							

Figure 6.9. Testing for Differences in Proportions

6.4. Analysis of Variance (ANOVA)

Up until this point, the focus has been on one-sample hypotheses testing or two-sample hypothesis testing. But what if there were more than two samples that need to be compared in the context of a single "factor" that differentiates them from each other? By holding the Type I error (significance level) at a constant level for all comparisons, one can perform statistical testing using a method called Analysis of Variance (ANOVA). If each sample is called a "group," then there are two major types of variations that occur when the means of each group are considered. The first is the variation between each group called "explained variation" and the second is the variation within the groups and is called "unexplained variation."

ANOVA allows a researcher to test for the existence of statistically significant differences among several group means, that are only different based on a single factor under consideration simultaneously, by using these two types of variations or variances. The assumptions underlying the ANOVA test are as follows:

1. The populations from which samples are taken are normal and have equal variances (σ^2).

2. Each sample is randomly and independently selected (there are no sampling biases)

3. The factor across which the groups are compared is a categorical variable

4. The observations in each group are numerical.

For instance, if one was interested in finding out if two treatments for controlling high blood pressure were effective or not, they could take samples that measure the blood pressure levels from people in first group receiving Treatment 1, from people in second group receiving Treatment 2, and from people in the third group who are not receiving any treatment at all for blood pressure. In order to test if the treatments are effective or not, the researcher can do an ANOVA to determine if the distribution of the high blood pressures in each group was the same or not.

Another thing to remember is that while ANOVA can be used for testing differences for how one factor (or categorical variable) behaviors vary from group to group, it can also be used for testing differences across multiple factors. The first one is called the One-Way or Single Factor ANOVA and the other one is called the Two-Way or Multiple Factor ANOVA. The requirements and assumptions for the interactions in the Two-Way ANOVA are beyond the scope of this book at this time, so the focus is on the One-way or single factor ANOVA methodology.

6.4.1. F-Distribution Basics

In order to test the null hypothesis that all the means of the populations represented by the samples are the same against the alternative hypothesis that at least two of the means are statistically different from each other, the F-distribution is employed. The F-distribution is named after Sir Ronald Fisher and is a representation of the ratio of explained versus unexplained variation, when considering multiple groups simultaneously.

$$F = \frac{Explained\ Variation}{Unexplained\ Variation}$$

Since the F-ratio considers variances, it is also used for other applications to compare the variances of two populations as a ratio of two independent Chi-square random variables with different degrees of freedom. This will be covered in more detail in Chapter 8 in Section 8.3. There are some basic characteristics of the F-distribution that need to be listed to ensure that one correctly employs the F-distribution for any testing, before delving into the steps of hypotheses testing through ANOVA. The general characteristics of the F-distribution are as follows:

1. The F-distribution consists of only non-negative values.

2. The F-distribution is not symmetrical

3. The *F*-distribution has two components in the degrees of freedom; first one based on the numerator, and a second one based on the denominator.

4. A different table is required for each combination of degrees of freedom and significance level.

5. The *F*-tables typically always give the right-tail value. For instance, Table C in Appendix shows select combinations of different numerator vs denominator degrees of freedom for significance level of $\alpha = 0.05$.

6.4.2. Steps of ANOVA

When doing Analysis of Variance, the goal is to identify whether the populations from which the samples are derived have the same normal distribution or not. Since it is already assumed that the population variances are the same, the test is primarily done on the means of the samples to estimate whether they all align or not. Thus, the null hypothesis (all means are the same) and the alternative hypothesis (at least two of the means are not the same) are always standardized and if *k* groups are considered for the ANOVA, they are defined as follows:

$$H_0: \mu_1 = \mu_2 = \mu_3 = \cdots = \mu_k$$
$$H_a: At\ least\ two\ means\ are\ not\ equal\ \mu_i \neq \mu_j\ for\ some\ i \neq j$$

Step 1. For $i = 1$ to k groups, with corresponding sample sizes of n_i, find the mean of each group ($\bar{X}_i$) and find the total mean of all observations across all groups ($\bar{X}_{TOTAL}$) using n_{TOTAL}

Step 2. Find 3 types of Variances
1. Total Variance: Total Sum of Squares SS$_{TOT}$

$$SS_{TOTAL} = \sum (X - \bar{X}_{TOTAL})^2$$

2. Explained variance: Between-group Sum of Squares SS$_{BETWEEN}$ for groups $i = 1$ to k

$$SS_{BETWEEN} = \sum n_i (\bar{X}_i - \bar{X}_{TOTAL})^2$$

3. Unexplained variance: Within-group Sum of Squares SS$_{WITHIN}$

$$SS_{WITHIN} = \sum (X_1 - \bar{X}_1)^2 + \sum (X_2 - \bar{X}_2)^2 + \cdots + \sum (X_k - \bar{X}_k)^2$$

Step 3. Find the Mean Squared (MS) Variances:
1. Between Mean Squared Variance with degrees of freedom = $(k - 1)$

$$MS_{BETWEEN} = \frac{SS_{BETWEEN}}{(k - 1)}$$

2. Within Mean Squared Variance with degrees of freedom = $(n_{TOTAL} - k)$

$$MS_{WITHIN} = \frac{SS_{WITHIN}}{(n_{TOTAL} - k)}$$

Step 4. Calculate the Test Statistic F_T as a ratio of the explained to unexplained variances:

$$F_T = \frac{MS_{BETWEEN}}{MS_{WITHIN}}$$

As one can see, the calculations for these various elements of the steps of hypotheses testing can become very tedious if one tries to do them by hand, especially if the sample sizes are large or if there are more than 3 samples to begin with. Thus, statistical software can be used to obtain the output for the ANOVA calculations. In Excel, the standard output table is as follows with the actual numbers instead of the explanations that are inserted in Figure 6.10:

Anova: Single Factor						
SUMMARY						
Groups	*Count*	*Sum*	*Average*	*Variance*		
X1	n1	Total of X1	Mean of X1	Variance of X1		
X2	n2	Total of X2	Mean of X2	Variance of X2		
X3	n3	Total of X3	Mean of X3	Variance of X3		
ANOVA						
Source of Variation	*SS*	*df*	*MS*	*F*	*P-value*	*F crit*
Between Groups	SSbetween	k - 1	SSbetween / (k - 1)	MSbetween/MSwithin	area below F	Critical F
Within Groups	SSwithin	n - k	SSwithin / (n - k)			
Total	SStotal	n - 1				

Figure 6.10. ANOVA output using Excel General Explanation

Example 6:8. ANOVA for 3 groups

A researcher is trying to identify the extent of weight reduction for three different types of weight loss diet programs (low calorie diet, low fat diet, and low carb diet) at a gym. The assumption is that since the members of the gym are all actively working out, the different populations of people following dietary weight loss regiments have the same variance. Perform a one-way ANOVA, given the following sample observations to test whether the extent of weight reduction differs by type of weight loss diets or not, using a 0.05 level of significance.

Low Cal	Low Fat	Low Carb
X1	X2	X3
7	7	7
7	8	9
5	8	7
4	9	8
6	5	8
3	8	14
9	7	10
10	10	11
5	11	5
2	2	6

Solution: One way to solve this problem is by using the Steps of Hypotheses Testing with manual calculation method and the other way is to solve it directly using the Excel in-built tool for One-Way ANOVA. Both methods are shown here.

$H_0: \mu_1 = \mu_2 = \mu_3$ or There is no difference in weight reduction by type of diet

H_a: *At least two means are not equal* or There is a difference in weight reduction by type of diet.

Step 1. For $i = 1$ to k groups, with corresponding sample sizes of n_i, find the mean of each group ($\bar{X}_i$) and find the total mean of all observations across all groups ($\bar{X}_{TOTAL}$) using n_{TOTAL}

Here, the $k = 3$ and the means of each group and total mean are as follows:

$$\bar{X}_1 = \frac{58}{10} = 5.8$$

$$\bar{X}_2 = \frac{75}{10} = 7.5$$

$$\bar{X}_3 = \frac{85}{10} = 8.5$$

$$\bar{X}_{TOTAL} = \frac{58 + 75 + 85}{30} = \frac{218}{30} = 7.267$$

Step 2. Find 3 types of Variances
1. Total Variance: Total Sum of Squares SS_TOT

$$SS_{TOTAL} = \sum (X - \bar{X}_{TOTAL})^2 = 215.867$$

2. Explained variance: Between-group Sum of Squares SS_BETWEEN for groups $i = 1$ to k

$$SS_{BETWEEN} = \sum n_i (\bar{X}_i - \bar{X}_{TOTAL})^2 = 37.267$$

3. Unexplained variance: Within-group Sum of Squares SS_WITHIN

$$SS_{WITHIN} = \sum (X_1 - \bar{X}_1)^2 + \sum (X_2 - \bar{X}_2)^2 + \cdots + \sum (X_k - \bar{X}_k)^2 = 178.6$$

The values of these are manually (using formulas) calculated as shown below:

	A	B	C	D	E	F	G	H	I	J	K	L	M	N
1	ANOVA: Testing the Means of 3 or more Groups Using F-test													
2		Ho: The means of all the groups are the same so there is no difference by type of treatment in output												
3		Ha: At least two of the groups have different means, so there is a difference by type of treatment in the output												
4		Low Cal	Low Fat	Low Carb			SS TOTAL				SS WITHIN			
5		X1	X2	X3		X1	X2	X3		X1	X2	X3		
6		7	7	7		0.071	0.071	0.071		1.44	0.25	2.25		
7		7	8	9		0.071	0.538	3.004		1.44	0.25	0.25		
8		5	8	7		5.138	0.538	0.071		0.64	0.25	2.25		
9		4	9	8		10.671	3.004	0.538		3.24	2.25	0.25		
10		6	5	8		1.604	5.138	0.538		0.04	6.25	0.25		
11		3	8	14		18.204	0.538	45.338		7.84	0.25	30.25		
12		9	7	10		3.004	0.071	7.471		10.24	0.25	2.25		
13		10	10	11		7.471	7.471	13.938		17.64	6.25	6.25		
14		5	11	5		5.138	13.938	5.138		0.64	12.25	12.25		
15		2	2	6		27.738	27.738	1.604		14.44	30.25	6.25		
16					TOTAL			SS TOTAL				SS WITHIN		
17	SIZE =	10	10	10	30			215.867	=SUM(F6:H15)			178.6	=SUM(J6:L15)	
18	SUM =	58	75	85	218									
19	MEAN =	5.8	7.5	8.5	7.267									
20	k =	3	=COUNT(B6:D6)					SS BETWEEN 37.267	=B17*(B19-E19)^2 + C17*(C19-E19)^2 +D17*(D19-E19)^2					
21	d.f. numerator =	2	=B20-1											

Step 3. Find the Mean Squared (MS) Variances:

1. Between Mean Squared Variance with degrees of freedom = $(k-1)$

$$MS_{BETWEEN} = \frac{SS_{BETWEEN}}{(k-1)} = \frac{37.267}{3-1} = 18.63$$

2. Within Mean Squared Variance with degrees of freedom = $(n_{TOTAL} - k)$

$$MS_{WITHIN} = \frac{SS_{WITHIN}}{(n_{TOTAL} - k)} = \frac{178.6}{30-3} = 6.615$$

Step 4. Calculate the Test Statistic F_T as a ratio of the explained to unexplained variances:

$$F_T = \frac{MS_{BETWEEN}}{MS_{WITHIN}} = \frac{18.63}{6.615} = 2.817$$

Step 5. Using the correct significance level of α, find the Critical Value of F_C with the numerator degrees of freedom = $(k-1)$ and denominator degrees of freedom = $(n_{TOTAL} - k)$ and identify the proper Rejection Region.

Here, the $\alpha = 0.05$, and the $d.f. = (3-1, 30-3) = (2, 27)$, using the F-table (Appendix Table C), one gets the $F_C = 3.354$ and the Rejection Region is marked in Blue in Figure 6.11.

	K	L	M	I
		Probability to the right		
D.f.2 ↓		1	2	
1		161.448	199.500	21
2		18.513	19.000	1
3		10.128	9.552	
25		4.242	3.385	
26		4.225	3.369	
27		4.210	3.354	
28		4.196	3.340	

Step 6. Compare the F_T with the F_C and decide whether to reject or fail to reject the null hypothesis in favor of the alternative hypothesis a significance level α. If $F_T < F_C$, fail to reject the null hypothesis, otherwise reject it.

Here the $F_T < F_C$ because 2.817 < 3.354, so fail to reject the H₀.

Step 7. Write the conclusion of the test in words based on the decision made in Step 6.

Thus, one can conclude that there is no difference in the weight reduction by type of diet at the 95% confidence level. Figure 6.11 shows the Excel formulas that can be used to help with the stepwise calculations if one chooses to pursue them manually.

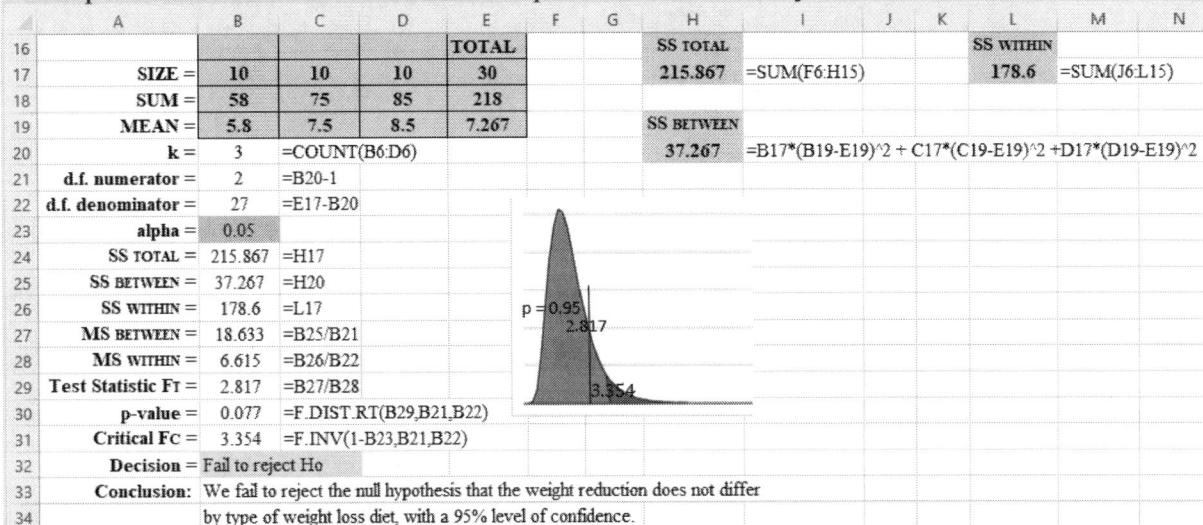

	A	B	C	D	E	F	G	H	I	J	K	L	M	N
16					TOTAL			SS TOTAL				SS WITHIN		
17	SIZE =	10	10	10	30			215.867	=SUM(F6:H15)			178.6	=SUM(J6:L15)	
18	SUM =	58	75	85	218									
19	MEAN =	5.8	7.5	8.5	7.267			SS BETWEEN						
20	k =	3	=COUNT(B6:D6)					37.267	=B17*(B19-E19)^2 + C17*(C19-E19)^2 +D17*(D19-E19)^2					
21	d.f. numerator =	2	=B20-1											
22	d.f. denominator =	27	=E17-B20											
23	alpha =	0.05												
24	SS TOTAL =	215.867	=H17											
25	SS BETWEEN =	37.267	=H20											
26	SS WITHIN =	178.6	=L17											
27	MS BETWEEN =	18.633	=B25/B21											
28	MS WITHIN =	6.615	=B26/B22											
29	Test Statistic F_T =	2.817	=B27/B28											
30	p-value =	0.077	=F.DIST.RT(B29,B21,B22)											
31	Critical F_C =	3.354	=F.INV(1-B23,B21,B22)											
32	Decision =	Fail to reject Ho												
33	Conclusion:	We fail to reject the null hypothesis that the weight reduction does not differ												
34		by type of weight loss diet, with a 95% level of confidence.												

Figure 6.11. ANOVA: Manual Calculations Using Excel Formulas

If one wanted to avoid calculating everything manually, there is a direct option in Excel under the Data Analysis → ANOVA: Single Factor option as shown below in Figure 6.12 on the top. At the bottom, is the Output that is provided by Excel.

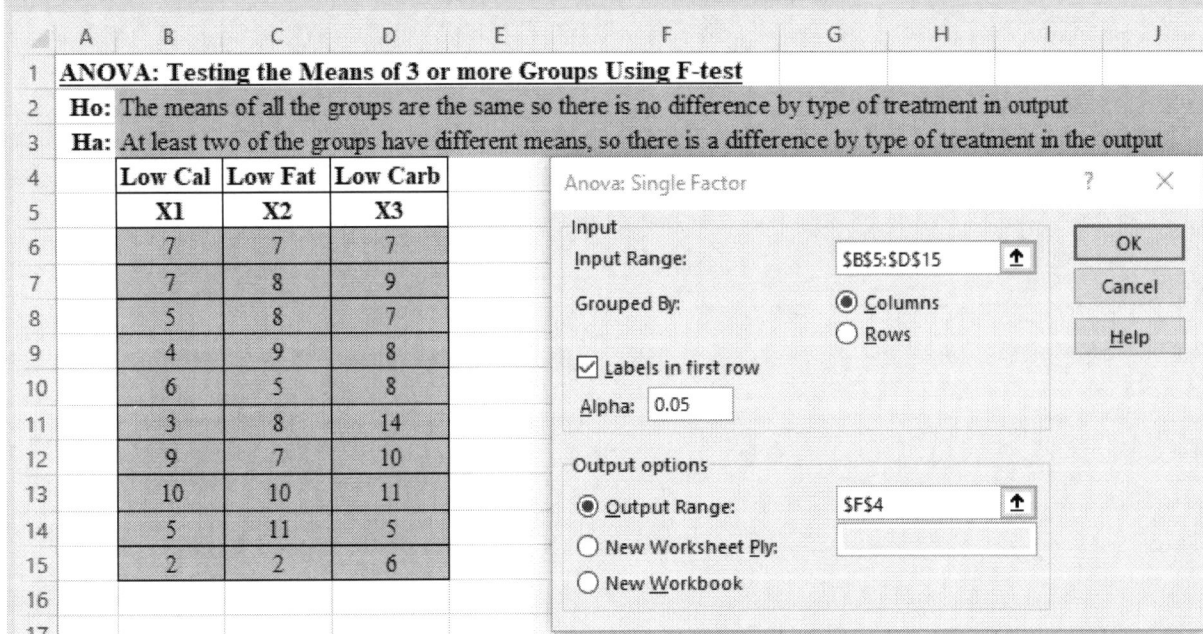

	A	B	C	D	E	F	G	H	I	J
1		ANOVA: Testing the Means of 3 or more Groups Using F-test								
2		Ho:	The means of all the groups are the same so there is no difference by type of treatment in output							
3		Ha:	At least two of the groups have different means, so there is a difference by type of treatment in the output							
4		Low Cal	Low Fat	Low Carb						
5		X1	X2	X3						
6		7	7	7						
7		7	8	9						
8		5	8	7						
9		4	9	8						
10		6	5	8						
11		3	8	14						
12		9	7	10						
13		10	10	11						
14		5	11	5						
15		2	2	6						
16										
17										

Anova: Single Factor

Input
Input Range: $B$5:$D$15
Grouped By: ● Columns ○ Rows
☑ Labels in first row
Alpha: 0.05

Output options
● Output Range: $F$4
○ New Worksheet Ply:
○ New Workbook

OK Cancel Help

ANOVA: Testing the Means of 3 or more Groups Using F-test

Ho: The means of all the groups are the same so there is no difference by type of treatment in output

Ha: At least two of the groups have different means, so there is a difference by type of treatment in the output

	Low Cal	Low Fat	Low Carb		Anova: Single Factor						
	X1	X2	X3								
	7	7	7		SUMMARY						
	7	8	9		*Groups*	*Count*	*Sum*	*Average*	*Variance*		
	5	8	7		X1	10	58	5.8	6.4		
	4	9	8		X2	10	75	7.5	6.5		
	6	5	8		X3	10	85	8.5	6.944444		
	3	8	14								
	9	7	10								
	10	10	11		ANOVA						
	5	11	5		*Source of Variation*	*SS*	*df*	*MS*	*F*	*P-value*	*F crit*
	2	2	6		Between Groups	37.26667	2	18.63333	2.816909	0.077427	3.354131
					Within Groups	178.6	27	6.614815			
					Total	215.8667	29				

This table will NOT automatically update: Have to manually run the Data Analysis to obtain this output.

Decision = Fail to reject Ho   =IF(J15<L15, "Fail to reject Ho", "Reject Ho")

Conclusion: We fail to reject the null hypothesis that the weight reduction does not differ by type of weight loss diet, with a 95% level of confidence.

Figure 6.12. Excel Inputs and Outputs for ANOVA: Single Factor

It is easy to obtain the output directly using Excel (or similar statistical software) instead of manually performing the calculations since variances can be cumbersome to calculate by hand or even by using basic formulas in Excel.

Chapter 7. Correlation and Regression Analyses

In the real world, there is a lot of interest in variables that appear to "move" together or have some sort of an obvious relationship with each other. The degree to which they are associated with each other is called "correlation." Sometimes, these variables are not actually "moving" together but are simply spuriously moving in the same direction. However, when two variables have a relationship, it is always better to test to identify if that relationship is causal or not; that is to say does one of the variables CAUSE the other variable to move in a certain direction? This type of causal analysis utilizes Regression methodology and requires one to identify which of the two variables is likely to be dependent on the other one. This chapter starts by discussing correlations and then presents the concept of regression analysis.

7.1. Correlation Coefficient

Scatter plots, as shown in Figure 7.1, can be used to identify if two variables are associated with each other or not, visually. Basics of Scatter Plots were discussed in Chapter 1 Section 1.3.3. In the figure on the left, as the value of the X-variable increases, there is a decrease in the *Y*-variable indicating a negative relationship whereas in the figure on the right, the values of both *X* and *Y* variables are increasing simultaneously.

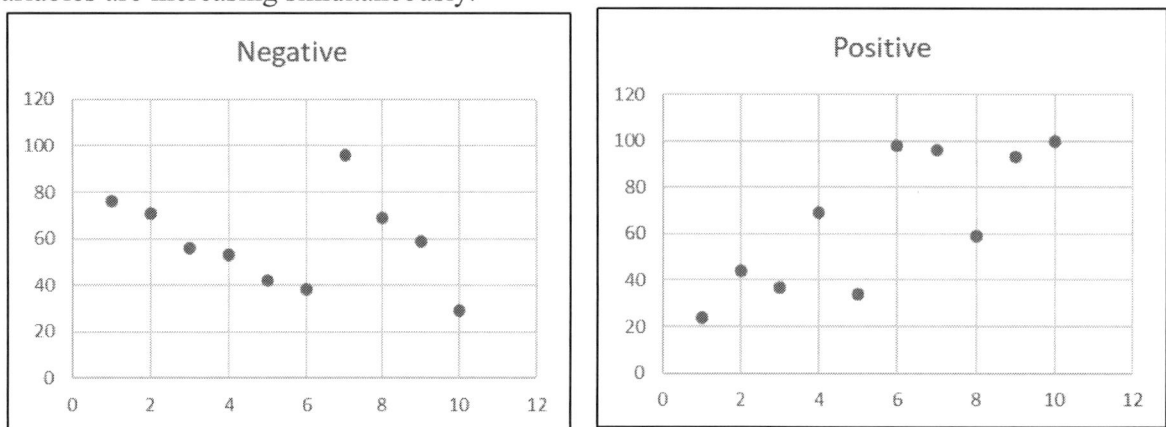

Figure 7.1. Negative and Positive Relationships

The relationship between the two variables of interest can be positive or it can be negative, but most importantly, it does not always have to be linear. However, the term "correlation," ALWAYS refers to a linear relationship using the population parameter ρ and it is estimated by using the formula for Pearson's Correlation Coefficient, r. Before discussing the formula for Pearson's r, it is important to list the requirements or assumptions under which the formula is considered to be valid. If these assumptions are violated, the reliability of the formula is suspect at best.

1. The Pearson's r only applies for testing the strength of linear relationships between two variables. If there are non-linear relationships, the Pearson's r value can be unreliable.

2. The data for both random variables, X and Y is interval data (not categorical or nominal) and the random variables are distributed normally and have the same number of observations.

3. Pearson's r can only be calculated between two variables at a time and can be tested using a t-test with $n - 2$ degrees of freedom for a sample size n

4. Pearson's r always takes the values between -1 and 1 and gives both the direction and the magnitude of the linear relationship between two variables such that:
   a. If $r = -1.0$, there is perfect negative correlation between X and Y
   b. If $-1.0 < r < -0.6$, there is a strong negative correlation between X and Y
   c. If $-0.6 < r < -0.3$, there is a moderate negative correlation between X and Y
   d. If $-0.3 < r \leq 0.3$, there is no correlation between X and Y
   e. If $0.3 < r < 0.6$, there is a moderate positive correlation between X and Y
   f. If $0.6 < r < 1.0$, there is a strong positive correlation between X and Y
   g. If $r = 1.0$, there is a perfect positive correlation between X and Y

The formula for Pearson's Correlation Coefficient (r) for Random Variables X and Y is:

$$r = \frac{SP}{\sqrt{SS_X SS_Y}} = \frac{\sum(X - \bar{X})(Y - \bar{Y})}{\sqrt{\sum(X - \bar{X})^2 \cdot \sum(Y - \bar{Y})^2}}$$

The steps of hypotheses testing can be followed in order to test for significance of the correlation r, where the null hypothesis is that there is no correlation ($r = 0$) between two variables and the alternative hypothesis is that there is a linear correlation between two variables ($r \neq 0$), the t-distribution is used with the degrees of freedom ($d.f. = n - 2$) and the test statistic is given by

$$t_T = \frac{r\sqrt{n - 2}}{\sqrt{1 - r^2}}$$

The steps for hypotheses testing are similar to the ones used for the t-test in Chapter 6:

Step 1. Clearly identify and state the Null Hypothesis (H_0) and Alternative Hypothesis (H_a)
Step 2. Specify the level of significance α (also called the acceptable risk of making a Type I error). If the H_0 is of the "not equal to" type, use $\alpha/2$ for two-tailed test
Step 3. Select and calculate the appropriate value of the Test Statistic using the following formula:

$$t_T = \frac{r\sqrt{n - 2}}{\sqrt{1 - r^2}}$$

Step 4. Determine the Critical Value (*CV*) of the t-distribution based on the level of α (or $\alpha/2$, as appropriate) and Degrees of freedom $n-2$. Clearly demarcate the Rejection Region (*RR*)

Step 5. Compare the Test Statistic to the Critical Value to identify whether the null hypothesis is rejected or not at the level of significance α. If the Test Statistic falls in the Rejection Region, reject the null hypothesis, otherwise fail to reject the null.

Step 6. Write a clear conclusion based on the determination made in Step 5.

Example 7:1. Finding and Testing Correlation Coefficient

A researcher is interested in finding out if the number of hours of electronic usage per day is correlated with the weight of a teenager and gathers information from 7 teenagers as given below. Calculate the correlation coefficient and test if the researcher's assumption is valid or not at a 0.10 level of significance.

Number of hours Electronics used	1.5	5	3.5	2.5	4	1.5	1
Weight in lbs	79	105	96	83	99	78	68

Solution: Follow the steps of hypothesis testing to solve this problem. But before doing that, calculate the correlation coefficient for X and Y in this case. Denote X = number of hours electronics used per day and Y = Weight in lbs. The formula for calculation of r is

$$r = \frac{SP}{\sqrt{SS_X SS_Y}} = \frac{\Sigma(X-\bar{X})(Y-\bar{Y})}{\sqrt{\Sigma(X-\bar{X})^2 \cdot \Sigma(Y-\bar{Y})^2}}$$

So, one must calculate the *SP*, SS_X, and SS_Y values.

	X	Y	(X-Xbar)	(Y-Ybar)	(X-Xbar)(Y-Ybar)	(X-Xbar)^2	(Y-Ybar)^2
	1.5	79	-1.21	-7.86	9.54	1.474	61.735
	5	105	2.29	18.14	41.47	5.224	329.163
	3.5	96	0.79	9.14	7.18	0.617	83.592
	2.5	83	-0.21	-3.86	0.83	0.046	14.878
	4	99	1.29	12.14	15.61	1.653	147.449
	1.5	78	-1.21	-8.86	10.76	1.474	78.449
	1	68	-1.71	-18.86	32.33	2.939	355.592
TOTAL =	19	608			117.71	13.43	1070.86
AVERAGE =	2.71	86.86			SP	SSx	Ssy

$$r = \frac{SP}{\sqrt{SS_X SS_Y}} = \frac{117.71}{\sqrt{13.43 \times 1070.86}} = 0.9815$$

Step 1. Clearly identify and state the Null Hypothesis (*Ho*) and Alternative Hypothesis (*Ha*)

    Ho: There is no correlation between X and Y

    Ha: There is a correlation between X and Y

Step 2. Specify the level of significance α (also called the acceptable risk of making a Type I error).

    Here the $\alpha = 0.10$, and a two-tailed test is being performed, so $\alpha/2 = 0.05$

Step 3. Select and calculate the appropriate value of the Test Statistic using the following formula:

$$t_T = \frac{r\sqrt{n-2}}{\sqrt{1-r^2}} = \frac{(0.98)\sqrt{7-2}}{\sqrt{1-(0.98)^2}} = \frac{2.19}{0.199} = 11.00$$

Step 4. Determine the Critical Value (*CV*) of the *t*-distribution based on the level of α/2 and Degrees of freedom *n* – 2. Clearly demarcate the Rejection Region (*RR*)

For Critical Value, look at *t*-tables (Table B in Appendix) for 0.05 and (*n* – 2 = 7 – 2 =) 5 degrees of freedom to obtain t_C = 2.015

	t-values corresponding to α and n						
cumu. Prob.	t (0.50)	t(0.75)	t(0.80)	t(0.85)	t(0.90)	t(0.95)	t(0.975)
α (or α/2)	0.50	0.25	0.20	0.15	0.10	0.05	0.025
df							
1	0.000	1.000	1.376	1.963	3.078	6.314	12.706
2	0.000	0.816	1.061	1.386	1.886	2.920	4.303
3	0.000	0.765	0.978	1.250	1.638	2.353	3.182
4	0.000	0.741	0.941	1.190	1.533	2.132	2.776
5	0.000	0.727	0.920	1.156	1.476	2.015	2.571
6	0.000	0.718	0.906	1.134	1.440	1.943	2.447

	A	B	C	D	E	F	G	H
1	**Correlation Coefficient and Hypothesis Testing**							
2								
3		**X**	**Y**	**(X-Xbar)**	**(Y-Ybar)**	**(X-Xbar)(Y-Ybar)**	**(X-Xbar)^2**	**(Y-Ybar)^2**
4		1.5	79	-1.21	-7.86	9.54	1.474	61.735
5		5	105	2.29	18.14	41.47	5.224	329.163
6		3.5	96	0.79	9.14	7.18	0.617	83.592
7		2.5	83	-0.21	-3.86	0.83	0.046	14.878
8		4	99	1.29	12.14	15.61	1.653	147.449
9		1.5	78	-1.21	-8.86	10.76	1.474	78.449
10		1	68	-1.71	-18.86	32.33	2.939	355.592
11	**TOTAL =**	19	608			117.71	13.43	1070.86
12	**AVERAGE =**	2.71	86.86			SP	SSx	Ssy
13								
14	**Corr. Coeff. r =**	0.9816	=PEARSON(B4:B10,C4:C10)					
15	**Hypothesis Testing**							
16	**Ho:** There is no correlation between X and Y							
17	**Ha:** There is a correlation between X and Y							
18	**Alpha =**	0.1						
19	**Number of Tails =**	2						
20	**Sample Size =**	7						
21	**Test Statistic**							
22	**tT =**	11.50	=B14*SQRT(B20-2)/SQRT(1 - B14^2)					
23	**Critical Value**							
24	**tc =**	2.015	=IF(B19=2, T.INV(1-B18/2, B20-2), T.INV(1-B18,B20-2))					
25	**Decision:**	Reject Ho	=IF(ABS(B24) < ABS(B22), "Reject Ho", "Fail to Reject Ho")					
26	**Conclusion:**	The correlation between X and Y is statistically and numerically significant at 90% confidence						

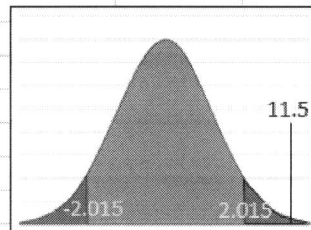

Figure 7.2. Correlation Coefficient and Hypothesis Testing for Example 7.1

Step 5. Compare the Test Statistic to the Critical Value to identify whether the null hypothesis is rejected or not at the level of significance α. If the Test Statistic falls in the Rejection Region, reject the null hypothesis, otherwise fail to reject the null.

As one can see in Figure 7.2, in the graph, the critical value lies in the blue Rejection Region, so one can reject the null hypothesis at 0.10 level of significance. Moreover, this can be confirmed by observing that $11.00 > 2.015$.

Step 6. Write a clear conclusion based on the determination made in Step 5.

Thus, one can conclude with a 90% confidence level that the correlation between X and Y is statistically significant. Given that the correlation value itself is very high (0.98), one can say that the correlation is also very strong.

Figure 7.2 shows the direct Excel formula to calculate the value of r (without needing the extra columns etc.) as well.

7.2. Regression Analysis

Assume that a professor wants to conduct a study to measure the effects of solving problems at home every week on the performance of a student in her statistics class. She collected data at random for 10 students on the number of hours spent in a week doing problem sets at home (X) and their scores in the class at the end of the semester (Y). The scores that the students had were 24, 44, 37, 69, 34, 98, 96, 59, 93, and 100. The immediate questions that would arise are as follows:

1. Why is there fluctuation in the scores for people in the class?

2. Why do some people perform better than the others?

3. Can some common characteristics of the people be identified based on the scores to explain at least some of the variation in the scores of students in the class?

4. A quick look at the data will show that the average score is 65.4 and the variance of the sample of scores (Y) is 886.3, and it has a standard deviation of 29.8. How much of this variability can be explained with the help of some external factor?

5. Is it possible that some variable such as the "number of hours studied per week" affects the scores?

One can use regression analysis to answer such questions. In fact, the goal of research in general is to explain why certain variables vary in a certain way! Regression analysis gives one the ability to quantifiably measure the relative importance of any variable. For the sake of simplicity, this section starts with what is called a *bivariate linear regression model*. In this type of model, there is one determining factor X, say the number of hours of study per week. Knowing the value of X for a student helps to explain the variation in Y across students. Thus, X is called the explanatory (or exogenous or predictor) variable and Y is referred to as the explained (or endogenous or predicted) variable. Consider the following data that the instructor collected to perform her test of the relationship between X and Y.

Table 7.1. Data for Bivariate Regression Analysis Illustration

Obs.	X = number of hours per week	Y = score on the final exam
1	1	24
2	2	44
3	3	37
4	4	69
5	5	34
6	6	98
7	7	96
8	8	59
9	9	93
10	10	100

7.2.1. Requirements for Bivariate Regression

1. Both (in bivariate analysis) variables are measured at interval level
2. Regression assumes a linear relationship between the variables X and Y. Various transformations of either Y or of X can be used if scatter plot shows a non-linear trend.
3. Sample members are chosen randomly to test significance of the model
4. To test significance, one assumes normality for both X and Y or else one would need to have a large sample.
5. The Regression Line always passes through the point $(\bar{X}, \bar{Y})$

7.2.2. Regression Model

Like correlation, a bivariate regression studies the strength of association between 2 variables. For instance, the final score and the number of hours of study per week. Here the score is the variable of interest and is called the dependent variable (Y) and the number of hours studying per week is the independent variable (X). A mathematical equation used to predict the value of dependent variable Y on the basis of independent variable X is written as:

$$Y = a + bX + e$$

In real words, this equation states the following: The final grade (Y) performance is a combination of the baseline grade (a), the total score contribution as a result of hours studied (bX) and some external error (e) that cannot be explained by either (a) or (bX).

- a = The baseline grade earned by all students even when $X = 0$ (no study hours). It is also called the vertical intercept, or Y-intercept because the line "cuts" the vertical axis at that point.

- b = The additional scored points for each hour of study per week. This term is also called the Regression Coefficient and represents the amount of change one expects in the Y for each increase of 1 unit of X. Thus, the difference in the final score between a student who studied 0 hours and a student who studied for 1 hour a week is expected to be b.

- e = The residual value (e), also known as the <u>Error Term</u> or Disturbance term or just <u>Residual</u> and is unpredictable and unique for each individual. This term the amount of final score that cannot be accounted for by a and bX. Thus, e represents the departure of a given student's grade form that which would be expected on the basis of the number of hours studied per week (X).

If the values of Y (scores) were plotted against the number of hours studied per week (X) from Table 7.1, the scatter plot would resemble the blue dots seen in Figure 7.3. Notice that there is an orange line that has been drawn through this scatter plot. This line is called the "Line of Fit" or the Regression Line, which is a representation of the linear estimate that one can make based on the available data in order to provide some prediction value for the equation.

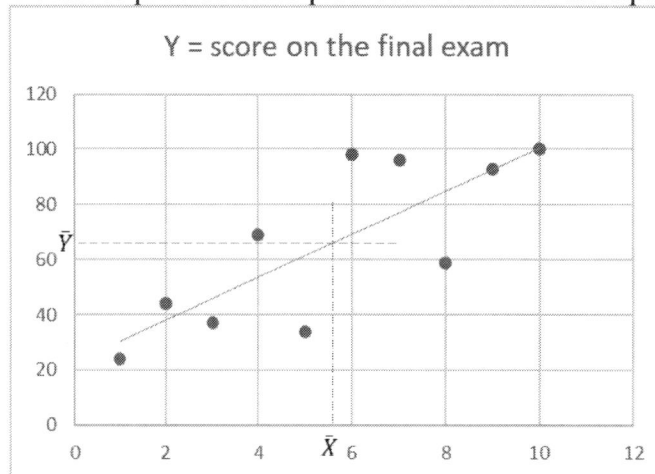

Figure 7.3. Scatter Plot of Score on the Final Exam

There appears to be a positive association between X and Y based on the graph. Regression involves placing or fitting a line through the scattered points. If one can estimate the parameters a and b, then the predicted value of Y, indicated as $\hat{Y}$ can be obtained, which can be written as:
$$\hat{Y} = a + bX$$

An important thing to note is that if one picks a specific value of X, say 5 hours of study per week, the corresponding observed Y-value or the final score of that individual is 34, but the corresponding point on the regression line which shows the expected or predicted score $\hat{Y}$ is 61.5 (See Figure 7.4). Thus, the estimated score is higher than the actual score by 27.5 points. This value of 27.5 is called the "error" (e) since that is the amount by which the prediction is "off" and in this case, it is an overprediction or a negative error since $e = Y - \hat{Y}$. Similarly, if one considers the X values from 1 to 10, there are corresponding values of e that can be obtained. Some of these errors are positive (underprediction) and some are negative (overprediction) such that the total of all errors is likely to be close to 0.

In Chapter 2, Section 2.2.3, there is a discussion on why deviations need to be squared in order to analyze the "spread" of a random variable. In this case, the error term e is the random variable and therefore, the Sum of Squared Errors (*SSE*), also called Sum of Squared Residuals (in software like Excel or STATA) needs to be minimized. Thus, the goal of regression analysis is to minimize the differences (or errors) between Y and $\hat{Y}$ by estimating the values of a (intercept) and b (slope) such that the Sum of Squared Errors (*SSE*) is minimized. This process of obtaining estimators for the slope (b) and the intercept (a) is called Ordinary Least Squares (OLS) method. Note that the regression line ALWAYS passes through the point $(\bar{X}, \bar{Y})$. The following steps are used for finding the regression line (or estimating the OLS regression model):

Step 1. The mean values of X and Y are calculated using the formulas:

$$\bar{X} = \frac{\sum X}{n}; \ \bar{Y} = \frac{\sum Y}{n}$$

From the illustration dataset (See Table 7.1), $\bar{X} = 5.5$; $\bar{Y} = 65.4$.

Step 2. Based on the obtained values of $\bar{X}$ and $\bar{Y}$, one can calculate different types of deviations given by the following formulas:

$$Sum \ of \ Product \ of \ deviations: SP = \sum(X - \bar{X})(Y - \bar{Y})$$
$$Sum \ of \ Squared \ X \ deviations: SS_X = \Sigma(X - \bar{X})^2$$
$$Sum \ of \ Squared \ Y \ deviations: SS_Y = \Sigma(Y - \bar{Y})^2$$

From the illustration dataset, as shown in Table 7.1, the corresponding SP, SS_X, and SS_Y values are:

$$SP = \sum(X - \bar{X})(Y - \bar{Y}) = 641$$
$$SS_X = \Sigma(X - \bar{X})^2 = 82.5$$
$$SS_Y = \Sigma(Y - \bar{Y})^2 = 7976.4$$

Step 3. The strength of the correlation coefficient between X and Y is essential to check before proceeding towards calculating slope and intercept. If there is no correlation between X and Y, establishing causation for a linear relationship might be futile. Remember that while correlation does NOT imply causation, for a causation to exist, an underlying correlation is essential (for linear relationships).

The Pearson's Correlation r calculated as follows, is greater than 0.6, demonstrating a strong correlation between X and Y in this sample:

$$r = \frac{SP}{\sqrt{SS_X \cdot SS_Y}} = \frac{641}{\sqrt{82.5 * 7976.4}} = 0.79$$

Step 4. The proportion of variation in Y that is determined or explained by X is represented by the <u>Coefficient of Determination</u>, R^2 or r^2. For the illustration, $R^2 = 0.79^2 = 0.6244$. Thus, 62.44% of fluctuations in the final score of students in this statistics class can be explained by the hours of study per week. <u>Coefficient of Non-determination</u> is the proportion of variation in Y that is not determined or explained by X and is defined as the value $(1 - R^2)$. Thus, in the example, 37.56% of the variation in the final scores is not explained by the number of hours that students studied per week. In multivariate analysis, since the correlation coefficient is not directly available due to large number of variables simultaneously being considered, the R^2 is calculated by using the following formula, which uses Sum of Squares (discussed later in this chapter):

$$R^2 = \frac{SS_{TOT} - SS_{RES}}{SS_{TOT}} = \frac{SS_{REG}}{SS_{TOT}}$$

Step 5. Using these deviations, one can calculate the slope b using the following equation:

$$b = \frac{SP}{SS_X} = \frac{\sum(X - \bar{X})(Y - \bar{Y})}{\sum(X - \bar{X})^2} = \frac{641}{82.5} = 7.77$$

Step 6. Once the slope is calculated, the vertical intercept a is calculated as follows:
$$a = \bar{Y} - b\bar{X} = 65.4 - (7.77)(5.5) = 22.67$$

Step 7. Once the slope and intercept are calculated, the equation for the Least Squares line becomes:
$$\hat{Y} = a + bX = 22.67 + 7.77X$$

The predicted values $\hat{Y}$ based on this equation can now be calculated for each value of X and these can be plotted on a graph as shown in Figure 7.4. The values are given in Table 7.3 in the next section of this chapter.

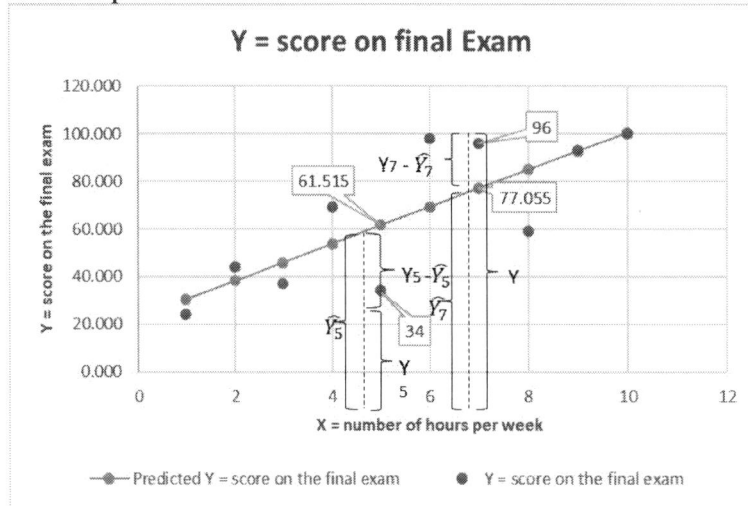

Figure 7.4. Trendline or Least Squares Regression Line

Table 7.2 shows the mechanical calculations for mean, variance, standard deviation, slope, intercept, r, R^2 using the basic Excel functions in the top half compared with the direct Excel functions that allow one to calculate all of these without creating additional columns or performing any manual calculations.

Table 7.2. Finding Slope and Intercept for Illustration Data in Regression Analysis

	A	B	C	D	E	F	G	H
1	Obs.	X = number of hours per week	Y = score on the final exam	X-Xbar	Y-Ybar	(X-Xbar)(Y-Ybar)	(X-Xbar)²	(Y-Ybar)²
2	1	1	24	-4.5	-41.4	186.3	20.25	1713.96
3	2	2	44	-3.5	-21.4	74.9	12.25	457.96
4	3	3	37	-2.5	-28.4	71	6.25	806.56
5	4	4	69	-1.5	3.6	-5.4	2.25	12.96
6	5	5	34	-0.5	-31.4	15.7	0.25	985.96
7	6	6	98	0.5	32.6	16.3	0.25	1062.76
8	7	7	96	1.5	30.6	45.9	2.25	936.36
9	8	8	59	2.5	-6.4	-16	6.25	40.96
10	9	9	93	3.5	27.6	96.6	12.25	761.76
11	10	10	100	4.5	34.6	155.7	20.25	1197.16
12	SUM	55	654			641	82.5	7976.4
13	AVERAGE	5.5	65.4			(SP)	(SSx)	(SSy)
14	Variance	9.2	886.3					
15	Std. Dev	3.0	29.8					
16								
17	slope b =	7.77	=F12/G12					
18	intercept a =	22.67	=C13-B17*B13					
19	Corr. Coeff. r =	0.79	=F12/SQRT(G12*H12)					
20	R-squared =	0.6244	=B19^2					
21								
22	1 - R-squared =	0.3756	=1-B20					

	A	B	C	
1	Obs.	X = number of hours per week	Y = score on the final exam	
2	1	1	24	
3	2	2	44	
4	3	3	37	
5	4	4	69	
6	5	5	34	
7	6	6	98	
8	7	7	96	
9	8	8	59	
10	9	9	93	
11	10	10	100	
12	SUM	55	654	
13	MEAN	5.5	65.4	
14	Variance	9.2	886.3	
15	Std. Dev	3.0	29.8	
16				
17	slope b =	7.77	=SLOPE(C2:C11,B2:B11)	
18	intercept a =	22.67	=INTERCEPT(C2:C11,B2:B11)	
19	Corr. Coeff. r =	0.79	=PEARSON(B2:B11,C2:C11)	
20	R-squared =	0.6244	=RSQ(C2:C11,B2:B11)	
21	1 - R-squared =	0.3756	=1-B20	

7.2.3. Interpretation of the Regression Line:

Interpretations of the components of the regression line can help in making predictions about the future or about the general population of students.

$$\hat{Y} = 22.67 + 7.77X$$

Y-intercept = 22.67: Even without studying a single hour per week, a student can be expected to get a 22.67 grade in class, on an average. Sometimes, the vertical or Y-intercept may not be really meaningful, and yet it is standard practice to include the intercept, it does serve the purpose of a baseline. For instance, theoretically, for a student attending class regularly, studying extra at home may not be the only criteria for doing well in class and a low grade of 22.67 could appear to be unreasonable and one could look at its significance (see Section 7.3) to determine how dependable this intercept is.

Regression Coefficient or slope = 7.77: For each additional hour studied per week, the expected final exam score increases by 7.77 points, on an average.

This equation can be used to make predictions as well. Assume that a student studies 11 hours per week. Thus, the expected grade of the student would be:

$$\hat{Y} = 22.67 + 7.77X = 22.67 + 7.77 * 11 = 108.14$$

This point (11, 108.14) can also be plotted on the regression line in the graph. However, one needs to be careful with the predictions using extremely high or unreasonable values of X. For instance, if one wanted to predict the score for an individual studying for 100 hours per week, the predicted score would be:

$$\hat{Y} = 22.67 + 7.77X = 22.67 + 7.77 * 100 = 799.67$$

Since the final score for the class is out of 100, 799.67 is a highly unrealistic score for the individual. Moreover, believing that a student studies over 100 hours per week of the semester is also unrealistic! This is merely the solution of the analytical problem. One must learn more about the random variable in this instance to be able to understand the story of what is happening here.

7.3. Post-Estimation for Regression Analysis

The goal of regression analysis is to estimate a Population Regression Model given by $Y = a + bX + e$ using available sample information to predict a Regression Line, given by $\hat{Y} = a + bX$ to fit a linear relationship which minimizes the error e, and allows one to make predictions for the outcomes of Y using values of X.

$$Y = a + bX + e$$
$$\hat{Y} = a + bX$$
$$\therefore Y = \hat{Y} + e$$
$$\therefore e = Y - \hat{Y}$$

The characteristics of e are as follows:
1. $\sum e = 0$ is the expected value of the sum of all errors
2. It is assumed that e is normally distributed with a standard deviation σ_e that is constant.
3. Each value of e is independent of any other value of e.

4. The only random variable in this model is the error term $e \sim N(0, \sigma_e)$.

Step 8. The goal of estimating the $\hat{Y}$ is to minimize the spread or variation in the errors by minimizing the Sum of the Squared Errors (SSE) or Sum of Squared Residuals (SS_{RES}):

$$SS_{RES} = \sum e^2 = \sum (Y - \hat{Y})^2$$

Two other important measurements of regression estimates are the Sum of Squares of Regression (SS_{REG}) defined as the sum of the squared differences between $\hat{Y}$ and the mean of Y and the Total Sum of Squares (SS_{TOT}) defined as the sum of the squared differences between Y and the mean of Y. Note that SS_{TOT} is the same as the Sum of Squared Deviations of Y (SS_Y) and the SS_{RES} is the same as the term SSE. The relationship between SS_{RES}, SS_{REG} and SS_{TOT} is given by:

$$SS_{TOT} = SS_{RES} + SS_{REG}$$
$$\sum (Y - \bar{Y})^2 = \sum (Y - \hat{Y})^2 + \sum (\hat{Y} - \bar{Y})^2$$

7.3.1. Mean Square Error and Standard Error of the Regression

Step 9. The Mean Squared Error (*MSE*) and Regression Standard Error (*SE*) calculations are required to identify if the actual model that is being estimated is statistically significant or not, similar to how standard deviations and standard errors were used to check for significance of variables and to test various hypotheses in Chapters 5 and 6.

Table 7.3. Estimates for SSres, SSreg and SStot for Regression Analysis

Obs.	X = number of hours per week	Y = score on the final exam	X^2	X.Y	Yhat = 22.67 + 7.77X	e	e^2	$(\text{Yhat - Ybar})^2$	$(\text{Y - Ybar})^2$
1	1	24	1	24	30.44	-6.44	41.43	1222.46	1713.96
2	2	44	4	88	38.21	5.79	33.57	739.51	457.96
3	3	37	9	111	45.98	-8.98	80.56	377.30	806.56
4	4	69	16	276	53.75	15.25	232.70	135.83	12.96
5	5	34	25	170	61.52	-27.52	757.08	15.09	985.96
6	6	98	36	588	69.28	28.72	824.56	15.09	1062.76
7	7	96	49	672	77.05	18.95	358.93	135.83	936.36
8	8	59	64	472	84.82	-25.82	666.89	377.30	40.96
9	9	93	81	837	92.59	0.41	0.16	739.51	761.76
10	10	100	100	1000	100.36	-0.36	0.13	1222.46	1197.16
SUM	55	654	385	4238	654	0.00	2996.02	4980.38	7976.40
							SSres	SSreg	SStot

n =	10	=COUNT(J2:J11)
k =	2	=COUNT(K2:L2)
MSE =	374.50	=Q12/(J16-J17)
s = SE =	19.35	=SQRT(J18)
F-test statistic =	13.299	=R12/J18
Alpha =	0.05	
F-critical value =	5.3177	=F.INV(1-J21,J17-1,J16-J17)
Standard Errors for Components		
Std. Error of a, sa =	13.22	=J19*SQRT(1/J16 + B13^2/G12)
Std. Error of b, sb =	2.13	=J19*SQRT(1/G12)

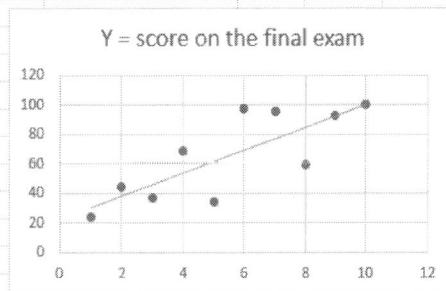

Y = score on the final exam

If k represents the total number of variables in a given regression, and the Sum of Squared Residuals (or Errors) is represented by SS_{RES} for a sample of size n, the MSE and the SE of the regression are defined as follows:

$$Mean\ Squared\ Error\ (MSE)\!:\ s^2 = \frac{SS_{RES}}{n-k}$$

$$Reg.\ Standard\ Error\ (SE)\!:\ s = \sqrt{MSE} = \sqrt{\frac{SS_{RES}}{n-k}}$$

The MSE and the SE for the grades and study hours example can be calculated based on Table 7.3. Based on the table, the $SS_{RES} = 2996.02$, $SS_{REG} = 4980.38$, and $SS_{TOTAL} = 7976.40$. Please note that if one rounded off the intercept and the slope during the calculations, the $SS_{RES} + SS_{REG}$ would only approximately be equal to the SS_{TOTAL} instead of being perfectly equal. There is a direct method in Excel to do the entire regression analysis simply based on the given values for X and Y, which will be covered towards the end of this section 7.3 in Table 7.4.

$$MSE\!:\ s^2 = \frac{SS_{RES}}{n-k} = \frac{2996.02}{10-2} = 374.5$$
$$Reg.\ Standard\ Error\!:\ s = \sqrt{MSE} = 19.35$$

7.3.2. Testing significance of components in the Regression Analysis:

The statistical significance of the correlation coefficient can be tested using the same method that was covered in Section 7.1 of this chapter using $(n-k)$ degrees of freedom, but typically this test is either done prior to estimating the regression or oftentimes, skipped in favor of statistical tests of the components and the model estimated.

$$H_0\!:\ r = 0$$
$$H_a\!:\ r \neq 0$$
$$t_T = \frac{r\sqrt{n-k}}{\sqrt{1-r^2}}$$

Step 10. The intercept a and the slope b estimated for the regression line can be tested for statistical significance by using the regression standard error s, after adjusting for the Sum of Squared deviations SS_X for the sample size n to get respective standard errors, s_a and s_b.

$$Std.\ Error\ of\ a\!:\ s_a = s\sqrt{\frac{1}{n} + \frac{\bar{X}^2}{SS_X}}$$

$$Std.\ Error\ of\ b\!:\ s_b = s\sqrt{\frac{1}{SS_X}}$$

For intercept a, the Null hypothesis, the Alternate Hypothesis, the Test Statistic, and the $(1-\alpha)\%$ Confidence Interval with degrees of freedom of $(n-k)$ are:

$$H_0\!:\ a = 0$$
$$H_a\!:\ a \neq 0;$$
$$t_T = \frac{a}{s_a}$$
$$100(1-\alpha)\%\ CI = a \pm t_{\alpha/2}s_a$$

For slope b, the Null hypothesis, the Alternate Hypothesis, the Test Statistic, and the $(1 - \alpha)\%$ Confidence Interval with degrees of freedom of $(n - k)$ are:

$$H_0: b = 0$$
$$H_a: b \neq 0$$
$$t_T = \frac{b}{s_b}$$
$$100(1 - \alpha)\% \ CI = b \pm t_{\alpha/2} s_b$$

Using the example for the grades and number of hours studied, the following Tests are performed for intercept a and slope b:
For intercept a:

$$s_a = s\sqrt{\frac{1}{n} + \frac{\bar{X}^2}{SS_X}} = 19.35 \times \sqrt{\frac{1}{10} + \frac{5.5^2}{82.5}} = 13.22$$

$$H_0: a = 0$$
$$H_a: a \neq 0$$
$$t_T = \frac{a}{s_a} = \frac{22.67}{13.22} = 1.72$$

For an $\alpha = 0.05$, and df = 8, the Critical t-value for two-tailed distribution $t_C = t_{0.025} = 2.306$. Since t_T is not in the rejection region ($t_T < t_C$), one will fail to reject $H_0: a = 0$ at a 95% confidence level. The confidence interval for a is calculated as follows:

$$100(1 - \alpha)\% \ CI = a \pm t_{\alpha/2} s_a = 22.67 \pm 2.306 * 13.22 = 22.67 \pm 30.49 = [-7.82, 53.16]$$

Thus, with 95% confidence level one can say that the true value of the intercept in the population is between -7.82 and 53.16. As is indicated by the significance test, this range is exceedingly broad and does not give any meaningful information.

For slope b:

$$s_b = s\sqrt{\frac{1}{SS_X}} = 19.35 \times \sqrt{\frac{1}{82.5}} = 2.13$$

$$H_0: b = 0$$
$$H_a: b \neq 0$$
$$t_T = \frac{b}{s_b} = \frac{7.77}{2.13} = 3.65$$

For an $\alpha = 0.05$, and df = 8, the Critical t-value for two-tailed distribution $t_C = t_{0.025} = 2.306$. Since t_T is in the rejection region ($t_T > t_C$), one can reject $H_0: b = 0$ at a 95% confidence level, implying that X (hours of study per week) is a significant determinant of Y (final grade in statistics). The confidence interval for b is calculated as follows:

$$100(1 - \alpha)\% \ CI = b \pm t_{\alpha/2} s_b = 7.77 \pm 2.306 * 2.13 = 7.77 \pm 4.91 = [2.86, 12.68]$$

Thus, one can say with 95% confidence that the true value of the slope is between 2.86 and 12.68. In real terms, this means that if a student studies for an additional hour per week, they can expect to increase their score on the final between 2.86 to 12.68 points!

One of my favorite instructors in statistics at the University of Texas at Dallas, Dr. Wim Vijverberg used to say in his class, *Techniques of Economic Research*, that "While we are convinced in our theoretical heart that b is non-zero, the rest of the world is skeptical and wants to hold on to the idea that b is zero. Therefore, we try to collect proof that at a 95 percent or 99 percent significance level, that the Null hypothesis of $b = 0$ should be rejected. If we do not find this evidence right away, we merely fail to reject the Null hypothesis until further notice, i.e. until we do find evidence that b is non-zero."

7.3.3. Significance of the Whole Model: F-test

Step 11. Based on the values of the *MSE* and the regression *SE*, it is possible to test whether the entire model that estimates the relationship between dependent and independent variables using the sample data is a good representation or estimate of the relationship between these variables in the population or not. This is not so crucial for models which are bivariate because the slope of the single independent variable (*X*) is all that requires to be tested. However, in multivariate analysis, a F-test is used to establish the validity off the model being estimated; that is to confirm whether the presumed relationships between various independent variables (*X*s) and the dependent variable *Y*, valid statistically or not. The following steps of Hypotheses Testing are followed:

Step 11.1. Clearly identify and state the Null Hypothesis (H_0) and Alternative Hypothesis (H_a)
      H_0: All the slopes in the regression are 0
      H_a: At least one of the slopes is not equal to 0
Step 11.2. Specify the level of significance α (the acceptable risk of making a Type I error).
Step 11.3. Select and calculate the value of the Test Statistic F_T using the following formula:

$$F_T = \frac{Explained\ Variation}{Mean\ Squared\ Error} = \frac{SS_{REG}}{MSE}$$

Step 11.4. Determine the Critical Value (*CV*) of the *F*-distribution based on the level of α and Degrees of freedom ($k - 1, n - k$). Clearly demarcate the Rejection Region (*RR*)

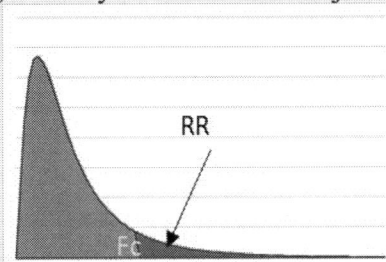

Step 11.5. Compare the Test Statistic to the Critical Value to identify whether the null hypothesis is rejected or not at the level of significance α. If the Test Statistic falls in the Rejection Region, reject the null hypothesis, otherwise fail to reject the null.
Step 11.6. Write a clear conclusion based on the determination made in Step 5.

For the illustration for grades (*Y*) and the number of hours studied per week (*X*), the

$$F_T = \frac{SS_{REG}}{MSE} = \frac{4980.38}{274.5} = 13.3$$

If $\alpha = 0.05$ and the degrees of freedom for the *F*-critical value are ($k - 1, n - k$) = (1, 8), one obtains Critical $F = F_C = F_{0.05} = 5.32$ from Table C in the Appendix. Thus, the value of $F_T >$

F_C, and the H0 can be rejected at a 95% level of confidence. Moreover, when the Excel method is used, the Critical Value of F is often not shared in the output. What is shared, however is the Significance F. If the value of the Significance F is less than 0.05, one can reject the null hypothesis at a 95% level of confidence as well.

D.f.2	Probability to the right of the value				α = 0.05 ← D.f.1	
	1	2	3	4	5	10
1	161.448	199.500	215.707	224.583	230.162	241.882
2	18.513	19.000	19.164	19.247	19.296	19.396
3	10.128	9.552	9.277	9.117	9.013	8.786
4	7.709	6.944	6.591	6.388	6.256	5.964
5	6.608	5.786	5.409	5.192	5.050	4.735
6	5.987	5.143	4.757	4.534	4.387	4.060
7	5.591	4.737	4.347	4.120	3.972	3.637
8	5.318	4.459	4.066	3.838	3.687	3.347

This implies that the regression model is dependable because the independent variable number of hours of study is able to meaningfully explain at least a part of the variation in the dependent variable to matter, statistically. Thus, the performed regression analysis indicates that hours of study per week has a statistically significant impact on class score at the 95% confidence level.

7.3.4. Confidence and Prediction Intervals for a given value of $X = X_0$:

If $s_{\hat{Y}}$ is defined as the standard error of predicted value $\hat{Y}$ for a specific value of $X = X_0$ and $s_{Y-\hat{Y}}$ is the standard error of $e = Y - \hat{Y}$ for the specific value of $X = X_0$, these values are calculated using the following formulas. The confidence intervals with degrees of freedom of $(n - k)$ can also be calculated using these standard errors.

$$s_{\hat{Y}} = s \sqrt{\frac{1}{n} + \frac{(X_0 - \bar{X})^2}{SS_X}}$$

$$s_{Y-\hat{Y}} = s \sqrt{1 + \frac{1}{n} + \frac{(X_0 - \bar{X})^2}{SS_X}}$$

$$100(1 - \alpha)\% \ CI \ of \ \hat{Y} = \hat{Y} \pm t_{\alpha/2} s_{\hat{Y}}$$

$$100(1 - \alpha)\% \ CI \ of \ \left(e = Y - \hat{Y}\right) = \hat{Y} \pm t_{\alpha/2} s_{Y-\hat{Y}}$$

In Table 7.4, the direct Regression inputs and Output using Data → Data Analysis → Regression function is given with manually marked values with arrows to demonstrate how the calculations using formulas given above can be automatically obtained through Excel without requiring any additional columns to be created. The Line Fit Plots also gives the scatter plot of Ys and predicted Ys, which can be customized as desired. Thus, in the example provided thereafter, the direct Excel method is going to be employed, instead of a stepwise calculation for all relevant estimates of the regression output.

Table 7.4. Direct Excel Inputs and Outputs using Data Analysis for Regression.

	A	B	C
1	Obs.	X = number of hours per week	Y = score on the final exam
2	1	1	24
3	2	2	44
4	3	3	37
5	4	4	69
6	5	5	34
7	6	6	98
8	7	7	96
9	8	8	59
10	9	9	93
11	10	10	100
12	SUM	55	654
13	MEAN	5.5	65.4
14	Variance	9.2	886.3
15	Std. Dev	3.0	29.8
16			

Regression dialog box:

- Input
  - Input Y Range: $C$1:$C$11
  - Input X Range: $B$1:$B$11
  - ☑ Labels ☐ Constant is Zero
  - ☐ Confidence Level: 95 %
- Output options
  - ⦿ Output Range: $E$1
  - ◯ New Worksheet Ply:
  - ◯ New Workbook
- Residuals
  - ☐ Residuals ☐ Residual Plots
  - ☐ Standardized Residuals ☐ Line Fit Plots
- Normal Probability
  - ☐ Normal Probability Plots

[OK] [Cancel] [Help]

SUMMARY OUTPUT

Regression Statistics

Multiple R	0.7902	r
R Square	0.6244	R^2
Adjusted R Square	0.5774	
Standard Error	19.3521	s
Observations	10	n

SSE   *MSE*

ANOVA

	df	SS	MS	F	Significance F
Regression	1	4980.376	4980.376	13.299	0.007
Residual	8	2996.024	374.503		
Total	9	7976.400			

	Coefficients	Standard Error	t Stat	P-value	Lower 95%	Upper 95%
					confidence interval	
Intercept	22.67	13.220	1.715	0.125	-7.82	53.15
X = number of hours per week	7.77	2.131	3.647	0.007	2.86	12.68

a   *b* *sa*   *sb*   *tTa* *tTb*

Line Fit Plot

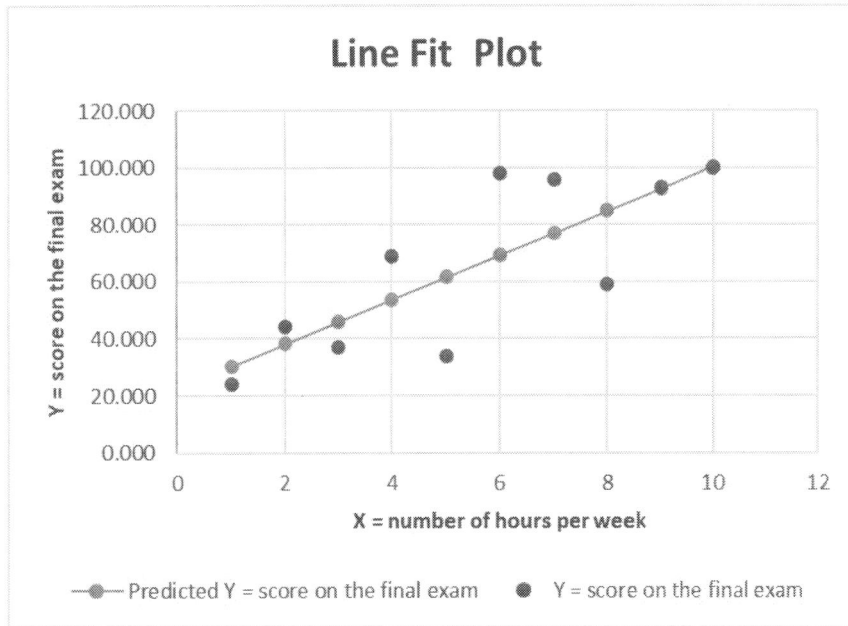

Example 7:2. Regression Analysis

Suppose a researcher wants to test if the mileage and the price of a used car are related to each other and wants to be able to predict the price of the car based upon its mileage. He takes a sample of 10 observations and finds the following. Predict what he expects the price of a car with 100,000 miles on it to be and test the model for significance.

MILES	PRICE
67937	6504
31959	16446
58028	10734
10529	16964
55593	9115
78661	10090
86785	9826
24110	8181
95947	-1933
72317	3434

Solution: The researcher is interested in the prices based upon the mileage, so Price is the dependent variable Y and the mileage is the independent variable, X. One can enter the relevant information in the Data Analysis, Regression Tab and obtain the corresponding output as shown in Figure 7.5. In this output, it can be seen that the correlation coefficient (Multiple R) is 0.721 and the coefficient of determination is 0.52, implying that around 52% of the variation in the price of cars can be explained by their mileage. Upon considering the Significance F value, it can be seen that Significance $F < 0.05$, implying that the model is statistically significant with a 95% confidence level. The estimated linear regression function is:

$$\hat{Y} = 17{,}291.79 - 0.1436X$$

	A	B
1	**X = MILES**	**Y = PRICE**
2	67937	6504
3	31959	16446
4	58028	10734
5	10529	16964
6	55593	9115
7	78661	10090
8	86785	9826
9	24110	8181
10	95947	-1933
11	72317	3434

Regression

Input
Input Y Range: $B$1:$B$11
Input X Range: $A$1:$A$11
☑ Labels   ☐ Constant is Zero
☐ Confidence Level: 95 %

Output options
◉ Output Range: $E$1
○ New Worksheet Ply:
○ New Workbook

Residuals
☑ Residuals   ☐ Residual Plots
☐ Standardized Residuals   ☑ Line Fit Plots

Normal Probability
☐ Normal Probability Plots

OK Cancel Help

SUMMARY OUTPUT

Regression Statistics	
Multiple R	0.721
R Square	0.520
Adjusted R Square	0.460
Standard Error	4108.401
Observations	10

ANOVA

	df	SS	MS	F	Significance F
Regression	1	146097709.6	146097709.6	8.656	0.0187
Residual	8	135031649.3	16878956.17		
Total	9	281129358.9			

	Coefficients	Standard Error	t Stat	P-value	Lower 95%	Upper 95%
Intercept	17291.79	3123.15	5.54	0.00	10089.80	24493.78
X = MILES	-0.143602	0.05	-2.94	0.02	-0.26	-0.03

RESIDUAL OUTPUT

Observation	Predicted Y = PRICE	Residuals
1	7535.93	-1031.93
2	12702.43	3743.57
3	8958.88	1775.12
4	15779.81	1184.19
5	9308.55	-193.55
6	5995.94	4094.06
7	4829.32	4996.68
8	13829.55	-5648.55
9	3513.65	-5446.65
10	6906.95	-3472.95

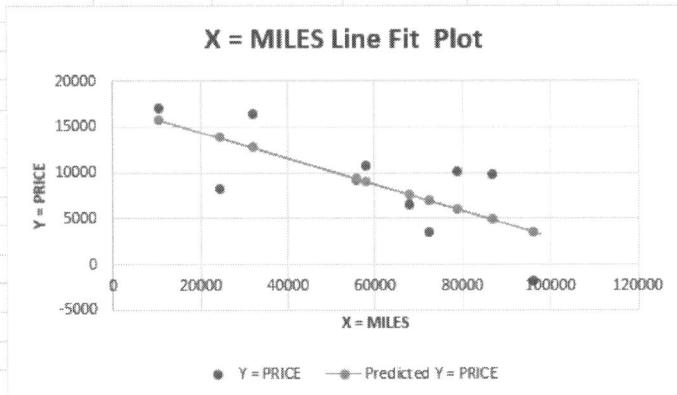

X = MILES Line Fit Plot

Figure 7.5. Regression Analysis Excel Output for Example 7.2.

The regression equation implies that the base price of a car is expected to be around $17,291.79 with a mileage of 0 for cars. For every additional mile that a car has on it, its price is expected to fall by $0.1436. The t-stats for both the intercept a and the slope b are significant at the 0.05 level, indicating that the mileage is indeed a significant contributor to the price of the car.

If a car has 100,000 miles on it, the X = 100,000. Entering this value into the estimated regression function, one gets an expected price of $3,291.79 for that car:
$$\hat{Y} = 17,291.79 - 0.1436X = 17291.79 - 0.1436 * 100000 = 2931.79$$

7.4. The General (multivariate) Approach

Consider a regression equation with two explanatory variables, X_1 and X_2. Thus, the endogenous variable Y is explained by these two exogenous variables. The linear approximation of the model is as follows:
$$Y = b_0 + b_1 X_1 + b_2 X_2 + \text{e}$$

In this model, b_0, b_1, and b_2 are the population parameters about which the researcher wants some information. They can be estimated using the method of Ordinary Least Squares (OLS) by using a sample. Thus, the predicted value of Y, indicated by $\hat{Y}$ can be computed as:
$$\hat{Y} = b_0 + b_1 X_1 + b_2 X_2 + \text{e}$$

The goal is always to minimize the difference between Y and $\hat{Y}$. Thus, one needs to estimate b_0, b_1, and b_2 such that the sum of squares of the error (*SSE*) is minimized. One can find the solution using the Regression Analysis function in Excel or other software. It is important to be careful that for a sample of n observations, there cannot be more than n-1 exogenous variables in the model, in principle. This model can be generalized with n-k degrees of freedom by using up to k exogenous variables $X_1, X_2, ..., X_k$ as follows:
$$Y = b_0 + b_1 X_1 + b_2 X_2 + \cdots + b_k X_k + \text{e}$$

All the tests of significance, confidence and prediction intervals that were covered for the bivariate analysis can be performed for the multivariate analysis with some adjustments in calculating the various sums of squares. Multivariate Analysis is best done using a statistical software package instead of manual calculations for so many variables and their interactions.

Example 7:3. Multivariate Regression Analysis

A production plant cost-control engineer is responsible for cost reduction. One of the costly items in his plant is the amount of water used by the production facilities each month. He decided to investigate water usage by collecting seventeen observations on his plant's water usage and other variables that he believes have an impact on the water usage. The collected variables are defined below along with the following table taken from page 352 (Draper & Smith, 1981) that shows the observations for each variable. Find the Linear Regression Equation and test for significance of the full model and each of the slopes of this equation.

Variable	Description
TEMP	Average monthly temperature (F)
PROD	Amount of production (M pounds)

DAYS   Number of plant operating days in the month
PERSONS   Number of persons on the monthly plant payroll
WATER   Monthly water usage (gallons)

WATER	TEMP	PROD	DAYS	PERSONS
3067	58.8	7107	21	129
2828	65.2	6373	22	141
2891	70.9	6796	22	153
2994	77.4	9208	20	166
3082	79.3	14792	25	193
3898	81	14564	23	189
3502	71.9	11964	20	175
3060	63.9	13526	23	186
3211	54.5	12656	20	190
3286	39.5	14119	20	187
3542	44.5	16691	22	195
3125	43.6	14571	19	206
3022	56	13619	22	198
2922	64.7	14575	22	192
3950	73	14556	21	191
4488	78.9	18573	21	200
3295	79.4	15618	22	200

Solution: Here, the dependent variable is *WATER* and the exogenous (independent) variables are *TEMP*, *PROD*, *DAYS*, and *PERSONS*. Thus, the regression model is given by:

$$WATER = b_0 + b_1 TEMP + b_2 PROD + b_3 DAYS + b_4 PERSONS + e$$

In Excel, it is possible to use multiple values of independent variables simultaneously (input into Data Analysis → Regression) to get the following output.

	A	B	C	D	E
1	**WATER**	**TEMP**	**PROD**	**DAYS**	**PERSONS**
2	3067	58.8	7107	21	129
3	2828	65.2	6373	22	141
4	2891	70.9	6796	22	153
5	2994	77.4	9208	20	166
6	3082	79.3	14792	25	193
7	3898	81	14564	23	189
8	3502	71.9	11964	20	175
9	3060	63.9	13526	23	186
10	3211	54.5	12656	20	190
11	3286	39.5	14119	20	187
12	3542	44.5	16691	22	195
13	3125	43.6	14571	19	206
14	3022	56	13619	22	198
15	2922	64.7	14575	22	192
16	3950	73	14556	21	191
17	4488	78.9	18573	21	200
18	3295	79.4	15618	22	200

Regression dialog

Input
- Input Y Range: $A$1:$A$18
- Input X Range: $B$1:$E$18
- ☑ Labels ☐ Constant is Zero
- ☐ Confidence Level: 95 %

Output options
- ◉ Output Range: $H$1
- ○ New Worksheet Ply:
- ○ New Workbook

Residuals
- ☐ Residuals ☐ Residual Plots
- ☐ Standardized Residuals ☐ Line Fit Plots

Normal Probability
- ☐ Normal Probability Plots

[OK] [Cancel] [Help]

SUMMARY OUTPUT

Regression Statistics	
Multiple R	0.8758
R Square	0.7670
Adjusted R Square	0.6894
Standard Error	248.9641
Observations	17

ANOVA

	df	SS	MS	F	Significance F
Regression	4	2448834.0	612208.50	9.877	0.0009
Residual	12	743797.5	61983.13		
Total	16	3192631.5			

	Coefficients	Standard Error	t Stat	P-value	Lower 95%	Upper 95%
Intercept	6360.34	1314.39	4.84	0.00	3496.52	9224.15
TEMP	13.87	5.16	2.69	0.02	2.63	25.11
PROD	0.21	0.05	4.65	0.00	0.11	0.31
DAYS	-126.69	48.02	-2.64	0.02	-231.32	-22.06
PERSONS	-21.82	7.28	-3.00	0.01	-37.69	-5.95

Figure 7.6. Input and Output for Multivariate Regression Analysis in Excel

Thus, based on these results the Linear Regression Equation for predicted *WATER* usage is:

$$\widehat{WATER} = 6360.34 + 13.87TEMP + 0.21PROD - 126.69DAYS - 21.81PERSONS$$

All of the slopes are significant at the 95% level because the p-values are below 0.05 for each one (or the t-Stat for each one is significant at 0.05 level). The entire model is also significant at 95% level, as observed from the F-test which shows a significance value of 0.0009, which is lower than 0.05. The R-square for the model indicates that 76.7% of the fluctuations in the *WATER* variable can be explained using the exogenous variables identified for this model. Thus, the model as well as all the slopes are significant in this example.

Table 7.5. Steps of Performing a Regression Analysis

Step 1. The mean values of X and Y are calculated using the formulas:

$$\bar{X} = \frac{\sum X}{n}; \ \bar{Y} = \frac{\sum Y}{n}$$

Step 2. Based on the obtained values of $\bar{X}$ and $\bar{Y}$, one can calculate different types of deviations given by the following formulas:

$$Sum \ of \ Product \ of \ deviations: SP = \sum(X - \bar{X})(Y - \bar{Y})$$
$$Sum \ of \ Squared \ X \ deviations: SS_X = \Sigma(X - \bar{X})^2$$
$$Sum \ of \ Squared \ Y \ deviations: SS_Y = \Sigma(Y - \bar{Y})^2$$

Step 3. Calculate the Pearson's Correlation r (and test it for significance, if required):

$$r = \frac{SP}{\sqrt{SS_X \cdot SS_Y}}$$

Step 4. <u>Coefficient of Determination: R^2 or r^2</u>

$$R^2 = \frac{SS_{TOT} - SS_{RES}}{SS_{TOT}} = \frac{SS_{REG}}{SS_{TOT}}$$

<u>Coefficient of Non-determination</u> $(1 - R^2)$.

Step 5. Using these deviations, one can calculate the slope b using the following equation:

$$b = \frac{SP}{SS_X} = \frac{\sum(X - \bar{X})(Y - \bar{Y})}{\sum(X - \bar{X})^2}$$

Step 6. Once the slope is calculated, the vertical intercept a is calculated as follows:

$$a = \bar{Y} - b\bar{X}$$

Step 7. Once the slope and intercept are calculated, the equation for the Least Squares line becomes:

$$\hat{Y} = a + bX$$

Step 8. Sum of Squares Calculations:

$$SS_{TOT} = SS_{RES} + SS_{REG}$$
$$\sum(Y - \bar{Y})^2 = \sum\left(Y - \hat{Y}\right)^2 + \sum\left(\hat{Y} - \bar{Y}\right)^2$$

Step 9. The Mean Squared Error (MSE) and Regression Standard Error (SE):

$$Mean \ Squared \ Error \ (MSE): s^2 = \frac{SS_{RES}}{n - k}$$

$$Reg. Standard \ Error \ (SE): s = \sqrt{MSE} = \sqrt{\frac{SS_{RES}}{n - k}}$$

Step 10. Statistical Significance for the intercept <u>a and</u> the slope

$$Std. Error \ of \ a: s_a = s\sqrt{\frac{1}{n} + \frac{\bar{X}^2}{SS_X}}; \ Std. Error \ of \ b: s_b = s\sqrt{\frac{1}{SS_X}}$$

For intercept a: $H_0: a = 0$; $H_a: a \neq 0$; $t_T = \frac{a}{s_a}$; $100(1 - \alpha)\% \ CI = a \pm t_{\alpha/2}s_a$

For slope b: $H_0: b = 0$; $H_a: b \neq 0$; $t_T = \frac{b}{s_b}$; $100(1 - \alpha)\% \ CI = b \pm t_{\alpha/2}s_b$

Step 11. F-Test for the Full Model with Degrees of Freedom $(k - 1, n - k)$

H_0: All the slopes in the regression are 0; H_a: At least one of the slopes is not equal to 0

$$F_T = \frac{Explained \ Variation}{Mean \ Squared \ Error} = \frac{SS_{REG}}{MSE}$$

Chapter 8. Chi-Squared Tests

The previous chapters have focused on various "parametric" tests for identifying whether the null hypothesis can be rejected or not, in favor of the alternative hypothesis. Parametric tests can only be applied if one has a normally (or close to normally) distributed population or if one has large sample sizes which allows one to estimate the parameters of the population by using the Central Limit Theorem. Moreover, the random variable(s) of interest is (are) all interval-level measures, which is to say that the data is not nominal or ranked but is representative of quantitative measurement alone. However, in the real world, data can be nominal or ranked and normality might not always hold. So, how would one test hypotheses that rely on nominal or ranked data in a quantitative manner? The answer to this question is found in the existence of non-parametric tests. It is important to remember that parametric tests are always more powerful than non-parametric tests because they rely on population "parameters" so whenever possible, they should be employed for hypotheses testing.

The biggest advantage of non-parametric tests is that they do not rely on any underlying distribution assumptions of the population, can be implemented on small samples, and focus on the median and other attributes of the data instead of the mean and standard deviation, which allows for nominal or ranked data to be considered. The most common type of non-parametric distribution that is used is called the Chi-squared (χ^2) Distribution and the types of tests covered in this chapter rely on it for testing the respective hypotheses. This chapter starts by covering one-way χ^2 tests such as the Goodness-of-fit test and the Single Variance test followed by a brief segue into F-test for Two Population Variances and then discussing Two-way χ^2 tests such as the Test of Independence, Test of Homogeneity, and the Median Test. The general table for the Chi-squared distribution is given in the Appendix as Table D and is used to identify the critical values of the χ^2 for the hypotheses tests. It is also worth noting that the formal non-parametric tests are of many types and specific versions of the tests are called by various names based upon the individuals who pioneered these tests. This book does not delve into those specific names or tests but focuses on the general concepts of non-parametric testing.

8.1. General Properties of Chi-Squared Distribution

The construction of the Chi-Squared Distribution is fascinating but is well beyond the scope of this book. However, it might help to see the formula for the Chi-Squared random variable to understand that it is a summation of various Z-scores at each degree of freedom included in the calculations of the Chi-Squared. Thus, if the random variable χ^2 is distributed over k degrees of freedom, then the formula of χ^2 is given as the sum of the squares of the corresponding Z values for each degree of freedom from 1 to k.

$$\chi^2 = Z_1^2 + Z_2^2 + \cdots + Z_k^2$$

As the formula indicates, the χ^2 is a combination of all squared terms implying that there are no negative values of χ^2 possible. The general characteristics of the curve are as follows:

1. The curve is non-symmetrical is always skewed to the right (long tail on the right and "hump" is on the left)

2. There is a different chi-square curve for each degree of freedom since the addition terms fluctuate based upon the degrees of freedom, k.

3. The test-statistic as well as the critical values of χ^2 are always positive.

4. When the degrees of freedom, k, are greater than 90, the χ^2 curve approximates a normal curve where the mean μ is given by the degrees of freedom, k, and the standard deviation $\sigma = \sqrt{2k}$

5. The mean μ is located just to the right of the peak (unlike the traditional normal distribution where the mean is exactly located at the peak of the distribution).

The steps for hypotheses testing using the Chi-squared Distribution are similar to the steps covered earlier in Chapter 6.

Step 1. Clearly identify and state the Null Hypothesis (H₀) and Alternative Hypothesis (Hₐ)
Step 2. Specify the level of significance α (also called the acceptable risk of making a Type I error). Note that using two-tailed analysis is typically avoided in Chi-squared distributions, unless specifically required or recommended.
Step 3. Select and calculate the appropriate value of the Test Statistic (χ_T^2)
Step 4. Determine the Critical Value (χ_C^2) based on the level of α and degrees of freedom k. Clearly demarcate the Rejection Region (RR)
Step 5. Compare the Test Statistic to the Critical Value to identify whether the null hypothesis is rejected or not at the level of significance α. If the Test Statistic falls in the Rejection Region, reject the null hypothesis, otherwise fail to reject the null.
Step 6. Write a clear conclusion based on the determination made in Step 5.

The calculations of the Test Statistic for the various types of one-way and two-way Chi-squared tests are given in Table 8.1.

Table 8.1. Test Statistic and Degrees of Freedom for Chi-Squared Tests

Chi-Squared Test	Degrees of Freedom	Test Statistic
One-Way Tests		
Goodness-of-Fit	$k - 1$ k = number of categories	$\chi_T^2 = \sum \dfrac{(O - E)^2}{E}$
Single Variance	$n - 1$ n = sample size	$\chi_T^2 = \dfrac{(n - 1)s^2}{\sigma^2}$
Two-Way Tests		
Independence	$(i - 1) \times (j - 1)$	$\chi_T^2 = \sum \dfrac{(O - E)^2}{E}$
Homogeneity	i = number of rows	
Median	j = number of columns	

8.2. One-way Chi-Squared Tests

There are two types of one-way chi-squared tests. They are called one-way tests because they deal with only a sample of only one type of random variable at a time. The two main one-way tests are the Goodness-of-Fit test that checks for observed versus expected frequencies of the random variable outcomes and the Single Variance test that checks for whether the variance in a sample corresponds correctly to the population variance or not.

8.2.1. Goodness-of-Fit Test

This test, also known as the Frequency test, is used to determine whether frequencies observed for the outcomes of a particular random variable differ statistically significantly from the hypothesized or expected outcomes for a given random variable distribution. Thus, if the expected frequency of each outcome is denoted by E and the corresponding observed frequency of each outcome by O for a total of k outcomes, the test statistic χ_T^2 is calculated using the following formula:

$$\chi_T^2 = \sum \frac{(O - E)^2}{E}$$

The critical value of χ_C^2 is found from the Chi-squared Table using degrees of freedom *df* = $(k - 1)$

Example 8:1. Goodness-of-Fit One-Way Chi-Squared Test

A researcher hypothesizes that the three major political positions (defined as conservative, moderate, liberal) are not represented equally in the media. He observes 45 news stories in a given week and finds that of these, 10 were favoring conservative positions, 12 were favoring moderate positions, and 23 were favoring liberal positions on political issues. Identify whether his hypothesis is valid at a 95% confidence level or not.

Solution: Follow the steps of the hypothesis testing to solve this problem. Note that a lot of the calculations in Chi-squared distributions are easier to perform in Excel than by hand.
Step 1. Clearly identify and state the Null Hypothesis (H_0) and Alternative Hypothesis (H_a)

H₀: All three political positions are equally represented in the media.
Hₐ: All three political positions are not equally represented in the media.

Step 2. Specify the level of significance α (also called the acceptable risk of making a Type I error). In this example, the confidence level is given to be 95% so the level of significance $\alpha = 0.05$.

Step 3. Select and calculate the appropriate value of the Test Statistic (χ_T^2)

In this example, if the media was equally representing all political positions, the expected frequencies for each category would be 15 or 1/3 of the total 45 news stories. One can create the following table based on the given information:

Position	O	E	O - E	(O - E)^2	((O - E)^2)/E
Conservative	10	15	-5	25	1.667
Moderate	12	15	-3	9	0.600
Liberal	23	15	8	64	4.267
TOTAL	45	45			6.533

$$\chi_T^2 = \sum \frac{(O - E)^2}{E} = 6.533$$

Step 4. Determine the Critical Value (χ_C^2) based on the level of α and degrees of freedom $k - 1$. Clearly demarcate the Rejection Region (RR)

Here there are 3 categories or positions, therefore the $k = 3$ and the degrees of freedom $d.f. = 3 - 1 = 2$ with an $\alpha = 0.05$. Note that in the Chi-squared table, this means that the blue region should be equal to 0.05 and the orange region would be 0.95. So, one would look at the table in the following manner:

d.f.	0.995	0.99	0.975	0.95	0.9	0.1	0.05	0.025	0.01	0.005
				Probability to the left of the value						
1	7.879	6.635	5.024	3.841	2.706	0.016	0.004	0.001	0.000	0.000
2	10.597	9.210	7.378	5.991	4.605	0.211	0.103	0.051	0.020	0.010
3	12.838	11.345	9.348	7.815	6.251	0.584	0.352	0.216	0.115	0.072

Thus, $\chi_C^2 = 5.991$

Step 5. Compare the Test Statistic to the Critical Value to identify whether the null hypothesis is rejected or not at the level of significance α. If the Test Statistic falls in the Rejection Region, reject the null hypothesis, otherwise fail to reject the null.

As one can see in Figure 8.1, the test statistic falls in the blue Rejection Region. Thus, one can reject the null hypothesis in this case at a 95% confidence level.

Step 6. Write a clear conclusion based on the determination made in Step 5.

At a 95% confidence level, one can reject the null hypothesis that all three political positions are equally represented in the media.

Figure 8.1 shows the Excel formulations used to solve this problem alongside the direct Chi-squared formula for the critical values. Note that there is a direct way to calculate the Test Statistic in Excel by using the CHISQ.INV.RT function in combination with CHISQ.TEST function without having to calculate anything except the Expected Frequencies.

	A	B	C	D	E	F	G	H	I
1	**Goodness-of-Fit One-way Chi-squared test**								
2									
3	Ho: All three political positions are equally represented in the media								
4	Ha: All three political posisitons are not equally represented in the media								
5	**Position**	**O**	**E**	**O - E**	**(O - E)^2**	**((O - E)^2)/E**			
6	**Conservative**	10	15	-5	25	1.667			
7	**Moderate**	12	15	-3	9	0.600			
8	**Liberal**	23	15	8	64	4.267			
9	**TOTAL**	**45**	**45**			**6.533**			
10									
11	χ_T^2 Test Statistic =	6.533	=CHISQ.INV.RT(CHISQ.TEST(B6:B8,C6:C8),(COUNT(B6:B8)-1))						
12	Significance α =	0.05							
13	1 - α =	0.95	=1-B12						
14	Number of rows k =	3							
15	egrees of freedom df =	2	=B14-1						
16	χ_C^2 Critical Value =	5.991	=CHISQ.INV(B13,B15)						
17	Decision:	Reject Ho		=IF(B11>B16, "Reject Ho", "Fail to Reject Ho")					
18	Conclusion:	Thus, at a 95% confidence level, we can reject the hypothesis that all three							
19		political positions are equally represented in the media							

Figure 8.1. Excel Solution for the Goodness-of-Fit Example.

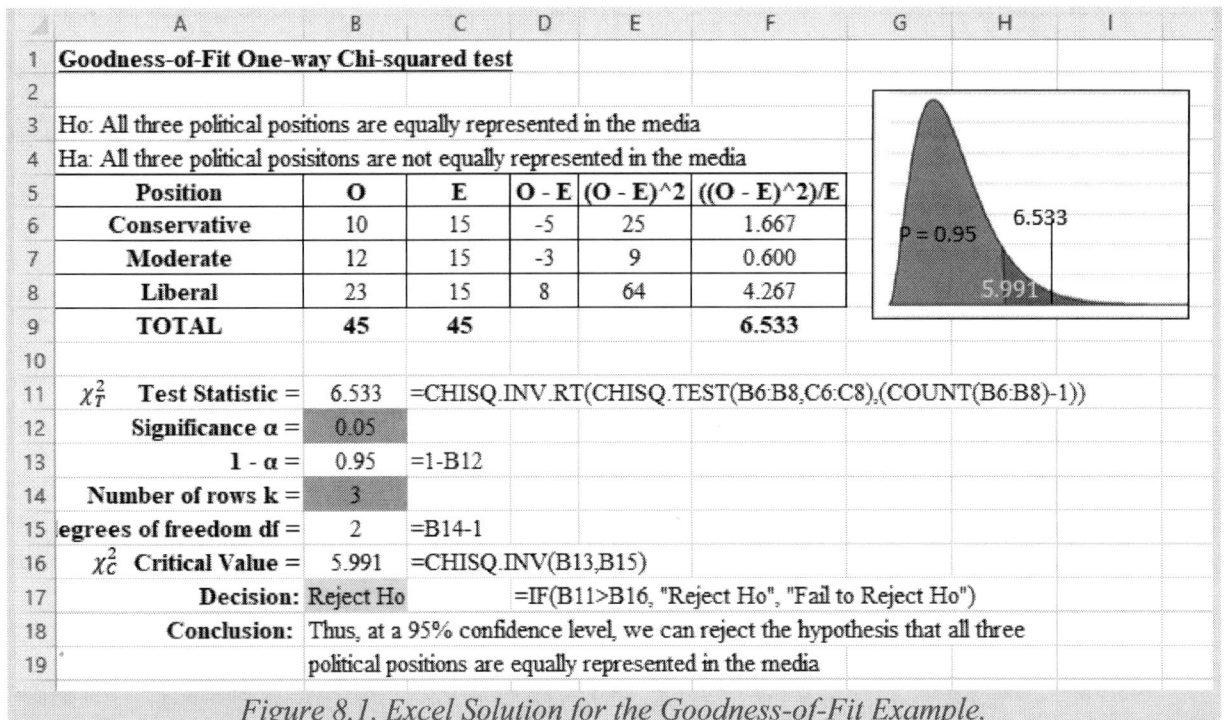

8.2.2. Single Variance Test

The single variance test allows one to identify whether the sample is truly representative of the population based upon its variance. This is similar to the difference of means tests that were covered in Section 6.2.1 in Chapter 6 that sought to identify whether a sample represented the population accurately based upon the mean values. If one looks at the formula for population variance (σ^2), it is the average of the squared deviations from the mean in a given population. Since this is a squared-term, one cannot use the usual Z-tables to test for comparison of two variances and instead use the Chi-Squared Distribution. It is important to note here that the underlying distribution of the random variable X, from which variances are calculated is a normal distribution. However, the random variable s^2 (variance of the sample) can be assumed to be distributed as a chi-squared distribution.

Thus, if one either knows or hypothesizes that the population variance is σ^2 and the obtained sample variance is s^2 from a sample of n observations, one can test for how closely the sample is representative of the population, in terms of its variability by using the following test statistic:

$$\chi_T^2 = \frac{(n-1)s^2}{\sigma^2}$$

The critical value of χ_C^2 is found from the Chi-squared Table using degrees of freedom $df = (n-1)$. In these types of examples, one can have a one-tailed or a two-tailed test depending upon how the hypotheses are set up. The three types of hypotheses sets used for single variance testing are given as follows and the Figure 8.2 shows the way the distributions and corresponding chi-squared values are graphed for each type:

$First\ type: H_0: s^2 \geq \sigma^2; H_a: s^2 < \sigma^2\ one-tailed\ test$
$Second\ type: H_0: s^2 \leq \sigma^2; H_a: s^2 > \sigma^2\ one-tailed\ test$

Third type: $H_0: s^2 = \sigma^2$; $H_a: s^2 \neq \sigma^2$ two $-$ tailed test

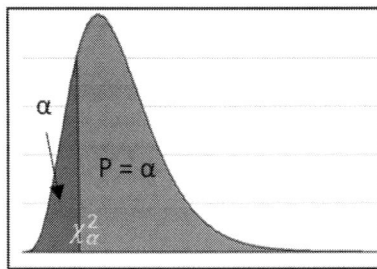
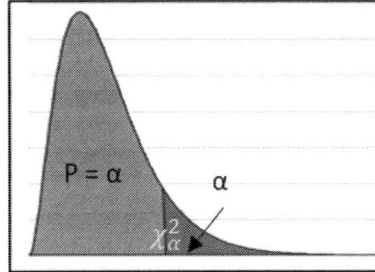
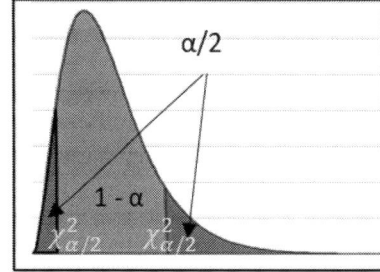

$H_0: s^2 \geq \sigma^2$
One-tailed α; RR in Blue

$H_0: s^2 \leq \sigma^2$
One-tailed α; RR in Blue

$H_0: s^2 = \sigma^2$
Two-tailed α/2; RR in Blue

Figure 8.2. Hypotheses for One-Tailed or Two-Tailed Chi Distributions

Moreover, keep in mind that by using the sample one is deriving certain conclusions about the population so if a hypothetical value of population variance σ^2 is to be compared with the true population, one can only do so by the use of the sample variance s^2 since one can actually calculate it to represent the population variance. A two-tailed test example is being considered here even though it is not common to use two-tailed Chi-squared tests in most cases, but it is interesting to learn how to apply it, when required.

Example 8:2. Single Variance Test

The standard deviation of heights for students in a school is 0.79 feet. A random sample of 25 students is taken, and the standard deviation of heights in the sample is 0.89 feet. Does the sample variation of heights correctly represent the variance of heights in the student population of the school? Test at a 0.10 level of significance.

Solution: In this case, one is being asked to compare variances of the heights of the sample and the height of the population. Since there is no clear indication of whether one is looking at "greater than" or "less than", one should assume that a two-tailed "not equal to" test is being expected. Now, one can apply the steps of hypotheses testing as given below.

Step 1. Clearly identify and state the Null Hypothesis (H_0) and Alternative Hypothesis (H_a)
$$H_0: s^2 = \sigma^2$$
$$H_a: s^2 \neq \sigma^2$$

Step 2. Specify the level of significance α (also called the acceptable risk of making a Type I error). In this example, the level of significance $\alpha = 0.10$ and for a two-tailed test the value of $\alpha/2 = 0.05$ (probability of each tail).

Step 3. Select and calculate the appropriate value of the Test Statistic (χ_T^2)
Here, the $n = 25$; $s = 0.89$ and $\sigma = 0.79$
$$\chi_T^2 = \frac{(n-1)s^2}{\sigma^2} = \frac{(25-1)0.89^2}{0.79^2} = 30.46$$
Step 4. Determine the Critical Values (χ_C^2) based on the level of α and degrees of freedom $n-1$. Clearly demarcate the Rejection Region (*RR*)

Since this is a two tailed test, and the total $\alpha = 0.10$, the first tail (left-handed tail) has $p = \alpha/2 = 0.05$ to the left of the first (lower) Chi-squared value. Similarly, the second tail (right-handed tail) as $p = 1 - \alpha/2 = 0.95$ to the left of the second (higher) Chi-squared value. Note that in the Chi-squared table, this means that each blue region should be equal to 0.05 and the orange region in the middle would be 0.90. So, one would look at the table in the following manner, for the degrees of freedom $df = n - 1 = 24$:

d.f.	Probability to the left of the value							
	0.995	0.99	0.975	0.95	0.9	0.1	0.05	0.025
1	7.879	6.635	5.024	3.841	2.706	0.016	0.004	0.001
2	10.597	9.210	7.378	5.991	4.605	0.211	0.103	0.051
3	12.838	11.345	9.348	7.815	6.251	0.584	0.352	0.216
4	14.860	13.277	11.143	9.488	7.779	1.064	0.711	0.484
5	16.750	15.086	12.833	11.070	9.236	1.610	1.145	0.831
6	18.548	16.812	14.449	12.592	10.645	2.204	1.635	1.237
7	20.278	18.475	16.013	14.067	12.017	2.833	2.167	1.690
8	21.955	20.090	17.535	15.507	13.362	3.490	2.733	2.180
9	23.589	21.666	19.023	16.919	14.684	4.168	3.325	2.700
10	25.188	23.209	20.483	18.307	15.987	4.865	3.940	3.247
11	26.757	24.725	21.920	19.675	17.275	5.578	4.575	3.816
12	28.300	26.217	23.337	21.026	18.549	6.304	5.226	4.404
13	29.819	27.688	24.736	22.362	19.812	7.042	5.892	5.009
14	31.319	29.141	26.119	23.685	21.064	7.790	6.571	5.629
15	32.801	30.578	27.488	24.996	22.307	8.547	7.261	6.262
16	34.267	32.000	28.845	26.296	23.542	9.312	7.962	6.908
17	35.718	33.409	30.191	27.587	24.769	10.085	8.672	7.564
18	37.156	34.805	31.526	28.869	25.989	10.865	9.390	8.231
19	38.582	36.191	32.852	30.144	27.204	11.651	10.117	8.907
20	39.997	37.566	34.170	31.410	28.412	12.443	10.851	9.591
21	41.401	38.932	35.479	32.671	29.615	13.240	11.591	10.283
22	42.796	40.289	36.781	33.924	30.813	14.041	12.338	10.982
23	44.181	41.638	38.076	35.172	32.007	14.848	13.091	11.689
24	45.559	42.980	39.364	36.415	33.196	15.659	13.848	12.401
25	46.928	44.314	40.646	37.652	34.382	16.473	14.611	13.120

Thus, the lower $\chi_c^2 = 13.848$ and the upper $\chi_c^2 = 36.415$

Step 5. Compare the Test Statistic to the Critical Value to identify whether the null hypothesis is rejected or not at the level of significance α. If the Test Statistic falls in the Rejection Region, reject the null hypothesis, otherwise fail to reject the null.

As seen in Figure 8.3, the test statistic falls in the orange region. Thus, one will fail to reject the null hypothesis in this case at a 90% confidence level.

Step 6. Write a clear conclusion based on the determination made in Step 5.

At a 90% confidence level, one fails to reject the null hypothesis that the variance of the sample is different than the variance of the heights in the student population at the school.
Figure 8.3 shows the Excel formulations used to solve this problem alongside the direct Chi-squared formula for the critical values. The NOTE at the bottom is important for future testing.

	A	B	C	D/E/F/G
1	**Single Variance one-way Chi-squared Test**			
3	Ho:		$s^2 = \sigma^2$	two-tailed test because "="
4	Ha:		$s^2 \neq \sigma^2$	
5	Alpha:		0.1	
6	1- alpha:		90%	=1-C5
7	Tails:		2	
8	Test Statistic:			
9		n =	25	
10		d.f. =	24	=C9-1
11		s =	0.89	
12		σ =	0.79	
13		χ^2_T =	30.46	=(C9-1)*C11^2 /C12^2
14		p-value =	0.830	=CHISQ.DIST(C13,C10, TRUE)
15	χ^2_C Critical Value =	left value	13.85	=IF(C7=2, CHISQ.INV(C5/2,C10), CHISQ.INV(C5, C10))
16		right value	36.42	=IF(C7=2, CHISQ.INV(1-C5/2,C10), CHISQ.INV(C6, C10))
17	Decision:	Fail to Reject Ho		=IF(C13<C15, "Reject Ho", IF(C13>C16, "Reject Ho", "Fail to Reject Ho"))
18	Conclusion:	Thus, at a 90% confidence level, we fail to reject the hypothesis that the variance		
19		in the sample is different from the variance in the student population for heights.		
20	NOTE: Only use the Green shaded Left Value, if it is a one-tailed test of the First Type "≥" in Ho			
21	Only use the Brown shaded Right Value, if is a one-tailed test of the Second Type with "≤" in Ho			

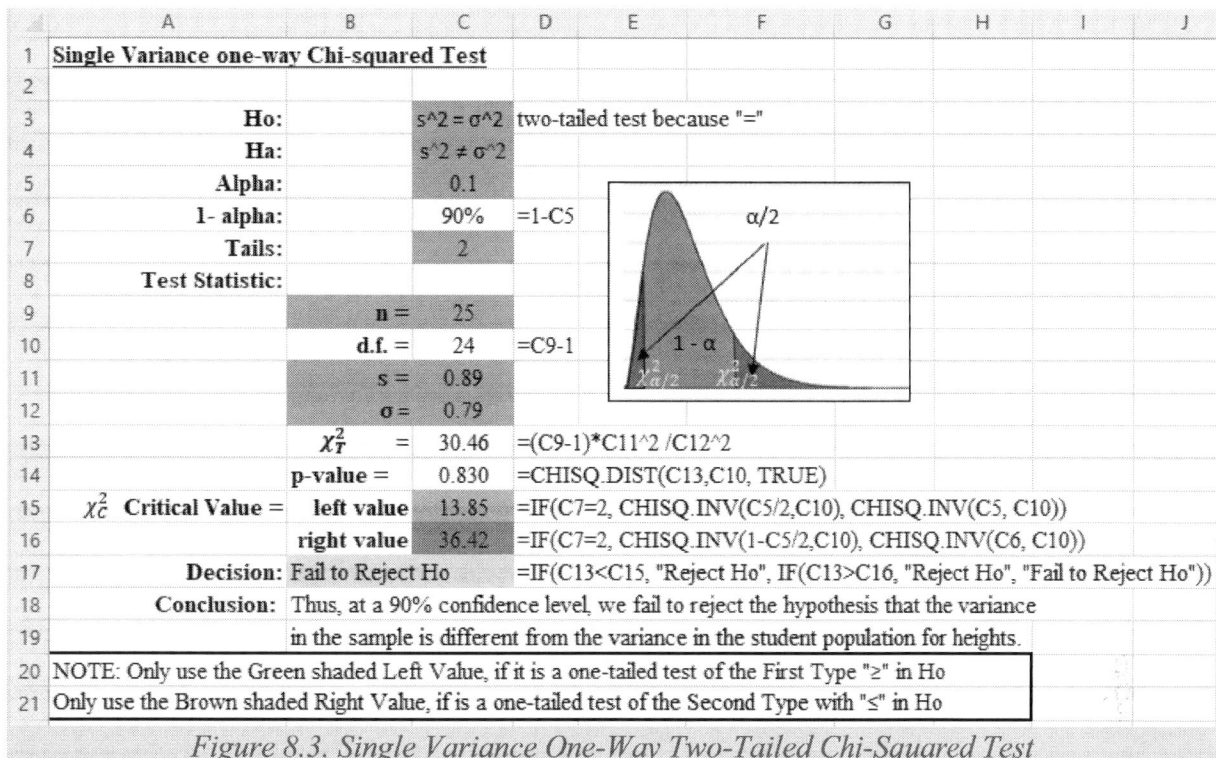

Figure 8.3. Single Variance One-Way Two-Tailed Chi-Squared Test

8.3. F-test for Two Population Variances

Even though this section does not directly apply to Chi-squared tests, it is included here since it directly ties into the Single Variance Testing done in Section 8.2.2. In Chapter 6, when the F-distribution was introduced under ANOVA, it was stated that the F-ratio is a ratio of two Chi-Squared values when the variances of two separate samples drawn from two distinct populations are considered. If only one population is being considered, the Chi-squared test for Single Variance (Section 8.2.2.) can be performed. However, if two populations are being considered, one must use the F-test. The assumptions required for testing two variances of different populations are:

1. The populations from which the 2 samples are drawn are normally distributed and each sample is assumed to be representative of the respective population in terms of mean as well as variance.

2. The populations are independent of each other

3. The variance of first population is denoted as σ_1^2, with the corresponding sample variance being s_1^2 and sample size being n_1. The variance of second population is denoted as σ_2^2, with the corresponding sample variance being s_2^2 and sample size being n_2. The F-ratio is given by the following formula, with degrees of freedom $d.f. = (n_1 - 1, n_2 - 1)$:

$$F = \frac{s_1^2/\sigma_1^2}{s_2^2/\sigma_2^2}$$

4. The null hypothesis for the two-variance test is that there is no difference in the variances of the two population, or that the F-ratio $= 1$. The alternative hypothesis is that the larger sample variance does indicate a larger population variance for the first population as compared to the second population (NOTE: Always pick the larger sample variance to represent the first population and the smaller sample variance to determine which population to mark as the second population – explanation given below)

5. Since the population variances are not always known, and samples are being used to test whether the population variances are close to each other or not, the Critical Value of F_C is obtained by using the level of significance α alongside the degrees of freedom $d.f. = (n_1 - 1, n_2 - 1)$ and the test statistic F_T is given by the following formula:

$$F_T = \frac{s_1^2}{s_2^2}$$

Notice how the F-ratio (given in point 3) in this case is similar to taking the ratio of the Chi-squared value of the Single Variance test for the first population in the numerator and the Chi-squared value of the Single Variance test for the second population in the denominator. Just like the Chi-squared test, there are three types of hypotheses that can be tested using the F-ratio and determining whether the two-tailed or the one-tailed test should be used is important. However, there is a way to always ensure that only the one-tailed test can be used by simply using the sample with the higher variance as the numerator (or it is the population being given the status of population 1). This is because if the value of F is close to one, the two population variances can be assumed to be closer to each other. If the bigger number is in the numerator, one only needs to consider the right-handed test for the F-statistic since the F-ratio would always be greater than 1. The usual steps of hypotheses testing can be applied to the Test of Two Variances.

Example 8:3. F-test of Two Variances

A random sample of 25 students is taken from School A, and the standard deviation of heights in the sample is 0.75 feet. Another random sample of 22 students is taken from School B and the standard deviation of heights in that sample is 0.89 feet. Do the populations of students at School A and School B have the same height variance? Test at 0.10 significance level.

Solution: In this case, one is being asked to compare variances of the heights of two samples, each taken from two different populations, respectively. Since there is no clear indication of whether one is looking at "greater than" or "less than," one should assume that a two-tailed "not equal to" test is being implemented. Now, one can apply the steps of hypotheses testing as given below.

Step 1. Clearly identify and state the Null Hypothesis (H_0) and Alternative Hypothesis (H_a)

$$H_0: \sigma_1^2 = \sigma_2^2$$
$$H_a: \sigma_1^2 \neq \sigma_2^2$$

Step 2. Specify the level of significance α (also called the acceptable risk of making a Type I error).

In this example, the level of significance $\alpha = 0.10$ for a two-tailed test, so the value of $\alpha/2 = 0.05$ (probability of each tail). However, if one makes sure to choose the higher sample variance as the first population (in this case School B which has std. dev. of 0.89), one only needs to find the right-hand tail value at significance level of 0.05.

Step 3. Select and calculate the appropriate value of the Test Statistic (F_T)

Here, the $s_1 = 0.89$, $n_1 = 22$; $s_2 = 0.75$, $n_2 = 25$

$$F_T = \frac{s_1^2}{s_2^2} = \frac{0.89^2}{0.75^2} = \frac{0.7921}{0.5625} = 1.408$$

Step 4. Determine the Critical Value (F_C) based on the level of α and degrees of freedom $d.f. = (n_1 - 1, n_2 - 1)$. Clearly demarcate the Rejection Region (RR)

Even though this is basically a two-tailed test, and the total $\alpha = 0.10$, one can focus on the second tail (right-handed tail) as $p = 1 - \alpha/2 = 0.95$ to the left of the Critical F since it was ensured that the F-ratio is greater than 1. Note that in the F-table, this means that blue region should be equal to 0.05 and the orange region would be 0.95. So, one would look at the table in the following manner, for the degrees of freedom $d.f. = (n_1 - 1, n_2 - 1) = (22 - 1, 25 - 1) = (21, 24)$

D.f.2	Probability to the right of the value					$\alpha = 0.05$	
						D.f.1	
	1	2	3	4	5	10	20
1	161.448	199.500	215.707	224.583	230.162	241.882	248.013
2	18.513	19.000	19.164	19.247	19.296	19.396	19.446
3	10.128	9.552	9.277	9.117	9.013	8.786	8.660
4	7.709	6.944	6.591	6.388	6.256	5.964	5.803
5	6.608	5.786	5.409	5.192	5.050	4.735	4.558
6	5.987	5.143	4.757	4.534	4.387	4.060	3.874
7	5.591	4.737	4.347	4.120	3.972	3.637	3.445
8	5.318	4.459	4.066	3.838	3.687	3.347	3.150
9	5.117	4.256	3.863	3.633	3.482	3.137	2.936
10	4.965	4.103	3.708	3.478	3.326	2.978	2.774
11	4.844	3.982	3.587	3.357	3.204	2.854	2.646
12	4.747	3.885	3.490	3.259	3.106	2.753	2.544
13	4.667	3.806	3.411	3.179	3.025	2.671	2.459
14	4.600	3.739	3.344	3.112	2.958	2.602	2.388
15	4.543	3.682	3.287	3.056	2.901	2.544	2.328
16	4.494	3.634	3.239	3.007	2.852	2.494	2.276
17	4.451	3.592	3.197	2.965	2.810	2.450	2.230
18	4.414	3.555	3.160	2.928	2.773	2.412	2.191
19	4.381	3.522	3.127	2.895	2.740	2.378	2.155
20	4.351	3.493	3.098	2.866	2.711	2.348	2.124
21	4.325	3.467	3.072	2.840	2.685	2.321	2.096
22	4.301	3.443	3.049	2.817	2.661	2.297	2.071
23	4.279	3.422	3.028	2.796	2.640	2.275	2.048
24	4.260	3.403	3.009	2.776	2.621	2.255	2.027

Thus, the $F_C = 2.027$

Note that the value of 20 is being checked instead of 21, since the F-table has limited choices for $d.f.$ in the numerator. The Excel formula will yield a more exact value of the Critical F.

Step 5. Compare the Test Statistic to the Critical Value to identify whether the null hypothesis is rejected or not at the level of significance α. If the Test Statistic falls in the Rejection Region, reject the null hypothesis, otherwise fail to reject the null.

As one can see in Figure 8.4, the test statistic falls in the orange region. Thus, one will fail to reject the null hypothesis in this case at a 90% confidence level.

Step 6. Write a clear conclusion based on the determination made in Step 5.

At a 90% confidence level, one fails to reject the null hypothesis that the variances of the heights of students at both schools are different from each other.

Figure 8.4 shows the Excel formulations used to solve this problem alongside the direct F formula for the critical values. NOTE that the degrees of freedom must be manually entered once one determines which sample (population) is being considered as number 1 (numerator).

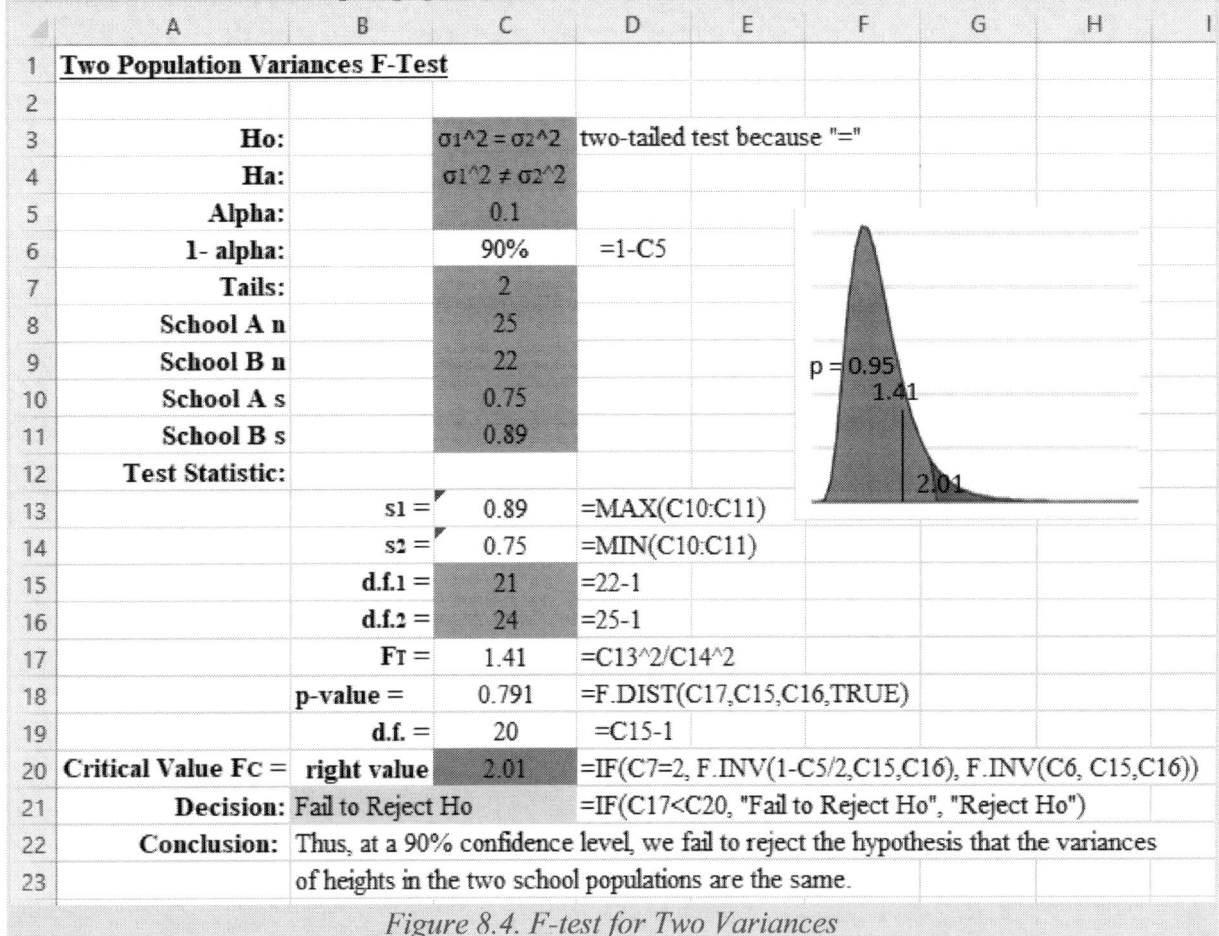

	A	B	C	D	E	F	G	H	I
1	**Two Population Variances F-Test**								
2									
3		Ho:	σ1^2 = σ2^2	two-tailed test because "="					
4		Ha:	σ1^2 ≠ σ2^2						
5		Alpha:	0.1						
6		1- alpha:	90%	=1-C5					
7		Tails:	2						
8		School A n	25						
9		School B n	22						
10		School A s	0.75						
11		School B s	0.89						
12		Test Statistic:							
13		s1 =	0.89	=MAX(C10:C11)					
14		s2 =	0.75	=MIN(C10:C11)					
15		d.f.1 =	21	=22-1					
16		d.f.2 =	24	=25-1					
17		FT =	1.41	=C13^2/C14^2					
18		p-value =	0.791	=F.DIST(C17,C15,C16,TRUE)					
19		d.f. =	20	=C15-1					
20	Critical Value Fc =	right value	2.01	=IF(C7=2, F.INV(1-C5/2,C15,C16), F.INV(C6, C15,C16))					
21		Decision:	Fail to Reject Ho	=IF(C17<C20, "Fail to Reject Ho", "Reject Ho")					
22		Conclusion:	Thus, at a 90% confidence level, we fail to reject the hypothesis that the variances						
23			of heights in the two school populations are the same.						

Figure 8.4. F-test for Two Variances

8.4. Two-way Chi-Squared Tests

When data is collected through random sampling for two categorical (or nominal) variables instead of one variable for the same group of observations, one can use cross-tabulations to organize the data. These cross-tabulations are also called Contingency Tables as covered in Section 1.2 of Chapter 1. Chi-squared tests are one of the few types of tests that can be used in cross-tabulations in order to test for independence of the two variables or to test whether there is homogeneity in two populations or not based on select characteristics.

In these contingency tables, relative frequencies for observed numbers of people that fell into each cross-tabulated category for two variables were covered. In Chi-Squared Two-Way tests, similar contingency tables are used to compare observed values with expected values in order to test for the relationship between the two categories of interest. However, it is essential to learn how to calculate the Expected Values, E_i for each cell in order to successfully carry out the Chi-Squared Two-Way tests. For finding the expected values, one would use the following formula:

$$E_i = \frac{n_{row} \times n_{column}}{n_{total}}$$

Thus, in the seatbelt usage and gender distribution for the 900 observations, one can find the Expected Values for each cell. For instance, since there are a total of 326 males and 405 people who always wear seat belts, one would find the "expected" number of males that always wear seatbelts as $= (326)(405)/900 = 146.7$. One can do this for all cells in all categories to get the following table of Expected Values, and if one compared it to the Original Observed Values table, one would find some differences. These differences are what are being "tested" in the Two-Way Chi-Squared Tests in this section of the chapter.

Observed Values

Gender	Always	Mostly	Sometimes	Rarely	Never	TOTAL
			Seat Belt Use			
Male	105	65	58	39	59	326
Female	300	110	65	44	55	574
TOTAL	405	175	123	83	114	900

Expected Values

Gender	Always	Mostly	Sometimes	Rarely	Never	TOTAL
			Seat Belt Use			
Male	146.7	63.4	44.6	30.1	41.3	326
Female	258.3	111.6	78.4	52.9	72.7	574
TOTAL	405	175	123	83	114	900

8.4.1. Tests of Independence and Homogeneity

These tests are similar to the Goodness-of-Fit Test that were covered earlier but is done for the Two-Way tables which consist of two variables in order to test if one of them is dependent on the other or not, for the Test of Independence. For the test of homogeneity, one compares two populations to each other to determine if their underlying distributions are the same or not. Both these tests fall into the same category in terms of approach and solution, so they are being considered together in this section. The primary difference is in terms of the way the null and alternative hypotheses are set up, so two separate examples are being demonstrated in this section. The goal, for either one of these tests, is to determine whether frequencies observed for the outcomes differ statistically significantly from the hypothesized or expected outcomes. If the number of columns is denoted by i and the number of rows are denoted by j, one would have a total of $i \times j$ outcomes. Thus, if one denoted expected frequency of each outcome by E and the corresponding observed frequency of each outcome by O, the test statistic χ_T^2 is calculated using the following formula:

$$\chi_T^2 = \sum \frac{(O - E)^2}{E}$$

The critical value of χ_C^2 is found from the Chi-squared Table using degrees of freedom $df = (i - 1) \times (j - 1)$.

This test is always a right-tailed test and the only requirement to successfully implement the test is that all the expected frequencies in each cell have at least five units. Note that in the test of homogeneity, there are two populations being compared with each other, so the number of rows, i is always equal to 2. Moreover, since this test hinges upon the number of expected frequencies so heavily, if the expected frequency of any cell in the table is greater than 5, but less than 10, one can apply the Yates' Correction to offset any errors in the calculation of the test statistic by using the following formulation:

$$\chi_T^2 = \sum \frac{(|O - E| - 0.5)^2}{E}$$

Example 8:4. Test of Independence
A researcher is interested in studying whether there is a relationship between ages and types of radio channels that individuals listen to in a given city. She randomly asks 85 people walking out of a store to choose their preferred radio broadcasts (music, news, or sports) and notes the age category they fall into (young, middle-aged, seniors). The following table shows the observed frequencies for each category. Conduct a Two-Way Chi-Squared test to identify if choice of radio broadcasts is independent of age at a 0.05 level of significance.

Age Groups

Preference	Young	Middle	Senior	TOTAL
Music	15	12	3	30
News	4	15	11	30
Sports	9	11	5	25
TOTAL	28	38	19	**85**

Solution: Follow the steps of the hypotheses testing to solve this problem. Note that a lot of the calculations in Chi-squared distributions are easier to perform in Excel than by hand.
Step 1. Clearly identify and state the Null Hypothesis (H_0) and Alternative Hypothesis (H_a)
H_0: Choice of radio broadcasts is independent of the age group of the individual.
H_a: Choice of radio broadcasts is not independent of the age group of the individual.

Step 2. Specify the level of significance α (also called the acceptable risk of making a Type I error). In this example, the level of significance $\alpha = 0.05$ and Two-Way tests are always right tailed.

Step 3. Select and calculate the appropriate value of the Test Statistic (χ_T^2)
One would need to calculate the Expected Frequencies for each category, first by using the formula $E_i = \frac{n_{row} \times n_{column}}{n_{total}}$ for each cell as shown in the table below:

Expected Frequencies

Age Groups

Preference	Young	Middle	Senior	TOTAL
Music	9.88	13.41	6.71	30
News	9.88	13.41	6.71	30
Sports	8.24	11.18	5.59	25
TOTAL	28	38	19	**85**

For each cell, one can now calculate the value of $\frac{(O-E)^2}{E}$ in order to create the following table. Note that the Yates' Correction is deliberately not being used (to minimize confusions) even though there are some expected frequencies higher than 5 but below 10. The sum of all these cell values, therefore, gives the Test Statistic χ_T^2

Calculation of Chi-Squared

	Age Groups			
Preference	**Young**	**Middle**	**Senior**	
Music	2.650	0.149	2.048	
News	3.501	0.188	2.750	
Sports	0.071	0.003	0.062	
				11.4217

$$\chi_T^2 = \sum \frac{(O-E)^2}{E} = 11.422$$

Step 4. Determine the Critical Value (χ_C^2) based on the level of α and degrees of freedom $df = (i-1) \times (j-1)$. Clearly demarcate the Rejection Region (*RR*)

Here there are 3 rows in the table, so $i = 3$, there are three columns in the table, so $j = 3$ and the degrees of freedom *d.f.* = (3-1)(3-1) = 4 with an $\alpha = 0.05$. Note that in the Chi-squared table, this means that the blue region should be equal to 0.05 and the orange region would be 0.95. So, one would look at the table in the following manner:

				Probab
d.f.	**0.995**	**0.99**	**0.975**	**0.95**
1	7.879	6.635	5.024	3.841
2	10.597	9.210	7.378	5.991
3	12.838	11.345	9.348	7.815
4	14.860	13.277	11.143	9.488

Thus, $\chi_C^2 = 9.488$

Step 5. Compare the Test Statistic to the Critical Value to identify whether the null hypothesis is rejected or not at the level of significance α. If the Test Statistic falls in the Rejection Region, reject the null hypothesis, otherwise fail to reject the null.

As one can see in Figure 8.5, the test statistic falls in the blue Rejection Region. Thus, one can reject the null hypothesis in this case at a 95% confidence level.

Step 6. Write a clear conclusion based on the determination made in Step 5.

At a 95% confidence level, one can reject the null hypothesis that choice of radio broadcasts is independent of the age group of the individual.

Figure 8.5 shows the Excel formulations used to solve this problem alongside the direct Chi-squared formula for the critical values. Note that there is a direct way to calculate the Test Statistic in Excel by using the CHISQ.INV.RT function in combination with CHISQ.TEST function without having to calculate anything except the Expected Frequencies.

	A	B	C	D	E	F	G	H	I	J	K
1	**Test of Independence: Two-Way Chi-Squared Test**										
2	Ho: Choice of Radio broadcast is independent of age group										
3	Ha: Choice of Radio broadcast is not independent of age group										
4		**Observed Frequencies**						**Expected Frequencies**			
5			**Age Groups**						**Age Groups**		
6	**Preference**	**Young**	**Middle**	**Senior**	**TOTAL**		**Preference**	**Young**	**Middle**	**Senior**	**TOTAL**
7	Music	15	12	3	30		Music	9.88	13.41	6.71	30
8	News	4	15	11	30		News	9.88	13.41	6.71	30
9	Sports	9	11	5	25		Sports	8.24	11.18	5.59	25
10	**TOTAL**	28	38	19	85		**TOTAL**	28	38	19	85
11											
12		**Calculation of Chi-Squared**									
13			**Age Groups**								
14	**Preference**	**Young**	**Middle**	**Senior**							
15	Music	2.650	0.149	2.048							
16	News	3.501	0.188	2.750							
17	Sports	0.071	0.003	0.062							
18					**11.4217**						
19	χ_T^2 Test Statistic =	11.422	=CHISQ.INV.RT(CHISQ.TEST(B7:D9,H7:J9),(COUNT(B7:B9)-1)*(COUNT(B7:D7)-1))								
20	Significance α =	0.05									
21	1 - α =	0.95	=1-B20								
22	Number of rows i =	3									
23	Number of columns j =	3									
24	degrees of freedom df =	4	=(B22-1)*(B23-1)								
25	χ_C^2 Critical Value =	9.488	=CHISQ.INV(B21,B24)								
26											
27	Decision:	Reject Ho	=IF(B19>B25, "Reject Ho", "Fail to Reject Ho")								
28	Conclusion:	Thus, at a 95% confidence level, we can reject the hypothesis choice of radio									
29		broadcasts is independent of the age group of the individual.									

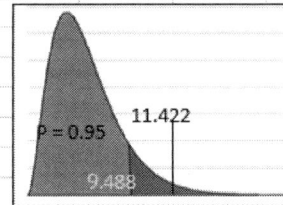

Figure 8.5. Two-Way Chi-Squared Test of Independence Excel Formulations

Example 8:5. Test of Homogeneity

Going back to the contingency table example that, it would be interesting to see if the two populations (males versus females) make different decisions when it comes to wearing their seatbelts while driving. The following table shows the observed frequencies for each category. Conduct a Two-Way Chi-Squared test to identify if males and female seatbelt wearing behaviors are different at a 0.01 level of significance.

Observed Frequencies

Seat Belt Use

Gender	Always	Mostly	Sometimes	Rarely	Never	TOTAL
Male	105	65	58	39	59	326
Female	300	110	65	44	55	574
TOTAL	405	175	123	83	114	900

Solution: Follow the steps of the hypotheses testing to solve this problem. Note that a lot of the calculations in Chi-squared distributions are easier to perform in Excel than by hand.
Step 1. Clearly identify and state the Null Hypothesis (Ho) and Alternative Hypothesis (Ha)
Ho: Distribution of seat belt wearing is the same for males versus females.
Ha: Distribution of seat belt wearing is not the same for males versus females.

Step 2. Specify the level of significance α (also called the acceptable risk of making a Type I error). In this example, the level of significance $\alpha = 0.01$ and Two-Way tests are always right tailed.

Step 3. Select and calculate the appropriate value of the Test Statistic (χ_T^2)
One would need to calculate the Expected Frequencies for each category, first by using the formula $E_i = \frac{n_{row} \times n_{column}}{n_{total}}$ for each cell as shown in the table below:

Expected Frequencies

Seat Belt Use

Gender	Always	Mostly	Sometimes	Rarely	Never	TOTAL
Male	146.70	63.39	44.55	30.06	41.29	326
Female	258.30	111.61	78.45	52.94	72.71	574
TOTAL	405.00	175.00	123.00	83.00	114.00	**900**

For each cell, one can now calculate the value of $\frac{(O-E)^2}{E}$ in order to create the following table. The sum of all these cell values, therefore, gives the Test Statistic χ_T^2

Calculation of Chi-Squared

Seat Belt Use

Gender	Always	Mostly	Sometimes	Rarely	Never
Male	11.853	0.041	4.058	2.656	7.593
Female	6.732	0.023	2.305	1.508	4.312
					41.082

$$\chi_T^2 = \sum \frac{(O-E)^2}{E} = 41.082$$

Step 4. Determine the Critical Value (χ_C^2) based on the level of α and degrees of freedom $df = (i-1) \times (j-1)$. Clearly demarcate the Rejection Region (RR)
   Here there are 2 rows in the table, so $i = 2$, there are five columns in the table, so $j = 5$ and the degrees of freedom d.f. $= (2-1)(5-1) = 4$ with an $\alpha = 0.01$. Note that in the Chi-squared table, this means that the blue region should be equal to 0.01 and the orange region would be 0.99. So, one would look at the table in the following manner:

d.f.	0.995	0.99	0.975
1	7.879	6.635	5.024
2	10.597	9.210	7.378
3	12.838	11.345	9.348
4	14.860	13.277	11.143
5	16.750	15.086	12.833

Thus, $\chi_C^2 = 13.277$

Step 5. Compare the Test Statistic to the Critical Value to identify whether the null hypothesis is rejected or not at the level of significance α. If the Test Statistic falls in the Rejection Region, reject the null hypothesis, otherwise fail to reject the null.

   As one can see in Figure 8.6, the test statistic falls in the blue Rejection Region. Thus, one can reject the null hypothesis in this case at a 99% confidence level.

Step 6. Write a clear conclusion based on the determination made in Step 5.

At a 99% confidence level, one can reject the null hypothesis that male and female populations have the same distribution in terms of seatbelt wearing habits.

Figure 8.6 shows the Excel formulations used to solve this problem alongside the direct Chi-squared formula for the critical values. Note that there is a direct way to calculate the Test Statistic in Excel by using the CHISQ.INV.RT function in combination with CHISQ.TEST function without having to calculate anything except the Expected Frequencies.

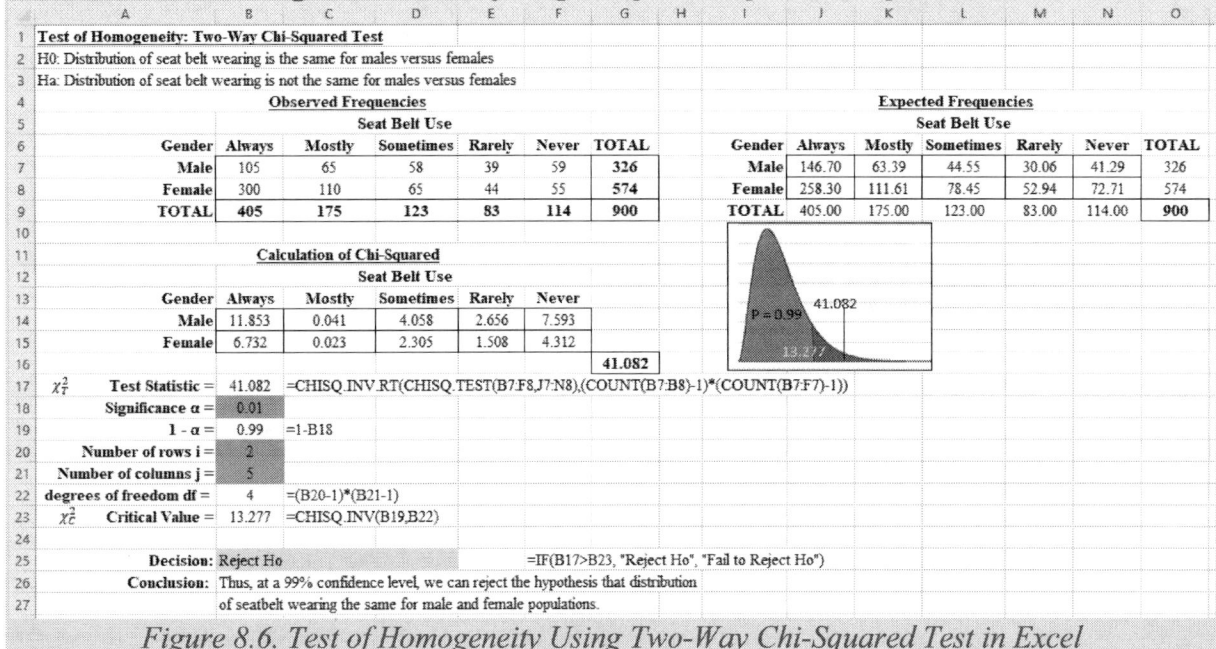

	A	B	C	D	E	F	G	H	I	J	K	L	M	N	O
1	Test of Homogeneity: Two-Way Chi-Squared Test														
2	H0: Distribution of seat belt wearing is the same for males versus females														
3	Ha: Distribution of seat belt wearing is not the same for males versus females														
4			Observed Frequencies								Expected Frequencies				
5			Seat Belt Use								Seat Belt Use				
6		Gender	Always	Mostly	Sometimes	Rarely	Never	TOTAL	Gender	Always	Mostly	Sometimes	Rarely	Never	TOTAL
7		Male	105	65	58	39	59	326	Male	146.70	63.39	44.55	30.06	41.29	326
8		Female	300	110	65	44	55	574	Female	258.30	111.61	78.45	52.94	72.71	574
9		TOTAL	405	175	123	83	114	900	TOTAL	405.00	175.00	123.00	83.00	114.00	900
10															
11			Calculation of Chi-Squared												
12			Seat Belt Use												
13		Gender	Always	Mostly	Sometimes	Rarely	Never								
14		Male	11.853	0.041	4.058	2.656	7.593								
15		Female	6.732	0.023	2.305	1.508	4.312								
16							41.082								
17	χ_T^2	Test Statistic =	41.082	=CHISQ.INV.RT(CHISQ.TEST(B7:F8,J7:N8),(COUNT(B7:B8)-1)*(COUNT(B7:F7)-1))											
18		Significance α =	0.01												
19		1 - α =	0.99	=1-B18											
20		Number of rows i =	2												
21		Number of columns j =	5												
22		degrees of freedom df =	4	=(B20-1)*(B21-1)											
23	χ_C^2	Critical Value =	13.277	=CHISQ.INV(B19,B22)											
24															
25		Decision:	Reject Ho				=IF(B17>B23, "Reject Ho", "Fail to Reject Ho")								
26		Conclusion:	Thus, at a 99% confidence level, we can reject the hypothesis that distribution												
27			of seatbelt wearing the same for male and female populations.												

Figure 8.6. Test of Homogeneity Using Two-Way Chi-Squared Test in Excel

8.4.2. Median Test

The Median Test is also based on a tweak from the Goodness-of-Fit and homogeneity tests where observations about an ordinal variable are taken from two different populations and since one does not have information about the mean, one could use the median to identify if there is a difference between the two populations or not by using Chi-Squared Tests. Start by gathering the data for the two samples and then finding the total observations for each of the values of the ordinal variable. Then, one would identify the median of the ordinal variable and create a table to identify how many observations in each sample lie above the median, and how many below the median. This table would be the Table of Observed Frequencies and thereafter one would proceed in the same manner as for the other Two-way tests (test of independence, test of homogeneity) with calculating the test statistic and identifying the critical values of the Chi-squared. An example will help to understand these steps better. Note that if the reader needs a refresher on how to find the Median for a Frequency Distribution, it was covered in Chapter 2, Section 2.1.2.

Example 8:6. Median Test

A researcher is trying to identify if there is a difference in the intensity of crimes that are committed against white or black victims in a city. She collects information regarding 19 white victims and 21 black victims. She uses a scale to measure the intensity of the crime committed (range from 1 to 5, with 1 being a crime resulting in no physical injury to 5 being the crime resulting in a fatality. Conduct a Median Test to identify if there is a difference between crimes committed against black and white victims in the city at a 0.05 level of significance. The information she has gathered is shared below:

Score	white victims	black victims
1	1	12
2	2	3
3	6	3
4	3	2
5	7	1
TOTAL	19	21

Solution: Follow the steps of the hypotheses testing to solve this problem. Note that a lot of the calculations in Chi-squared distributions are easier to perform in Excel than by hand.

Step 1. Clearly identify and state the Null Hypothesis (H₀) and Alternative Hypothesis (Hₐ)
H_0: There is no difference in intensity of crimes committed towards white or black victims.
H_a: There is a difference in intensity of crimes committed towards white or black victims.

Step 2. Specify the level of significance α (also called the acceptable risk of making a Type I error). In this example, the level of significance $\alpha = 0.05$ and Two-Way tests are always right tailed.

Step 3. Select and calculate the appropriate value of the Test Statistic (χ_T^2)
In this example, the Median Test is being implemented, which requires one to create the Table of Observed Frequencies first by finding the median score for the total of all victims.

Score	white victims	black victims	TOTAL	Cumu. Freq.
1	1	12	13	13
2	2	3	5	18
3	6	3	9	27
4	3	2	5	32
5	7	1	8	40
TOTAL	19	21	40	

Based on this, one can see that the crime intensity score of the $40/2 = 20^{th}$ victim is a 3. Thus, the median intensity of the sample of 40 victims is 3. Based on this one can create the table of observed frequencies using the number of victims whose crime intensity was higher than the median value and those whose crime intensity was not higher than the median for each race.

Observed Frequencies

	white	black	TOTAL
Higher than Median	10	3	13
Not Higher than Median	9	18	27
TOTAL	19	21	40

Now, one would need to calculate the Expected Frequencies for each category, first by using the formula $E_i = \frac{n_{row} \times n_{column}}{n_{total}}$ for each cell as shown in the table below:

Expected Frequencies

	white	black	TOTAL
Higher than Median	6.18	6.83	13
Not Higher than Median	12.83	14.18	27
TOTAL	19	21	**40**

For each cell, one can now calculate the value of $\frac{(O-E)^2}{E}$ in order to create the following table. The sum of all these cell values, therefore, gives the Test Statistic χ_T^2

Calculation of Chi-Squared

	white	black
Higher than Median	2.369	2.144
Not Higher than Median	1.141	1.032
		6.686

$$\chi_T^2 = \sum \frac{(O-E)^2}{E} = 6.686$$

Step 4. Determine the Critical Value (χ_C^2) based on the level of α and degrees of freedom $df = (i-1) \times (j-1)$. Clearly demarcate the Rejection Region (RR)

Here there are 2 rows in the table, so $i = 2$, there are 2 columns in the table, so $j = 2$ and the degrees of freedom d.f. = (2-1)(2-1) = 1 with an $\alpha = 0.05$. Note that in the Chi-squared table, this means that the blue region should be equal to 0.05 and the orange region would be 0.95. So, one would look at the table in the following manner:

				Probability to the	
d.f.	**0.995**	**0.99**	**0.975**	**0.95**	**0.9**
1	7.879	6.635	5.024	3.841	2.706
2	10.597	9.210	7.378	5.991	4.605

Thus, $\chi_C^2 = 3.841$

Step 5. Compare the Test Statistic to the Critical Value to identify whether the null hypothesis is rejected or not at the level of significance α. If the Test Statistic falls in the Rejection Region, reject the null hypothesis, otherwise fail to reject the null.

As one can see in Figure 8.7, the test statistic falls in the blue Rejection Region. Thus, one can reject the null hypothesis in this case at a 95% confidence level.

Step 6. Write a clear conclusion based on the determination made in Step 5.
At a 95% confidence level, one can reject the null hypothesis that black and white victims face the same intensity of crime in the city.

Figure 8.7 shows the Excel formulations used to solve this problem alongside the direct Chi-squared formula for the critical values. Note that there is a direct way to calculate the Test Statistic in Excel by using the CHISQ.INV.RT function in combination with CHISQ.TEST function without having to calculate anything except the Expected Frequencies

	A	B	C	D	E	F	G	H	I
10	Median Score =	3	Score of the 40/2 = 20th observation						
11									
12	Ho: There is no difference in intensity of crimes commited towards white or black victims								
13	Ha: There is a difference in intensity of crimes commited towards white or black victims								
14									
15		**Observed Frequencies**					**Expected Frequencies**		
16		white	black	TOTAL			white	black	TOTAL
17	**Higher than Median**	10	3	13		**Higher than Median**	6.18	6.83	13
18	**Not Higher than Median**	9	18	27		**Not Higher than Median**	12.83	14.18	27
19	**TOTAL**	19	21	40		**TOTAL**	19	21	40
20									
21		**Calculation of Chi-Squared**							
22		white	black						
23	**Higher than Median**	2.369	2.144						
24	**Not Higher than Median**	1.141	1.032						
25				**6.686**					
26	χ_T^2 Test Statistic =	6.686		=CHISQ.INV.RT(CHISQ.TEST(B17:C18,G17:H18),(COUNT(B17:B18)-1)*(COUNT(B17:C17)-1))					
27	Significance α =	0.05							
28	1 - α =	0.95		=1-B27					
29	Number of rows i =	2							
30	Number of columns j =	2							
31	degrees of freedom df =	1		=(B29-1)*(B30-1)					
32	χ_C^2 Critical Value =	3.841		=CHISQ.INV(B28,B31)					
33									
34	Decision:	Reject Ho			=IF(B26>B32, "Reject Ho", "Fail to Reject Ho")				
35	Conclusion:	Thus, at a 95% confidence level, we can reject the hypothesis that there is							
36		no difference in crime intensity against white or black victims.							

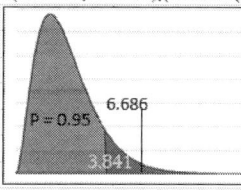

Figure 8.7. Median Test Two-Way Chi-squared Using Excel Formulas.

Appendix: Common Statistical Tables

Table A. *Z*-Table for Probability Calculations in Standard Normal Distribution

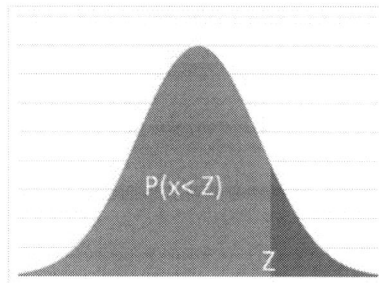

Standard Normal Distribution Z-Table showing P(x < Z)									
Z-value	0.00	0.01	0.02	0.03	0.04	0.05	0.06	0.07	0.08	0.09
0.0	0.5000	0.5040	0.5080	0.5120	0.5160	0.5199	0.5239	0.5279	0.5319	0.5359
0.1	0.5398	0.5438	0.5478	0.5517	0.5557	0.5596	0.5636	0.5675	0.5714	0.5753
0.2	0.5793	0.5832	0.5871	0.5910	0.5948	0.5987	0.6026	0.6064	0.6103	0.6141
0.3	0.6179	0.6217	0.6255	0.6293	0.6331	0.6368	0.6406	0.6443	0.6480	0.6517
0.4	0.6554	0.6591	0.6628	0.6664	0.6700	0.6736	0.6772	0.6808	0.6844	0.6879
0.5	0.6915	0.6950	0.6985	0.7019	0.7054	0.7088	0.7123	0.7157	0.7190	0.7224
0.6	0.7257	0.7291	0.7324	0.7357	0.7389	0.7422	0.7454	0.7486	0.7517	0.7549
0.7	0.7580	0.7611	0.7642	0.7673	0.7704	0.7734	0.7764	0.7794	0.7823	0.7852
0.8	0.7881	0.7910	0.7939	0.7967	0.7995	0.8023	0.8051	0.8078	0.8106	0.8133
0.9	0.8159	0.8186	0.8212	0.8238	0.8264	0.8289	0.8315	0.8340	0.8365	0.8389
1.0	0.8413	0.8438	0.8461	0.8485	0.8508	0.8531	0.8554	0.8577	0.8599	0.8621
1.1	0.8643	0.8665	0.8686	0.8708	0.8729	0.8749	0.8770	0.8790	0.8810	0.8830
1.2	0.8849	0.8869	0.8888	0.8907	0.8925	0.8944	0.8962	0.8980	0.8997	0.9015
1.3	0.9032	0.9049	0.9066	0.9082	0.9099	0.9115	0.9131	0.9147	0.9162	0.9177
1.4	0.9192	0.9207	0.9222	0.9236	0.9251	0.9265	0.9279	0.9292	0.9306	0.9319
1.5	0.9332	0.9345	0.9357	0.9370	0.9382	0.9394	0.9406	0.9418	0.9429	0.9441
1.6	0.9452	0.9463	0.9474	0.9484	0.9495	0.9505	0.9515	0.9525	0.9535	0.9545
1.7	0.9554	0.9564	0.9573	0.9582	0.9591	0.9599	0.9608	0.9616	0.9625	0.9633
1.8	0.9641	0.9649	0.9656	0.9664	0.9671	0.9678	0.9686	0.9693	0.9699	0.9706
1.9	0.9713	0.9719	0.9726	0.9732	0.9738	0.9744	0.9750	0.9756	0.9761	0.9767
2.0	0.9772	0.9778	0.9783	0.9788	0.9793	0.9798	0.9803	0.9808	0.9812	0.9817
2.1	0.9821	0.9826	0.9830	0.9834	0.9838	0.9842	0.9846	0.9850	0.9854	0.9857
2.2	0.9861	0.9864	0.9868	0.9871	0.9875	0.9878	0.9881	0.9884	0.9887	0.9890
2.3	0.9893	0.9896	0.9898	0.9901	0.9904	0.9906	0.9909	0.9911	0.9913	0.9916
2.4	0.9918	0.9920	0.9922	0.9925	0.9927	0.9929	0.9931	0.9932	0.9934	0.9936
2.5	0.9938	0.9940	0.9941	0.9943	0.9945	0.9946	0.9948	0.9949	0.9951	0.9952
2.6	0.9953	0.9955	0.9956	0.9957	0.9959	0.9960	0.9961	0.9962	0.9963	0.9964
2.7	0.9965	0.9966	0.9967	0.9968	0.9969	0.9970	0.9971	0.9972	0.9973	0.9974
2.8	0.9974	0.9975	0.9976	0.9977	0.9977	0.9978	0.9979	0.9979	0.9980	0.9981
2.9	0.9981	0.9982	0.9982	0.9983	0.9984	0.9984	0.9985	0.9985	0.9986	0.9986

Table B. *t*-table for Probabilities and Degrees of Freedom

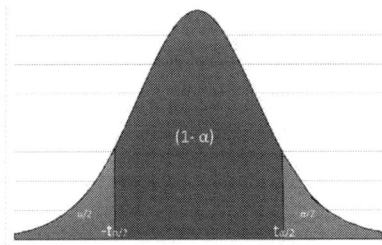

					t-values corresponding to α and n						
cumu. Prob.	t (0.50)	t(0.75)	t(0.80)	t(0.85)	t(0.90)	t(0.95)	t(0.975)	t(0.99)	9(0.995)	t(0.999)	t(0.9995)
α (or α/2)	0.50	0.25	0.20	0.15	0.10	0.05	0.025	0.01	0.005	0.001	0.0005
df											
1	0.000	1.000	1.376	1.963	3.078	6.314	12.706	31.821	63.657	318.309	636.619
2	0.000	0.816	1.061	1.386	1.886	2.920	4.303	6.965	9.925	22.327	31.599
3	0.000	0.765	0.978	1.250	1.638	2.353	3.182	4.541	5.841	10.215	12.924
4	0.000	0.741	0.941	1.190	1.533	2.132	2.776	3.747	4.604	7.173	8.610
5	0.000	0.727	0.920	1.156	1.476	2.015	2.571	3.365	4.032	5.893	6.869
6	0.000	0.718	0.906	1.134	1.440	1.943	2.447	3.143	3.707	5.208	5.959
7	0.000	0.711	0.896	1.119	1.415	1.895	2.365	2.998	3.499	4.785	5.408
8	0.000	0.706	0.889	1.108	1.397	1.860	2.306	2.896	3.355	4.501	5.041
9	0.000	0.703	0.883	1.100	1.383	1.833	2.262	2.821	3.250	4.297	4.781
10	0.000	0.700	0.879	1.093	1.372	1.812	2.228	2.764	3.169	4.144	4.587
11	0.000	0.697	0.876	1.088	1.363	1.796	2.201	2.718	3.106	4.025	4.437
12	0.000	0.695	0.873	1.083	1.356	1.782	2.179	2.681	3.055	3.930	4.318
13	0.000	0.694	0.870	1.079	1.350	1.771	2.160	2.650	3.012	3.852	4.221
14	0.000	0.692	0.868	1.076	1.345	1.761	2.145	2.624	2.977	3.787	4.140
15	0.000	0.691	0.866	1.074	1.341	1.753	2.131	2.602	2.947	3.733	4.073
16	0.000	0.690	0.865	1.071	1.337	1.746	2.120	2.583	2.921	3.686	4.015
17	0.000	0.689	0.863	1.069	1.333	1.740	2.110	2.567	2.898	3.646	3.965
18	0.000	0.688	0.862	1.067	1.330	1.734	2.101	2.552	2.878	3.610	3.922
19	0.000	0.688	0.861	1.066	1.328	1.729	2.093	2.539	2.861	3.579	3.883
20	0.000	0.687	0.860	1.064	1.325	1.725	2.086	2.528	2.845	3.552	3.850
21	0.000	0.686	0.859	1.063	1.323	1.721	2.080	2.518	2.831	3.527	3.819
22	0.000	0.686	0.858	1.061	1.321	1.717	2.074	2.508	2.819	3.505	3.792
23	0.000	0.685	0.858	1.060	1.319	1.714	2.069	2.500	2.807	3.485	3.768
24	0.000	0.685	0.857	1.059	1.318	1.711	2.064	2.492	2.797	3.467	3.745
25	0.000	0.684	0.856	1.058	1.316	1.708	2.060	2.485	2.787	3.450	3.725
26	0.000	0.684	0.856	1.058	1.315	1.706	2.056	2.479	2.779	3.435	3.707
27	0.000	0.684	0.855	1.057	1.314	1.703	2.052	2.473	2.771	3.421	3.690
28	0.000	0.683	0.855	1.056	1.313	1.701	2.048	2.467	2.763	3.408	3.674
29	0.000	0.683	0.854	1.055	1.311	1.699	2.045	2.462	2.756	3.396	3.659
30	0.000	0.683	0.854	1.055	1.310	1.697	2.042	2.457	2.750	3.385	3.646
100	0.000	0.677	0.845	1.042	1.290	1.660	1.984	2.364	2.626	3.174	3.390
Z-values	0.000	0.674	0.842	1.036	1.282	1.645	1.960	2.326	2.576	3.090	3.291

Table C. F-values for $\alpha = 0.05$

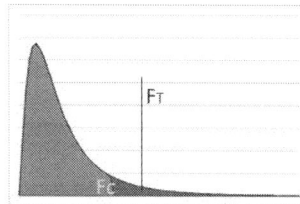

D.f.2	Probability to the right of the value					$\alpha = 0.05$				
					← D.f.1 →					
	1	2	3	4	5	10	20	50	60	120
1	161.448	199.500	215.707	224.583	230.162	241.882	248.013	251.774	252.196	253.253
2	18.513	19.000	19.164	19.247	19.296	19.396	19.446	19.476	19.479	19.487
3	10.128	9.552	9.277	9.117	9.013	8.786	8.660	8.581	8.572	8.549
4	7.709	6.944	6.591	6.388	6.256	5.964	5.803	5.699	5.688	5.658
5	6.608	5.786	5.409	5.192	5.050	4.735	4.558	4.444	4.431	4.398
6	5.987	5.143	4.757	4.534	4.387	4.060	3.874	3.754	3.740	3.705
7	5.591	4.737	4.347	4.120	3.972	3.637	3.445	3.319	3.304	3.267
8	5.318	4.459	4.066	3.838	3.687	3.347	3.150	3.020	3.005	2.967
9	5.117	4.256	3.863	3.633	3.482	3.137	2.936	2.803	2.787	2.748
10	4.965	4.103	3.708	3.478	3.326	2.978	2.774	2.637	2.621	2.580
11	4.844	3.982	3.587	3.357	3.204	2.854	2.646	2.507	2.490	2.448
12	4.747	3.885	3.490	3.259	3.106	2.753	2.544	2.401	2.384	2.341
13	4.667	3.806	3.411	3.179	3.025	2.671	2.459	2.314	2.297	2.252
14	4.600	3.739	3.344	3.112	2.958	2.602	2.388	2.241	2.223	2.178
15	4.543	3.682	3.287	3.056	2.901	2.544	2.328	2.178	2.160	2.114
16	4.494	3.634	3.239	3.007	2.852	2.494	2.276	2.124	2.106	2.059
17	4.451	3.592	3.197	2.965	2.810	2.450	2.230	2.077	2.058	2.011
18	4.414	3.555	3.160	2.928	2.773	2.412	2.191	2.035	2.017	1.968
19	4.381	3.522	3.127	2.895	2.740	2.378	2.155	1.999	1.980	1.930
20	4.351	3.493	3.098	2.866	2.711	2.348	2.124	1.966	1.946	1.896
21	4.325	3.467	3.072	2.840	2.685	2.321	2.096	1.936	1.916	1.866
22	4.301	3.443	3.049	2.817	2.661	2.297	2.071	1.909	1.889	1.838
23	4.279	3.422	3.028	2.796	2.640	2.275	2.048	1.885	1.865	1.813
24	4.260	3.403	3.009	2.776	2.621	2.255	2.027	1.863	1.842	1.790
25	4.242	3.385	2.991	2.759	2.603	2.236	2.007	1.842	1.822	1.768
26	4.225	3.369	2.975	2.743	2.587	2.220	1.990	1.823	1.803	1.749
27	4.210	3.354	2.960	2.728	2.572	2.204	1.974	1.806	1.785	1.731
28	4.196	3.340	2.947	2.714	2.558	2.190	1.959	1.790	1.769	1.714
29	4.183	3.328	2.934	2.701	2.545	2.177	1.945	1.775	1.754	1.698
30	4.171	3.316	2.922	2.690	2.534	2.165	1.932	1.761	1.740	1.683
31	4.160	3.305	2.911	2.679	2.523	2.153	1.920	1.748	1.726	1.670
32	4.149	3.295	2.901	2.668	2.512	2.142	1.908	1.736	1.714	1.657
33	4.139	3.285	2.892	2.659	2.503	2.133	1.898	1.724	1.702	1.645
34	4.130	3.276	2.883	2.650	2.494	2.123	1.888	1.713	1.691	1.633
35	4.121	3.267	2.874	2.641	2.485	2.114	1.878	1.703	1.681	1.623
36	4.113	3.259	2.866	2.634	2.477	2.106	1.870	1.694	1.671	1.612
37	4.105	3.252	2.859	2.626	2.470	2.098	1.861	1.685	1.662	1.603
38	4.098	3.245	2.852	2.619	2.463	2.091	1.853	1.676	1.653	1.594
39	4.091	3.238	2.845	2.612	2.456	2.084	1.846	1.668	1.645	1.585
40	4.085	3.232	2.839	2.606	2.449	2.077	1.839	1.660	1.637	1.577
41	4.079	3.226	2.833	2.600	2.443	2.071	1.832	1.653	1.630	1.569
42	4.073	3.220	2.827	2.594	2.438	2.065	1.826	1.646	1.623	1.561
43	4.067	3.214	2.822	2.589	2.432	2.059	1.820	1.639	1.616	1.554
44	4.062	3.209	2.816	2.584	2.427	2.054	1.814	1.633	1.609	1.547
45	4.057	3.204	2.812	2.579	2.422	2.049	1.808	1.626	1.603	1.541

Table D. Chi-Squared Values given p and d.f.

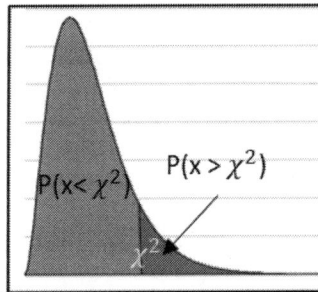

d.f.	Probability to the left of the value									
	0.995	0.99	0.975	0.95	0.9	0.1	0.05	0.025	0.01	0.005
1	7.879	6.635	5.024	3.841	2.706	0.016	0.004	0.001	0.000	0.000
2	10.597	9.210	7.378	5.991	4.605	0.211	0.103	0.051	0.020	0.010
3	12.838	11.345	9.348	7.815	6.251	0.584	0.352	0.216	0.115	0.072
4	14.860	13.277	11.143	9.488	7.779	1.064	0.711	0.484	0.297	0.207
5	16.750	15.086	12.833	11.070	9.236	1.610	1.145	0.831	0.554	0.412
6	18.548	16.812	14.449	12.592	10.645	2.204	1.635	1.237	0.872	0.676
7	20.278	18.475	16.013	14.067	12.017	2.833	2.167	1.690	1.239	0.989
8	21.955	20.090	17.535	15.507	13.362	3.490	2.733	2.180	1.646	1.344
9	23.589	21.666	19.023	16.919	14.684	4.168	3.325	2.700	2.088	1.735
10	25.188	23.209	20.483	18.307	15.987	4.865	3.940	3.247	2.558	2.156
11	26.757	24.725	21.920	19.675	17.275	5.578	4.575	3.816	3.053	2.603
12	28.300	26.217	23.337	21.026	18.549	6.304	5.226	4.404	3.571	3.074
13	29.819	27.688	24.736	22.362	19.812	7.042	5.892	5.009	4.107	3.565
14	31.319	29.141	26.119	23.685	21.064	7.790	6.571	5.629	4.660	4.075
15	32.801	30.578	27.488	24.996	22.307	8.547	7.261	6.262	5.229	4.601
16	34.267	32.000	28.845	26.296	23.542	9.312	7.962	6.908	5.812	5.142
17	35.718	33.409	30.191	27.587	24.769	10.085	8.672	7.564	6.408	5.697
18	37.156	34.805	31.526	28.869	25.989	10.865	9.390	8.231	7.015	6.265
19	38.582	36.191	32.852	30.144	27.204	11.651	10.117	8.907	7.633	6.844
20	39.997	37.566	34.170	31.410	28.412	12.443	10.851	9.591	8.260	7.434
21	41.401	38.932	35.479	32.671	29.615	13.240	11.591	10.283	8.897	8.034
22	42.796	40.289	36.781	33.924	30.813	14.041	12.338	10.982	9.542	8.643
23	44.181	41.638	38.076	35.172	32.007	14.848	13.091	11.689	10.196	9.260
24	45.559	42.980	39.364	36.415	33.196	15.659	13.848	12.401	10.856	9.886
25	46.928	44.314	40.646	37.652	34.382	16.473	14.611	13.120	11.524	10.520
26	48.290	45.642	41.923	38.885	35.563	17.292	15.379	13.844	12.198	11.160
27	49.645	46.963	43.195	40.113	36.741	18.114	16.151	14.573	12.879	11.808
28	50.993	48.278	44.461	41.337	37.916	18.939	16.928	15.308	13.565	12.461
29	52.336	49.588	45.722	42.557	39.087	19.768	17.708	16.047	14.256	13.121
30	53.672	50.892	46.979	43.773	40.256	20.599	18.493	16.791	14.953	13.787

About the Book

This book is primarily written for individuals and managers who are learning the basics of statistics for business applications. The goal of this book is to introduce readers to the basic statistical analysis and the tools required to succeed in the world of datasets. This book covers the fundamentals of statistics, probability distributions, data analysis, and regression analysis using simple and stepwise approaches to solving problems using MS Excel tools. This book covers descriptive and inferential statistics in eight chapters. The first two chapters introduce basic types of functions, research methods, what hypothesis testing means, different types of data, how to present data using tables and graphs, and how to describe data in numerical terms by focusing on the measures of central tendency and variability. The next three chapters introduce the reader to the world of probability calculations before crossing over to the inferential world of statistics. The inferential world of statistics allows one to enhance their decision-making skills by learning about various types of distributions, sampling, and testing options armed with the descriptive statistical tools to draw meaningful inferences. The last three chapters of the book bring everything together as they explore the nuances of relationships between two or more variables and discuss methods to identify if and how they interact with each other.

About the Author

Dr. Kruti Dholakia Lehenbauer

Dr. Kruti Lehenbauer has been teaching classes in Business, Economics, and Statistics at the undergraduate and graduate levels since 2006 as a full-time professor and lives in San Antonio with her family. She has an extensive background in economics, statistics, public policy, and political economy. She has also provided consulting services to banks and other institutions since 2011 and consistently finds that data-based decisions lead to optimal outcomes for everyone!

Printed in Great Britain
by Amazon

32500365R00110